ACKNOWLEDGMENTS

This book is a collection of stories about the early days of rodeo. It was gathered from dozens of personal interviews of people who were involved with rodeo from the beginning to the present day. The variety and length of the interviews vary. They include contestants, stock contractors, family members, announcers and fans. We would like to thank those people who contributed their time and supplied the information included in these pages.

This book is dedicated to my folks, Bud and Karola Jory

PHOTO CREDITS

TABLE OF CONTENTS

AN ORAL HISTORY OF RODEO

FROM

PENDLETON

TO

CALGARY

by
Doug and Cathy Jory

ISBN: 0-9722309-0-4

Printed by Maverick Publications, Inc.
P.O. Box 5007 · Bend, OR 97708

INTRODUCTION

"Whatever happened to ol' what's his name?" That was a phrase I heard repeatedly when I was a boy visiting my dad at the Mustanger barns at the Pendleton Round-Up grounds in the late 1940s. There was a warm-up shack located next to the Indian Village where the cowboys congregated when they were in town, and just inside the door was a pot-bellied stove that was never allowed to go out through the winter. They'd gather around the stove and tell their stories, and inevitably the conversation would start out with—"Whatever happened to ol' what's his name?"

In 1996, Cathy and I were going through some family papers and we discovered a trunk with nearly 500 old rodeo pictures that had been in the family since 1910 and the first Pendleton Round-Up. Looking over the pictures reminded me of the cowboys sitting around the warm-up shack, talking about the past.

The pictures covered the period from 1910 to 1929. My grandparents, Ben and Mildred Jory were involved in rodeo back in the early days. Ben competed at Pendleton in 1910 and later became a stock contractor and rodeo promoter. Mildred traveled with him, and together, they put on shows all over the Northwest.

It was Cathy's idea that we try to find out something about the people in the pictures. We realized that most of them were gone, but surely they had relatives we could talk to about their lives. We spent the next six years traveling around the Northwest in our spare time interviewing people for this book. We were asked repeatedly why more people weren't doing this. "In a few years all of the old timers will be gone. It's a shame that someone isn't recording it."

A few of the people in the interviews are family members, and several are long-time friends. Although I didn't get to know my grandfather, Ben, I heard stories about him, and when the opportunity came to put this book of interviews together, I naturally included him in it. Lary Daniels was married to Ben's youngest daughter, Maxine. Lary was well known in rodeo circles as being one of the toughest competitors around; his daughter, MonteCre was a trick rider in the early 1950s. Bill Sylvester lived with my family when he was fourteen on a small ranch near Baker, Oregon. Bill later followed rodeo to Madison Square Garden and back in the company of Bud Linderman and some of the biggest names in rodeo.

Our initial effort at interviews outside of our area was at the National Finals Rodeo in Las Vegas in 1996. We attended the Turtles' convention held at the Aladdin Hotel & Casino. The Turtles are the forerunner of the Professional Rodeo Cowboys' Association. They began in 1936 in an attempt to legitimize the cowboy's right for more money and fairer treatment by rodeo promoters. The Turtles helped set the standards that govern modern rodeo today. The convention provided a great opportunity to meet some of the original members and to conduct interviews.

On our trip home we planned to stop in Ely to visit Wylie Carroll and his wife, Altha. Shortly after discovering the collection, The Oregonian had written a feature article on the pictures, and Wylie had called us asking for information on his distant cousin, Roy Moss, the 1911 winner of the steer roping at the Pendleton Round-Up; later, with Wylie's help we managed to contact Lyle Moss in Sweet Home, Oregon for more information on Roy Moss and the Moss family.

Fifty miles south of Ely we had a flat tire and a radiator problem and spent a couple of hours alongside the highway wrestling with the bracket to get the spare tire loose. A man stopped in a pickup and told us that he would call the Highway Patrol at the next town, 57 miles in the opposite direction. The call, instead of going to Las Vegas went to Salt Lake City, then to Las Vegas. Las Vegas called Ely. A patrolman met us at the edge of town and told us that the Nevada Highway Patrol doesn't patrol the highways at night. Stranded in December on the Nevada desert at midnight is something I wouldn't wish on anyone. It reminded me of Mark Twain's tale about getting lost in a snowstorm on his way to Carson City and waking up fifteen steps from a stage station. It gets cold out there under the stars. The towns along highway 93 heading north from Las Vegas have city limit signs giving the elevation rather than the population, and all of them are over 7,000 feet.

Following a good night's sleep at a motel and a quick breakfast, we called Wylie and Altha and drove over to visit. They met us in the front yard and invited us inside where we spent the next hour or so talking about Wylie's experiences prospecting throughout the state of Nevada. Wylie wasn't involved in rodeo, but he knew a lot who were. He ran wild horses in the Nevada desert and followed a Geiger counter for years hunting elusive uranium readings from one end of the state to the other. "I got cancer from these darn bombs and underground blasts. From the Mercury Test Site. We were hunting uranium by plane. We couldn't find any commercial grade uranium in the state of Nevada. I was picking up hot stuff all over from the big bomb blasts. I'd send it in and have it assayed. It wasn't uranium; it was fall-out. So there's no uranium here, just hot stuff clear up to Ely. Deer are dying like flies down around Caliente. It can't keep going this way."

Looking back over his life, Wylie reminisced about his days chasing wild horses: "I trapped lots of mustangs in the '50s and '60s, but the BLM won't let you do it anymore. The way we run wild horses was you run 'em a few times with a plane until you know just about where they were gonna go. Then you make 'em think they're getting away from you. Then you charge 'em and get the Judas Horse, and he leads them into a corral.

"You take the Judas Horse out in a trailer. Then you turn him loose with the wild ones and he leads them into the corral."

Wylie escorted us out to our van when we were ready to leave, and just before we drove off I told him that we'd be keeping in touch. "The next time we'll get the real story," I jokingly told him. "This was just a warm-up."

"That's okay with me, Amigo," Wylie said as he waved goodbye.

We carried our entire collection of pictures with us on our trips and started out the interviews by going over them and talking about rodeo. Nearly everyone involved with early rodeo is gone, and a typical response was: "That was a little before my time." But there were a lot of memories of those people, which led to other incidents in their own lives. Some stories, like the Bartlemays', came from family history written down by relatives; others were spur-of-the-moment encounters and provided only brief glimpses, like talking to Lyle Moss on the phone at a nursing home in Sweet Home, Oregon.

They told their stories the way they felt like telling them. When Muggs Bentley and Guy Cash started talking during an interview at Grangeville, Idaho, we just sat back and listened while the two old friends reminisced. It was like taking a day off.

Some interviews fell into place while others fizzled out completely. Even though some interviews failed to develop, it wasn't because of lack of interest or "try". Invariably, people referred us to others. Like Cathy says, "They passed us around like an old suitcase."

There was always something promising just over the hill—"Buck Tiffin lived in Weiser, Idaho", someone said. "Don't forget Ed McCarty. I remember once we was down in Palm Springs together"... "C. C. Coe, now there was someone worth remembering."

There were two types of people we encountered while conducting interviews for the book—those who didn't want to have anything to do with it, and people who loved the idea. We were informed by several people at the onset that they wouldn't have anything to do "with another journalistic rodeo book."

Sometimes we had a tape recorder with us, and occasionally we resorted to hurried notes scribbled on a piece of scrap paper. We interviewed Harold Hartle, long-time Pendleton resident at a laundromat with a hand-held tape recorder during an impromptu hour-long conversation; and it took over a year to conduct the Colfax interviews at Bob Hickman's saddle shop. During that year, waiting for the Yakima Canutt museum dedication and talking to Bob by phone, we were too late when the opportunity finally came to interview Marlo Ochs. Marlo had died.

The Hall of Fame in Pendleton was particularly helpful. Jack Sweek, the director, invited us down one afternoon to look at our rodeo pictures and arranged for an interview with Monk Carden, the winner of the oldest rodeo clown award at every convention he attends. Monk is whip sharp at 92, and is a walking encyclopedia of Pendleton history, along with being a very engaging and interesting man.

We made two trips to Alturas, California to interview Reba Perry Roberts Blakely. Reba lived a varied and exciting life and was a top cowgirl during the period known as the Golden Age of rodeo, the

Introduction

1920s. She rode racehorses for C. B. Irwin, traveled the vaudeville circuit, and was present on the fateful day in 1929 when Bonnie McCarroll was killed by a saddle bronc in the arena at Pendleton. In Reba's view, cowgirls were something special.

In the mid-1970s, Reba rented an apartment in Pendleton for a couple of months to research some articles for "Ketchpen" magazine and spent quite a lot of time going over family history with my mother, Karola Jory. It seemed ironic that twenty-five years later we would find ourselves knocking on her door at a nursing home and talking about her life in rodeo.

When Reba retired from rodeo, she became an authority on the subject, writing countless articles for magazines. She had two patrons during those years—the Will Rogers Institute; and her friend for many years, New York socialite Kay Swift, who married Fay Hubbard, a cowboy from central Washington. Reba is a member of the Cowgirl Hall of Fame in Fort Worth, Texas.

The first Pendleton Round-Up in 1910 featured Northwest Bucking, which was won by a local boy by the name of Bert Kelly. Bronc riding has always been the specialty of Northwest cowboys. They excelled in the riding events while the Southwest has generally produced the top ropers, such as Bob Crosby and Carl Arnold. Wayne Davis, a bronc riding champion from Enterprise, Oregon explains how bronc riding took precedence over other events with local cowboys. He explains the difference between riding in the Northwest and riding in the world competition. Many bronc riders carried world champion reputations but weren't acknowledged as world champs. Wayne explains how that came about. He won the "World" in 1938 at Pendleton.

Many of the well-known cowboys from earlier eras, Hoot Gibson, Hugh Strickland, and Bob Crosby were still around when Stub Bartlemay, Turk Greenough, Pete Knight, and Wayne Davis were just beginning their rodeo careers. Every ten years or so another group of cowboys comes along to replace the generation before them. Ask a cowboy when he rodeoed, and he'll probably start by telling you that he was in the same era as Deb Copenhaver or before or after Casey Tibbs. Muggs Bentley, who rode on a saddlehorse behind his uncle in the first parade at Grangeville Border Days in Idaho in 1912, remembers the day "when I realized that I couldn't compete with the kids anymore." And Bill Sylvester's comments on Jerry Ambler near the end of his riding days are a reminder that even the best can't do what they love forever. I recall Bill Sylvester calling my folks in Pendleton on the phone in the 1960s and crying about not knowing any of the "kids" at a rodeo. From Bert Kelly's first bronc ride in Pendleton to the last time Jerry Ambler got on a saddle bronc marks the beginning and the end of different eras.

Throughout these interviews we came to realize that we were gathering history as well as stories from people. The Spain Brothers Rodeo Company, for example, describes a rodeo in the mining camps at Sumpter in the Blue Mountains of Eastern Oregon. This was several years before the Pendleton Round-Up began. King Spain points out that it might have been the first rodeo held in the Northwest.

There are several references to "ranch" rodeos. Sid and Art Seale held bucking contests on the ranch near Condon, Oregon. Stub Bartlemay rode the bucking horse "Philippi" near the Bartlemay ranch on the Columbia and big money changed hands on the bets wagered; Monk Carden, a Pendleton resident, was on hand when Bob Askin won a side-bet on the bronc "No-Name" following the show. Tony Vey also had an annual rodeo at his ranch on Butter Creek. Les and Mildred Riley, stock contractors from Central Ferry, Washington, put on a rodeo at their place in Eastern Washington; and Larry and Wanda Hickman, from Colfax, Washington, remembered when they were growing up that all of the neighborhood kids would meet at their place on Sunday when their folks had gone off to church and put on a rodeo; the grown-ups never could explain why the family cow wouldn't give any milk the next day.

Fritz Zuger remembers the first college rodeo held in the Northwest. He was a member of the first Washington State College rodeo team. Bob Chambers' account of a rodeo held at Fort Riley, Kansas with the U.S. Cavalry is another unpublicized chapter in rodeo history; later, Bob served with Merrill's Marauders in the jungles of Burma where G. I.'s put on exhibition rodeos to relieve the boredom, and many in the audience were Japanese soldiers.

Reg Kesler, in the final interview of the book, gives a good glimpse of Canadian rodeo history. Although not one of its early pioneers, as a modern stock contractor and promoter he knows the sport thoroughly and is an articulate spokesman for professional rodeo, both in Canada and the U. S.

Since the interviews depend so heavily on photos for illustration, something should be said about their history. The pictures contained in this book, known as "real-time photos" were taken primarily by three main photographers of the period—W. S. Bowman, who had a studio in Pendleton; Marcell of Portland; and Ralph Doubleday, the most prolific rodeo photographer of his day. It's estimated that Doubleday produced over thirty million postcards during the more than forty years that he followed rodeo. He accomplished the feat with an antiquated seven-by-seven-inch-plate portrait Graflex camera that he carried until he retired due to blindness in 1954.

Ralph Doubleday was a pioneer in rodeo photography, and his name became synonymous with arena action throughout the country. He was considered not only the best in the business, but a publicist for the sport of rodeo that was just taking hold. He became a fixture at Pendleton and covered the Round-Up for many years. He was a friend of my grandfather, Karl "Junk" Walters, a Pacific Coast league baseball player who lived in Pendleton in the 1920s. Doubleday wasn't above playing favorites. Cathy and I were studying the pictures when she spotted a familiar face in the front row of the crowd. It was Karl Walters, smiling big for the camera; and naturally, it was Doubleday taking the picture.

Highlighted is Karl 'Junk' Walters

The original idea behind this book was to furnish some information on the people in the pictures. The pictures covered the era from 1910 to 1929, the year of the great stock market crash; however, the interviews continued beyond that era, and we followed up on them regardless of where they led. We received help from numerous people with pictures; some were loaned to us and others were given to us outright. Eventually, however, the day arrived when we had to call a temporary halt to the interviews and focus on putting the book together. It was a hard thing to do. For several years we had been privileged to associate with a group of people we thoroughly enjoyed and respected. It was like stepping back in time. We realized that the past certainly does have value and should not be easily forgotten.

KING SPAIN

King Spain is the son of Fred Spain and nephew of John Spain, the winner of the 1911 saddle bronc championship at the Pendleton Round-Up. Although John Spain was declared the winner over the Negro cowboy George Fletcher and the legendary Jackson Sundown, a Nez Perce Indian from Cul-de-Sac, Idaho, many in the crowd thought that the local George Fletcher had won. Jackson Sundown, one of the all time favorites at the Round-Up later became the bronc riding champion in 1916.

King has a letter sent to the Spain Brothers in 1909 by the livestock director of the Pendleton Round-Up, Til Taylor asking them to supply bucking horses for the first Round-Up. Fred and John Spain trailed their bucking string 85 miles from Telocaset to Pendleton to be on hand.

———————

Spain Brothers Rodeo Co.
as told by King Spain

When the folks came into this country, they went to the Willamette Valley first. John Spain was born at Cottage Grove, Oregon in 1881. Fred was born before they got there. He was born back East somewhere.

When my dad an' his brother, John were kids they got to see Buffalo Bill Cody's Wild West Show. Boy, that fired those boys up. They wanted to have a Wild West Show of their own. That was great.

Anyway, when they got back here to Eastern Oregon where they were raised, the country was full of wild horses. About all they did was chase them damn wild horses an' catch an' break 'em. They'd sell 'em to the cavalry. Fred and John made a drive in 1902

1

with two other fellas. They made the drive from Malheur to almost the Canadian border. There was a big remount station there. They took 600 head of horses up there for a man named Harlan Stewart. They were old time cowboys, the real article. They either rode or had to walk, an' they didn't like walkin'.

The first rodeo the Spain Brothers ever put on was in 1904, in Sumpter, Oregon. They put it on for the miners. It was a Fourth of July celebration. They didn't have an arena or anything. They just led their buckin' horses up there, the four of 'em, my dad, John and the same two fellas they went to Canada with. They went up there an' rode buckin' horses an' then just passed the hat to the miners for their pay.

That was the year my mother an' dad were married, an' they forgot to tell her they were goin' to be gone for several days. Of course, she was madder than hops when they got back. She was about ready to divorce my dad, I think. Anyway that was their first show. That's pretty early, 1904. They also helped out greatly with the Eastern Oregon Livestock Show at Union an' the Wasco Co. Fair at The Dalles. An' they put on a big rodeo up towards Tacoma, Washington, at Sedro Woolley. I don't know if that's the right name, but they put on a big show for three days and got paid $800, all in $20 gold pieces. They did real well. They hauled everybody up there in boxcars by train.

They had a little light spring wagon with their camp gear an' bedrolls. They went to a lot of shows just leadin' their stock an' haulin' their stuff in the wagon. They made a lot of shows in Oregon, Washington, an' Idaho that way. They didn't have horse trailers an' all that fancy stuff, an' there weren't many fences. That was from around 1904 to about 1915. That was about the span of their rodeo business.

The Spain Brothers put on the first two shows ever at the Wasco Co. Fair at The Dalles, Oregon. That was in 1914. They got awful nice letters from the people, congratulating them on putting on a nice clean show. There wasn't any drinking to speak of, an' they kept everything pretty well in line. They had some of the old timers there. Hoot Gibson was there. Any number of them.

When they put on a rodeo, they just went out an' got an outfit together an' contacted cowboys to get 'em to come. They sent out an' got guys that they knew were good.

They had quite a buckin' string. They had about the first one in the Northwest that I know of. Actually, it was before rodeos,

2

really. They were really wild horse hunters, an' when they got one that bucked real good, they hung onto him.

I have some old letters that are quite interesting. One, from Tillman Taylor, the sheriff from Pendleton who was killed in the jailbreak. It was written in 1909 asking my dad an' John if they would bring some of their buckin' horses over to the first Pendleton Round-Up, which they did. They brought over a relay string, an buckin' horses, an' everything. The letter is quite a nice thing to hang on to.

John an' my dad had the honor of leadin' the first Westward Ho Parade at the Pendleton Round-Up.

In about 1915 or 1916, they were at the Pendleton Round-Up with their horses, relay string, pony express, an' stagecoach team along with their buckin' horses.

Ol' C. B. Irwin came up to my dad an' said: "Fred, you got a pretty good string o' horses, what'll you take for 'em?"

An Dad, just out of his gourd, said $15,000.

The old fella just whipped out his checkbook an' bought 'em out right there.

C. B. Irwin was an interestin' guy. I seen him many times. In later years, they used to present him with a pair of Levi's, bib overalls, at the Round-Up. My God, they was big enough for four men to crawl into. He came right after the Buffalo Bill Wild West Show, actually, an' he put on shows all over the U. S. He was big time. He had a circus outfit, an' he had all the rollin' stock, an' he moved it all by rail. He brought his big ol' tent, cook, cookin' outfit, an' he took care of his crew right there, wherever they was havin' a rodeo. He was quite a friend of Charles Russell an' Will Rogers. He was big time. That little outfit he bought from my dad an' John, that didn't amount to nothin'.

When he bought out the outfit, Dad an' John was put out of the rodeo business, but both of 'em competed for a long time afterward. My dad was still contestin' in 1929 in the bulldoggin' in Oregon City when that show went broke.

The guy that was runnin' the show was the sheriff, an' somehow the money disappeared. Dad had $3000 comin'. He didn't get any of it.

They all lost out. But they had a banquet that was kind of funny an' kind of sad, in a way. They put on a banquet for the cowboys an' their families, an' the fella that was Emcee-in' the thing introduced my dad as the "Granddaddy" of 'em all. Dad got madder than hell. He was well over fifty years old, but he was still bulldoggin' steers. That really ticked my dad off.

Dad had to go to Portland to his sister, Mabel Beauchet, to borrow money to get home on.

John Spain won the Championship of the Northwest Bronc Ridin' in Pendleton in 1911. It wasn't a popular win because George

4

Fletcher, a Negro, an' Jackson Sundown, a Nez Perce Indian, were ridin' against him. "Nigger" George Fletcher was said to have made an awful fine ride, but they didn't give it to him. They wouldn't even give poor "Nigger" George a number to put on. I don't think they were about to do a Negro any favors in those days. They was pretty tough.

Jackson Sundown

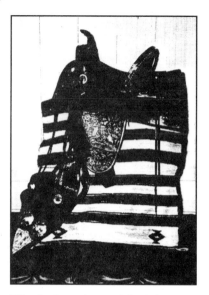

"That's the prize saddle John was presented with in 1911 in Pendleton. My grandson has it located. A fella has it in Kansas. He's trying to get it but isn't havin' much luck. He wants to get it back in the family where it belongs."

John won it that year. That Kesey fella, or whatever that author's name was, wrote a book on the bronc ridin' that year, an' he made a big hullabaloo out of the last-go-'round. Actually, it was the first go-'round. He had John Spain comin' from Tennessee. He'd never been to Tennessee. They was gonna make a motion picture of it. It was to be about John, George Fletcher, an' Jackson Sundown. They was gonna cast John as a very undesirable person. They had him as a racist an' a bigot. But he wasn't. He was a fine man. The worst language he or my dad ever used was 'dod donnit'. He was nothin' like they tried to make him out to be. An' they wanted to cast Willie Nelson as John Spain. I said no! No to the movie. Can you imagine Willie Nelson as John Spain?

John was ridin' the stagecoach once at the Pendleton Round-Up, an' he was hangin' from the side. I don't know who was drivin' the coach, but it upset right on him, on the side that he was on. Everybody in the crowd just gasped, afraid he was killed.

6

He come up on the other side after the dust cleared an' waved his hat at the crowd. He wasn't hurt a bit, but it was a spectacular wreck.

John was big an' stout. He wasn't a pretty rider, but they couldn't buck him off. He was usually in the money on the wild horse race. He'd just snug one of those danged horses an' get on an' make him go wherever he wanted him to go.

John was given the opportunity to go over to England with the Tex Austin Rodeo, but he didn't take it. He went instead with an outfit in a vaudeville deal. I don't know what it was, but they were going in a ship by sea, either from San Francisco to Portland or vice-versa. They got into bad weather an' had to kick a bunch of the livestock overboard. My dad said one big horse followed the ship for miles before he drowned.

They lost John, didn't know where in the world he was. They finally found him down in the engine room. He was down there to get warm. They came near havin' a shipwreck.

He went back to Boston once. He got a girl-friend he met on the vaudeville tour. She was from Boston, from a wealthy family, an' he went back there to see her. He was pretty serious about her, but he could see he was a fish out of water back there. They had a big Southern mansion; they might even of had slaves, probably not. He come home after that. He didn't get involved with her too far.

John was only 47 when he died. That's awful young. He got sick at North Powder where he was living in 1928. I don't know exactly how he got to Hot Lake, near La Grande, but he got there to the hospital late in the evening. He'd lost a lot of blood from bleedin' ulcers. Instead of callin' in a doctor an' gettin' him a blood transfusion, they let him wait till mornin, an' he was dead in the mornin'. It was kinda unnecessary, actually. They could of saved him if they'd given him a transfusion, probably.

Fred Spain wasn't particularly religious, but he was raised with a kind of religious background. He left home when he was 11 years old. He got mad at his dad an' step-mother. Some of the Sprays, his grandparents from Union, kind of watched out for him. The Sprays was his mother's people. He never went home after that.

He was ridin' a horse when his dad caught up with him when he run away from home. His dad started leadin' him back home, an' Dad reached over an' slipped the bridle off his horse. He'd taught his horse to follow his lead with his knees. He slipped away, an' his dad couldn't catch him. They lived in the lower Grande Ronde Valley then.

My dad won the bulldoggin' in Pendleton one year, but he got disqualified because he softened up a steer or two, an' when Roy Raley asked him about it, Dad wouldn't lie to him. He said 'yes,' he'd tapped him a few times; so he was out of it, an' his name wasn't even on the records for the best time on three steers. Those kind of things I always laid to Buffalo Vernon, cause he came up from Texas, an' he's the one that probably bulldogged the first steers around this country. I just laid it to ol' Buff Vernon for tunin' dad in on softenin' up one of those steers a little bit. They gave it to Sam Garrett. He was posted as the winner in that year. He deserved it. I think it was around 1913, along in there.

Yakima Canutt, when he was just a kid, I'd say probably 17 or 18 years old, was real horse crazy. My folks took him to Telocaset to their ranch, an' he stayed all winter an' they helped him become a cowboy. The first rodeo he competed in they called him Enos, an' that wasn't too good a name to stick in a program, so my folks called him Yak, since he was from around Yakima.

Dad was back in Madison Square Garden one time. A restaurant would seat the cowboys all next to the windows so the pedestrians walkin' up an' down the street could see 'em. And that Tex Richards, the big promoter, gave 'em all tickets to the ringside at Madison Square Garden to the Godfrey-Tate fight. Two big Negroes fought. And they got ringside seats to that. Dad never quit talkin' about that. He thought that was wonderful.

There was a group of cowboys who went into the service in World War I from right there in Pendleton. Dad had a letter from Lee Caldwell when he was fightin' in the war in France. He told Dad about hittin' a shell hole just like he was bulldoggin' a steer. Somebody was after him in an airplane. He sent dad a piece of fuselage off a German plane that had been shot down. He sent it to Dad along with the story.

Dad was in the cattle business. He went broke in 1921 or 1922 when the bottom fell out of everything after the war. He lost everything, an' never did get it back.

After that, my dad was ridin' fire patrol an' saltin' cattle for Benson Cattle Co. out of Union, Oregon, an' he was doin' a lot of ridin' every day. Sid Seale would bring over some colts every spring to Dad, an' he would use 'em all summer, an' by the time he got through with his ridin', he had 'em broke. Sid would come an' get 'em. That saved our bacon because times were so darn hard. There wasn't no jobs. Wasn't hardly nothin'. Dad had that little ridin' job, but it didn't pay much.

I can show you a tree up in the Little Catherine Creek area that he carved "Fred Spain, Sept. 1931" in that tree.

I ride up there an' look at it ever once in awhile. It's just as plain... standin' up there on a knob, an' he could see all around. He built a ladder, an' the ladder is still standin' there. Since 1931, mind you. He could get up there an' look all around the country an' see if there was any smoke.

Benson sold out to the Davis Brothers, but that came later. They had a thousand acres of land up there, an' he'd ride across it every day to a certain area an' then come back. I use to ride it with him a lot.

I remember once when I was a kid, I was sittin' in a box stall down at the Round-Up grounds there in Pendleton. The cowboys had a blanket spread out on some straw bales an' a bunch of 'em were playin' poker. Ol' Jesse Stahl, the Negro, was runnin' the game. He kept on reachin' out an' takin' a rake-off from each pot. Funniest thing to me, an' I've always remembered it. One of the cowboys spoke up an' said: "Jesse, you old s.o.b., you take one more drag out of that pot an' I'm gonna black both your eyes." Oh, that was funny. That cowboy figured he was takin' too much drag. Everybody just laughed. It eased a lot of the tension behind the chutes. It did slow him down some on the drag.

"They were the last of the real old time Cowboys."
L - R: Hugh Strickland, Ray Bell, Howard Tegland, Yakima Canutt,
Mike Hastings

DOLLY BOSTWICK

Dolly Bostwick is the great niece of Bert Kelly, winner of the 1910 saddle bronc riding in Pendleton. Dolly and her husband Jim make their home in Pendleton. They shared some of the family history in the form of early newspaper articles and Round-Up programs with us and shed some light on the brief career of a famous Round-Up personality.

Bert Kelly
as told by Dolly Bostwick
Pendleton, Oregon

WINNING THE CHAMPIONSHIP OF THE NORTHWEST, ...G CONTEST. AND THE $250 SADDLE. PRESENTED BY AT THE ROUND UP, PENDLETON Or.

Bert Kelly was raised on the Kelly place down towards College Place, Washington. He won what was called the Northwest Bucking Contest at the first Pendleton Round-Up in 1910.

Bert's brothers were racehorse people, especially Roy, Joe Kelly's father. Joe must be 80 years old now. Joe was a young fella at the time. He could ride. It seemed like Roy always won the races; several cousins rode racehorses too. I wasn't even born when Bert died, so I didn't know much about him, other than what the folks had told me. Bert had worked with the Drumhellers in Walla Walla. They owned racehorses and land near Walla Walla.

There were 8 boys and 2 girls in Bert's family. My mother and aunt could ride just as good as the boys. Grandfather Joseph Kelly was born in Canada, but his family grew up on the same piece of property where Joe Kelly lives today. Grandpa Kelly went to Texas when he was only 16 years old. He was all over Texas and Kansas before he settled down at the old Kelly place in Washington. Bert's father and mother were married in 1883; Washington didn't even become a state until 1889. It was still a Territory back then.

We have an old program of the 1912 Pendleton Round-Up. It was published in "The Daily Live Wire". Bert Kelly came in 8th in the Pony Express race. Boy, he was dragging that day, wasn't he? Lew Minor of Wallowa is in it. There's a picture of the Westward Ho Pageant.

There was an army of cowboys. All the cowboys, the stars and all, used to ride downtown in the parade.

Here's some of the names from the program: Dick McGinnis on Brown Eyes; Lucian Williams on Kirk; Chester Byers lost to a steer; Tex McLeod on Sock Eye; Lewis Mosely on Sunfish Molly; Nacrisse McKay on Smithy; Glen Cox on Brown Eyes; Dick Parker on Annie; G. R. Moss "Pulled leather on Sullivan." Ben Jory was third on Blue Devil in Catch, Saddle and Ride event. Bert Kelly won the Spud Race with 7 spuds. I don't know what a spud race is, but I'm so proud of him.

There was a Slow Mule race. The last mule won $5.00.

The rules in the bronc riding were simple: Each contestant to ride any horse and as often as the judges may deem necessary to determine winner.

They didn't have chutes in those days. They were just tied to snubbing horses, and the cowboys just mounted them from the ground and took off.

Entered in the Cowgirls' relay race were Bertha Blancett, Ella Lazinka, Hazel Walker, Tillie Baldwin, and Miss Auggie.

Our kids get a kick out of dragging this stuff out. They get these clippings out and they probably wore them out more than anybody.

Bert won a saddle in 1910 for the Northwest Bucking contest. We always called it in the family the Silver Saddle or The Saddle. There was a rumor going around for awhile that he sold it.

Bert's bridle with the silver bit was stolen at the last Round-Up from the Hall of Fame. The family was just sick about it.

Bert died at the age of 29 in 1914. He was 25 years old when he won in Pendleton. He died of consumption.

GIRLS RELAY RACE PENDLETON ROUND-UP 1925
(DOUBLEDAY) (10)

JOE KELLY

Joe Kelly lives at the original home ranch near College Place, Washington. Joe is a nephew of Bert Kelly, the saddle bronc champion at the first Pendleton Round-Up in 1910. Several generations of the Kelly family have been involved in rodeo in Eastern Oregon and Washington. Joe Kelly was an early member of the Walla Walla Wagonwheelers and the Pioneer Posse, two riding clubs that dominate the pony express and relay races held each year at the Round-Up.

I was born in 1915 at the Vet's hospital in Walla Walla. The old one burned down, and I was the first person born in the new hospital. They wanted to send me through school, but my folks wouldn't let me. I imagine I would have got a pretty good education out of it.

I used to train horses for several guys in Pendleton, and I run a public stable for 25 years. My uncles, my dad, myself, my kids, and my grandkids have all been part of rodeo, have been, and still are.

When I first started riding at the Pendleton Round-Up, they contracted me. I worked all the events that I could in the racing end of it.

When you take the spurs out of some of them buckin' horses, they could run pretty good. Some of 'em had thoroughbred blood in 'em, especially now. When I was racing, all I done was hang on. The horse knew what he was supposed to do.

I rode for the Walla Walla Wagonwheelers for a long time; and I rode for the Pioneer Posse in the Pendleton Round-Up. When they ran at the State Championship here in Washington, I'd go back to the Walla Walla Wagonwheelers.

I helped start the Walla Walla Wagonwheelers, and I was a leading rider for the Posse. My uncle was the Wagonmaster. He

14

told me: "If I gotta be Wagonmaster, I gotta have somebody I can trust."

So I started the Wagonwheelers. Bill Harter an' Francis Hobson and some of those guys an' myself got together and built the Pioneer Posse. There was a big meeting to make the race rules. I was the only one who knew how to "drag out." When you have relay races, you "drag out." When they started the Posse, they limited the draggin' out. You had to stay in a certain area, a boxed area. The new rule was made against me.

I used to ride against Jim Bloom a lot. We run horses together. I started with quarter horses, and then I switched over to thoroughbreds.

Lots of times I'd be at the Fairgrounds in Walla Walla, and ropers would come in early, and maybe they'd want to drink or do something else, but they had to have their horses worked, so they'd sit there, an' I'd rope calves for 'em off their horses.

Fay Hubbard run horses too. I'll never forget, he had a two horse trailer with no roof on it. He had a piece of iron on the top, kind of a border; it was loose. And believe it or not, one of his wheels flew off, so he took a chain an' tied that one axle up with the chain, an' that's the way he hauled his horses for better than a year. Most of the time they wouldn't quite touch the ground. The heck of it was, when he hauled two horses, this piece of iron that was on the top was loose an' flappin'. It would hit those horses on the back, but he never seemed to have any trouble.

In Spokane, Washington, a little later on, he was runnin' horses, an' somehow or other, he got his horses stabled on Sprague Ave. It was downtown across from a bar. He drank coffee, but he loved to dance. He kept them horses up there on a vacant lot right across from the bar. It was called the "Double Clutch" bar. That was in the '50s.

I knew Bob Crosby. I would come closer to knowin' the ropers than any of them. I was always sittin' down there on the west end in Pendleton where all the ropers an' doggers an steer ropers came out.

I knew King Merritt. He was a steer roper. The same bunch came around about every year. I remember the race rider, the red headed girl, Ella Lazinka.

Dad knew all those guys. He knew Yakima Canutt an' Buffalo Brady, the fancy roper. He knew all those guys, every one of 'em.

My dad knew darn near all of the Indians down there at the Round-Up grounds. He'd go down there when the show started an' he never came home 'till it was over. He'd go stay with the Indians—sleep in the tepees an' have fun.

Dad said one time there was a guy on a buckin' horse that bucked clear across the arena, down past the grandstands, and bucked off. He took off his hat, waved to the crowd, an' fell over dead. That was in Pendleton.

I've always had a lot of fun at the Pendleton Round-Up.

One year they had two or three strings of race horses, an' they didn't have riders for 'em. A contractor called me to come over. He had some nice horses. They was broke sons-a-guns. He said, "My string had to stand in the barn. You gotta get down here tomorrow."

I told him I hadn't picked up a saddle for more than a year and that I was gonna be a little rusty.

He said, "You get down here. You'll be all right."

He beat me that day, an' I beat him the next two days on his own horses.

I remember Lary Daniels. He was pretty happy the last time I saw him. Both of his horses won down there at Sundown race track in Kennewick, Washington. I've known Lary ever since he was a kid. I knew him when he had a bar in Lewiston, Idaho. I won the ropin' there one year.

Lary was good to me, but he could be a nasty little son-of-a-gun, an' he didn't care. He was a funny guy. He'd go out an' whip you or get whipped, an' the next night you'd go out an' drink an' party together. He was just that type. I don't think Lary ever did hold a grudge. He told me one time 'Joe, I fight to win.' He didn't care how, just any way to get it done. I remember one time he broke off a bottle and used it like a curry comb on a guy's face.

Lary ran into a big guy, and I mean BIG—maybe twenty-five years old. I didn't get to see the fight, but I seen Lary the next day. Lary hated smokin'. He just got the crap hammered out of him, an', of course, he wouldn't admit it. The next day he was talkin' to me: "I saw those cigarettes in his pocket, an' I knew sooner or later I'd get to him," he told me.

I'll never forget that. Lary was a good egg.

I remember the time he had two horses down at Kennewick. They both won at Sundown.

I've got news for you. He wasn't too smooth. He'd use a machine on his horses too; in fact, the last two days them horses run, I know at least one of 'em was packin'—a bug, a battery. They absolutely wouldn't run that fast.

Fact is, in Walla Walla one time, a kid jockey dropped one comin' back to the stands from the saddle, an' Lary kicked it clear up to the finish line.

Those were good times.

SAM SEALE

Sam Seale is the son of Sid Seale, one of the original stock contractors for the first Pendleton Round-Up in 1910. Sam lives on the old Seale ranch near Condon, Oregon. Sam's father, Sid, and uncles Art and Walt were early participants in the Round-Up, and in 1969 Sid and Walt were the Grand Marshals of the Westward Ho Parade.

Sid Seale
as told by Sam Seale
Arlington, Oregon

Walt Seale, my dad's brother was contracted to supply horses for the Yukon Expo in Seattle in 1909. Walt wrote to my dad, Sid Seale, who was living in Arizona, and asked him to come back home and help him gather the horses. They were gathering them from the Horse Heaven Hills and around Arlington, Oregon.

They sent the wild horses from Arlington on a train to Seattle. They had to drive 'em through the city of Seattle. The horses were wild, and the only thing they recognized were the horses those guys were on. They followed those horses and didn't have any problems at all.

They had a pavilion where they kept the horses, up near where the University of Washington is now. They had electric lights, something new back then. Somebody walked in, in the middle of the night and turned on the lights, and the horses stampeded. My dad said that was the worst thing that happened. They were gathering horses all over Seattle.

It lasted all summer and into the fall. The guy's name who was putting on the show was Jim Gabriel. We have a group picture, and it has him in it. One of the other guys was Tom Mix.

They drove the horses back to Arlington from Seattle through the Cascades. I remember we were up at Sunnyside, Washington once and my dad said, "This is the place, when we were driving the horses back that one of the horses recognized this spot." They had been through there some time before when they shipped them from Arlington. He recognized the spot, and as soon as he saw it, he knew where he was and just lined out for home at Arlington.

At the age of 14, my dad started cowboyin'. He was around Arlington for a year or so, and then when he was 16 he went down to Burns and got a job at the "P" Ranch. That was quite a few years after Pete French was killed, but Bill Hanley was runnin' it. That was the old Pete French ranch. Mike Hanley, from over in Jordan Valley, was his grandson or great grandson.

My dad was down there for awhile, and then he went to work down in Nevada. I think he was on a ranch in Arizona when Walt wrote to him in 1909 to come up and help with the horses for the show in Seattle.

After he came back up here to Arlington, he returned to the ranch in Condon. He would go down to Harney County and help with the roundup in the fall. He'd ride horseback from here down there. That was quite a ride.

I was in the army, stationed in Germany, and I got acquainted with this guy from California, who was kind of interested in horses. He asked me if I ever heard of a guy named Charlie Couch. I never knew him, but I wrote home and asked my dad, and he knew him well. He was from the Burns country. He was a foreman for Bill Brown, who raised a lot of horses.

I've got a picture of my dad. A good picture of him and Maime Saunders, a Roman Rider. One up at Spokane, Washington, and then we've got a group picture with Art Seale at Nell, British Columbia. There's a bunch of cowboys lined up: Art Acord, Del and Bertha Blancett, and some others. Polly Helmes looked at it and said that it was kind of a who's who of early rodeo.

The Electric Power Company, a Co-Op in the Columbia Basin has a magazine they call "Rural Life." About 1970 they came out here and interviewed my dad, and they had a picture with the article about him along with some of the old pictures.

They used to have little rodeos here at the ranch. Local guys used to come out and find out how good, as riders they were. A few people came out to watch.

My dad kind of got involved in his business. I don't remember going to the Round-Up as a kid. My dad was pretty busy. I do remember that he went up in 1960. They had the 50-year reunion of the Pendleton Round-Up, and he went to that.

In 1969, he and Walt, his brother, were the Grand Marshals of the Westward Ho Parade.

JOE CANNON

Joe Cannon is the son of Darrell Cannon, the all-around champion at Pendleton in 1921. Joe is a veterinarian in Bonsall, California. During a succinct phone conversation of less than half-an-hour, Joe Cannon outlined some of the highlights of his memories of his father.

**Darrell Cannon
as told by Joe Cannon
Bonsall, California**

Dad was born in Heppner, Oregon. There's a little museum there. I scattered my dad's ashes back up on the mountainside there, and I stopped in at the museum. There's a bit there about the family, not a lot. I was planning that when I went through all of his stuff that I'd donate it to the museum because I like it and I've got a lot of interest in it; so I thought that it was as good a place as any for it.

My dad went to local rodeos. He had a saddle he won at Dayton, Washington, but nothing out of that area—Central Washington and Oregon.

He told me about being in the Pendleton Round-Up. He was entered in the Wild Horse race, and his team went out and spooked 'em and picked out the lead mare, and, sure enough, they go in and rope her and throw the saddle on her, and once around the arena they go. She didn't buck a jump; she just ran. Well, comes the second day and some of the other competitors were onto him, and, as the story goes, my dad's mugger got the rope on this mare, and he had to fight some other people off to keep them from getting this mare. My dad's mugger won, and they got the saddle on her and around they went again, and they won the whole thing.

He told a lot of stories about swimming horses across the Snake River. They had to go a bit east to accomplish that. It was all of that Eastern Oregon and Washington area. The main property was in Walla Walla, and they had a lot of wheat farming there. I remember him telling about the 30-40 head of horses pulling the equipment to harvest. Their operations ranged pretty wide.

They would round up wild horses every spring. They would keep those 5 years old and older and break them. But I remember him talking about swimming the horses across the Snake River. That was a big event. The Snake was a free flowing river in those days, and no matter what time of year, or what spot you picked, it was quite an adventure.

Another story that comes to mind...he was a relay rider for the Drumhellers in Walla Walla. He only weighed around 125 pounds at the most, and all the horses were thoroughbreds. One year he was undefeated, and he held a world's record. I can't remember what it was. It was a really popular event in those days, relay races, and they had both men and women riders. Here was this little kid with no beard at all; so, they dressed him up as a woman, and he raced as a woman. He wore a long skirt and boots. It was entertainment. It was circus.

One old photo...one of my favorite pictures was when my dad was 14. That would be 1911. He was riding exhibitions at those rodeos. This kid was getting paid a hundred dollars a day for riding

broncs. He was billed as the 12-year-old wonder. Of course, he was really 14.

One picture I have shows him wearing angora chaps. The wool on those chaps is almost as long as his legs. He's got this horse with all four feet off the ground. He's got his hat in his hand, and he's riding the hide off this bronc, and he's waving at the crowd...at 14.

He won the bronc riding in Pendleton in 1921. I have nothing to substantiate any of this, but the stories that he told me; but he wasn't the kind of person who would make up something like that. He loved a good story, but I don't think that he'd stretch it. He was little and as tough as nails. Somehow he got onto the rodeo circuit at 14. That's when he left home and started making the hundred dollars a day riding broncs.

I asked him what he did with all that money, the hundred dollars a day, when I was a teenager, but he never would answer me. He was a unique person, and it was certainly a different world then.

LYLE MOSS

Lyle Moss is 91 years old. He worked for 15 years with the Forest Service, and later spent 30 years with Farmer's Insurance in Lakeview, Oregon. Lyle is related to Roy Moss, early steer roping champion at Pendleton.

Roy Moss
as told by Lyle Moss
Sweet Home, Oregon

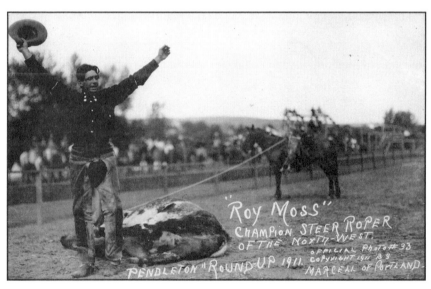

Roy Moss come down here and lived about a year. He got in with my kid brother. They had a pack string that they used for various people. We lived in Sisters, Oregon. They had five or six pack horses, and they kept 'em busy. I was still on the old Moss home ranch. I stayed with my dad on that. My kid brother went on this other spree with Roy Moss. Sweet Home was the site of the old home ranch. Just out of town there.

Roy Moss worked in the movies quite a lot. He was a stunt rider. And he won the world championship bronc riding one year. He was noted for riding a buckin' horse with one foot out of the stirrup.

He was in Hollywood and worked in the movies for several years. I got the names of the movies he was in around somewhere. Anyway, he was with this rodeo outfit and made some pictures. He was the star rider.

He was kind of a loner. He didn't mix much with other cowboys, but he outrode all of 'em. He was just a small guy, about 140 pounds.

The Mosses were quite prominent people, original ranchers in this part of the country. McCagy Moss was the father of Roy Moss. Roy was married a couple of times. He brought his second wife over to Lakeview and camped a day or two when he was on his honeymoon. He was quite a wild guy, that Roy.

They camped with the other Mosses for awhile. We killed 'em a deer. I think I killed it. We got deer for most of them people. In fact, I've killed more deer than a lot of people have seen; but nobody kept track of all that stuff.

Everybody is trying for information on the Mosses. I didn't record it. It was just tales that we had in our minds. Roy Moss followed a lot of those rodeos. And he was quite a character. In fact, he might have been running from the law a time or two.

He wore a six-shooter. He was a guy who wore one 'a them an' used it when needed.

Could he make you laugh? Well, not laugh so much as you cried. People didn't run over Roy Moss any. He took care.

25

RICK STEBER

Rick Steber has written more than twenty books. He re-sides near Prineville, Oregon, with his wife Kristi and sons Seneca and Dusty. "Wild Horse Rider", his biography of Lew Minor, the 1912 winner of the saddle bronc riding at the Pendleton Round-Up is quoted along with Rick's interview.

———————————————

"Ladies and Gentlemen! The Kit Carson Wild West Show has the distinct pleasure of presenting to you, Windmill, the finest bucking horse on the face of the earth. Each town we visit we make the same proposition—fifty dollars to any man who can ride Windmill. Before today no man has collected. Perhaps we have a gentleman in the audience who thinks he can ride this horse. If so, let him step forward."

Heads turned and eyes looked at Lew but he stayed where he was, draped nonchalantly in his place.

"Come now. Fifty dollars. There must be one individual who feels man enough to give it a go. Any takers?"

Lew stalled, people were almost to the point of calling his name before he finally accepted the challenge and casually descended the bleachers and hopped over the railing. As his heels struck the dirt the crowd cheered. Many had seen him buck McDonald's horses down Main Street and stories of some of his most memorable rides in Nevada had found their way up and circulated.

"We do have a contestant." The announcer asked Lew off to the side, "What's your name?"

"Lew Minor."

"This brave young man is Lew Minor." The applause swelled. "Let's give him a great big hand." It swelled more. He spoke to Lew again. "You're from around here I guess."

"Wallowa."

From Pendleton to Calgary

"Ladies and Gentlemen, from right here in Wallowa your own Lew Minor. Say, Lew, is your life insurance paid up? Just joking, just joking. Boys, help him up."

Windmill generally lost his rider with a twisting spin, either left or right, and a reverse counter-spin. Lew kept a low center of gravity and knew from experience what Windmill was going to do even before the horse did. The contest was not won on brute strength but on quickness and balance.

"Sir, that was sensational, an eye-popping ride," gushed the announcer who also was show manager. "I would like to offer you employment with the Kit Carson Wild West Show. You would tour with us, be our star attraction."

Lew took the fifty dollars and put it in his pocket. And just that quickly made up his mind.

The crowd greeted the announcement, "The Kit Carson Wild West Show is proud to announce its latest star, Lew Minor," with a rousing cheer of, "Lew! Lew! Lew!"

... from Wild Horse Rider, by Rick Steber.

When I was living up in Northeastern Oregon, people would always tell me Lew Minor stories, stories about this cowboy and how great of a rider he was back in the early days, and I went up to talk to him. It was a real hot July day. I went up to his place, and I'd heard all these stories about this cowboy that won the World's Championship. The thing that set him apart from a lot of guys was that he was this big, tall, rangy guy, and when he spurred a horse, he really spurred him. He had a lot of power to him. He had this length to his body where most cowboys didn't.

In my mind, that's who I saw, this nineteen year old kid out there that could really ride broncs. When I went up to his place, he lived out of Wallowa on Promise Road, I went to his place on a hot July day and out came this old man. He was in his late 80s, and he was all broken up. I told him I wanted to hear some of the old stories about his life. He took me over behind this log barn in the shade, and we sat on a bale of hay, right next to each other. We leaned up against the cool of those logs, and he started telling me these stories—young buck stories about when he was in his prime. He made those stories come alive; once you understood the rhythm, once you understood the words, then it all flowed together. But it was such a contradiction—the young buck and the old man.

Then, right at that point, and I usually don't do it that way, I knew that I had to tell that story.

And then how to tell the story was another thing. I interviewed him over a seven-year period, and during that period he killed his last elk. He was really proud of it. He went out and killed that elk, and it damned near killed him. He gradually went downhill. Every time I would go up there, and I went as often as I could, I was always expecting that I was going to be the one who found him dead. The only other one that came around there was Jiggs Silvers, from Martin. He'd go up there and more or less look after him.

One time I went out there, and it was a cold day. A storm was blowing, and it was snowing. I got there, and the front door of the cabin was open. I hollered, and there wasn't any answer. I walked in, and the house was cold. I went into the bedroom and checked on the other side of the bed, and he wasn't there. They tell me that most people die in the bathroom. I hated to go into the bathroom, but I finally went in, and he wasn't there either. He must have gone down outside somewhere, I thought, and I found him out there by the cabin.

He'd sold his cattle off, one at a time, and he'd had to kill his last horse. He had this little flock of chickens left, and he'd go out and sprinkle grain for them. He didn't have a coat on, and he had a light shirt, and it was partway open. He was just kind of losing it.

They finally put him in the hospital, but he didn't last very long. The thing he kept saying was, "I don't know why I'm still alive. All my friends are dead."

Other times he'd say, "Ah, she's a great life, she is. I was born in a little log cabin here in the Wallowa valley. When I was a boy, there wasn't no railroads; there wasn't no cars. I've lived a different kind of life. I was lucky. I've broke horses, I've rode rodeos and street carnivals, and now everything's changed where it just don't seem possible. When I'm dead and gone, it'll be just like I was never here at all."

I told him that a little part of him would remain in the book. A lot of people really like that book, "Wild Horse Rider."

Another thing that I thought was interesting about Lew was that here he was, the very best in the world on that particular day, or during that particular era, and it was right when the automobile was taking over, and here he was, the very best at something at a time when the eras were changing.

MILDRED MILEY

Mildred Miley was a princess on the 1930 Pendleton Round-Up Court. She is 85 years old and is taking a computer class at Walla Walla Community College. She is active in civic affairs in her home town of Athena, Oregon.

If it depended on the locals, there probably wouldn't have been much of a rodeo in the beginning. There were a lot of people from Nevada, Arizona, and places like that.

I remember that we didn't have cars back then. We used to take Daddy's. We had an old truck. Stafford and I went to the Round-Up together. Father wouldn't have let me go if it weren't for my brother.

You could usually tell who my father was by the way he slanted his hat.

Pendleton was a little clique then, and probably still is today.

I remember old Fox Hastings. She was two axe handles wide in the rear-end. She had a pet steer with knobs on the horns.

We all had our favorites, but I'd have to see the names to remember who they were. Nobody had any money. First the Depression, then the War.

In the 1920s the arena was beautiful. There were red and green shirts everywhere—blue and yellow silk with hand painted bucking horses on the back. Then all of a sudden they started wearing white shirts. White shirts marked the new era for me. It was nice, but not as colorful. Henry Collins from Pendleton was President of the Round-Up. Anyway, it was a wonderful collection of shirts.

I was on the Round-Up court in 1930. We got to go to La Grande and stayed at the Sacajewea hotel. Then we went to Baker and made an appearance at the American Legion convention. We didn't go to the Rose Parade in Portland. That year the Queen was Lois McEntire.

29

The princesses, besides myself, were Annabel Varga, Virginia Sturgis and Annabel Tullock. We were the first ones to ride into the arena, but we didn't have to jump the fence. Back then only the Queen rode in front of the stands. I remember that Lois rode a palomino horse.

We were given white satin shirts with black trim. We borrowed our boots and hats and had to give them back right after the photo session.

HAROLD HARTLE

Harold Hartle is a lifelong resident of the Pendleton area, and has very clear memories of the early days of the Round-Up. Harold lived and worked on ranches all of his life and still drove Cat while in his 70s.

My first Round-Up was in 1914. I was seven years old. In those days they didn't have announcing. They had a pole in front of the grandstand, maybe 15 feet high, with a crow's nest on top of that, and they announced everything through a horn.

I went with my folks. In those days, I was a country boy and didn't know much about the town. I was going to school at that time in Holdman, several miles north of Pendleton. I was born in Helix in 1907.

Dad farmed in Juniper Canyon. When I was old enough to go to school, we moved to Holdman. I went the first three years of my schooling there, and then World War I started April 6, 1917. We moved to Pendleton that spring, and from then on I got to see all the Round-Ups. I saw my first one in 1914, and I saw at least one show until we got to town, and then I saw more of them. In later years I got to go to all four days of the Round-Up.

I never did work for the Round-Up, but I worked with the Westward Ho Parade for more than 20 years. I remember Ben Jory and his oxen when they were in the Parade. I remember when Charles Tullis started with the 12 mule team; later on, I think it was in 1937, he had trouble with his combine driver, so he canned him, sold his mules and bought a Cat. After that, his freight team was gone from the parade.

But the Round-Up got another freight team organized. Jim Hill drove it first; later, Hank Arkel was the driver of the mule team.

My dad had mules. I drove combine with from 21 head to 33 head on combine and 12 head on a plow. I hauled wheat with 8 head. I knew mules! A lot of people had 10 to 12, but my dad had 8 head on hauling teams; but we ran four, eight-head teams; that would be 32 head, and two wagons with each team.

They were needing a driver for that freight team with the Round-Up. Ray Schuning was the director at the time, and he knew I had worked with mules all my life. So, he told the board of directors that I could handle that freight team, but he was the only one who thought so. I didn't get the job. I could have driven the team.

You get to know the team, and the team has got to know you. That's when Louis Umbarger was keeping them at his place. All I had to do was go out to Umbargers' and work with the team a week or so before Round-Up.

I remember Lee Caldwell, Jackson Sundown, "Nigger" George Fletcher. Yakima Canutt went on to the movies and was a director. He became quite famous. Tommy Grimes was a roper; Bob Crosby was a great roper. He roped steers and calves. He won the championship here in Pendleton several times. He wasn't a fancy dresser. He wore an old floppy hat and work clothes, but he was a great roper. I've got pictures of Hugh Strickland and Yakima Canutt taken back in the 1920s. Montie Montana was a trick roper.

Ray McCarroll was a bulldogger, and so was Frank McCarroll. Frank's wife, Bonnie McCarroll was killed in the bucking contest on the first day of the 1929 Round-Up. I didn't see that myself. In those days the women rode with their stirrups tied underneath the horse so they stayed put. Maybe that had something to do with it.

Another woman, Mabel Strickland was quite a rider. I knew her when she was just a teenager. She grew up on the Walla Walla River between Wallula and Lowden, Washington. Dad had some mules down there in a pasture belonging to John Douglas. When it came time to round 'em up, Mabel had a little pony from the Douglas' livery stable, and she went out and helped Dad round up those mules. During the Round-Up here in Pendleton, Mabel was riding relay races. Her name was DeLong then. Whenever she would come around the track my dad would stand up and yell "Come on Mabel!."

My dad, Bill Hartle, farmed with mules. Like my dad, a lot of farmers didn't have pasture, so when they didn't need the mules, they would turn them out into John Douglas' pasture.

From Pendleton to Calgary

I think Mabel grew up in Lowden. That's where Hugh Strickland came from, and I think that's where they got together and got married. Hugh Strickland was a great roper and bronc rider.

Mabel also did some exhibition roping. I saw her. Fox Hastings bulldogged. There's some stories that those two competed, but I don't know that for sure. Mabel, Lorena Trickey, Kittie Canutt, and Vera McGinnis were all relay riders.

Ella Lazinka...I didn't get to see her ride, but I knew her personally. I saw her a time or two and talked with her. They had a ranch in the Ukiah area. When she got old enough to go to school, her folks moved to town. They had their home on Emigrant across from the Methodist church.

When she got hurt in one of the first relay races held here at the Round-Up, the arena had a wooden fence, and she was entered in a relay race. Her horse crowded that fence, and a 2 X 4 was on top; a sliver in that 2 X 4 caught her on the leg and ripped her leg pretty bad. She was laid up for quite awhile. Her mother stopped her racing after that. She was never allowed to race again.

In those days, there was an old expression: "Bite 'em on the lip!"

When the bulldogger downed his steer, he had to keep that steer down and then throw his hands up in the air. The way they kept their steer down was to get ahold of their lip with your teeth and bear down. I saw that happen right in front of me. I remember when the guy got through, he climbed over the fence and spit real good. In bulldogging, the steers came out just about where they

33

do now. They had a barricade set up so when they came out, they took off right down the track. They didn't hardly ever catch them until they got in front of the grandstands where most of the people were. There weren't any seats on the north side of the Round-Up grounds back then. Believe me, those steers were big!

George Fletcher grew up here. The Indians helped him a lot. He lived with the Indians. He got to be quite a bronc rider. They never would allow George Fletcher to win because he was colored. They tell the story that one night someone grabbed George's hat off his head, and they took it and cut it into little bitty pieces and sold it to everybody who'd buy it, and they gave the money to George. I saw him ride. He was what they called a sloppy rider. He made those horses look tough. But he was always still on the horse when they blew the whistle.

In those days, they picked the judges from whomever they wanted. I remember one year that Lee Caldwell won the championship in the bronc riding. They didn't want a local boy to win, so he had to ride three horses in the same day before they'd give it to him.

I saw a guy get burned to death in the arena one year. It happened right in front of me. Not many people know about that. There's only one guy besides me who knows about it, who actually saw it happen. I'm not sure of the year, but it was either 1917 or 1918 that it happened. Now, in those days the trick riders and fancy ropers filled in between acts in front of the grandstands. This guy had an act that he claimed he'd done before. I didn't see him pour the gas on himself, but when I first saw him, we were sitting on the east turn on the east side of the grandstands. When I first saw him, him and the horse was both on fire.

The idea was that when he passed the grandstand, the fire would be blowing back, and by the time he reached the other end, the fire would be out.

Well, it didn't do that. When I first saw him, he was on fire and the horse was on fire and spinning around. He got excited and didn't run straight.

Like any guy that's burning, he jumped off the horse and started running straight down the track. There was two fellas sitting on the arena fence. They jumped off and grabbed him as he came running by; they threw him on the ground, and they rolled him around, trying to put the fire out. But he got away and started down the track again, and when he came by us they were still trying to catch him. He finally went down, and he never got up. He was gone.

I think he inhaled the flames. About that time somebody noticed the horse. Its mane and tail were on fire. Somebody yelled to get the fire out, and someone rushed up and put it out.

What I think the rider done was that he put the gas on himself, but he estimated wrong, and when he lit it, that excited the horse and he just stood there and didn't run. It all flared up. A guy by the name of Chet Victor was the only other man alive who saw it happen that I know of. His brother-in-law was one of the men sitting on the fence.

They used to have a standing race here in Pendleton, but it was discontinued a long time ago. You drove two horses like a team, and they was buckled together so they wouldn't spread out. As the race started, the rider was on the left horse; when they got going, the rider crawled up and stood with one foot on each horse's back.

Hoot Gibson was from down around Echo somewhere. When he came up here for the first time to the Round-Up, he had to borrow the money for entrance fees, and he wound up being the all-around Champion.

Hoot Gibson was one of the earliest performers. I never got to see him because he was a little before my time, but he came back to Pendleton again in the '20s, and they made a movie with him in it here. Part of the movie was a chariot race.

Ben Swaggert raised race horses back then. They called them Creamolines. Now they call them Palominos. Hoot Gibson had four head of these creamoline horses, and they ran a race in the movie. Hoot had the inside lane in the race. Another guy had a team of bay horses, I think. They were coming around the track with a car, with the top down in front of them, with a camera that was taking in the action. When they went by me, the guy on the outside was having a heck of a time holding that bay team back. He was going to beat Hoot, and Hoot had to win the race. Everybody was hollering, afraid Hoot wasn't going to win it; of course, the other guy held out, and he won.

In another movie, Hoot was to ride in the bucking contest at the Round-Up. Somebody had kidnapped him, and he was tied up in a cabin. The cabin was at the head of the old Lee Street Bridge, which is 8th Street now. It was on top of the hill, and he was supposed to be tied up in the cabin.

He got away and came running down the hill. There was an Indian standing there they called Chief Tall Pine. Glen Bushie was his real name. He was supposed to be an Indian. He had feathers on him. The Indian had a car parked right there at the Lee Street Bridge, and here comes Hoot, running down the street. He jumps into that car and takes off, leaving the Indian standing there. Now he's headed for the Round-Up grounds to be in the bucking contest!

It shows him driving down the street. It shows him driving down different streets, but he crosses that Lee Street Bridge three times. They tried to make Pendleton look like a big town.

He got to the Round-Up and rode in the bucking contest. But he never really rode in the contest. Another boy who lived up the river, part Indian, did the riding. The movie company hired him to ride the bucking horse. They paid him $25.00 for every horse that he'd climb on. He boasted around town that he had a good job working for the movies. Later, it showed Hoot on a horse, but it wasn't no bucking horse.

Hoot came back to Pendleton in later years. He was the Grand Marshal of the parade one year. I think he made something like 150 movies. I remember in my early days of going to the movies that Hoot Gibson was the one you wanted to see. I never saw him in the Round-Up, only in those pictures. I was still in school at the time.

BILL SHAW

Bill Shaw is a local rancher in the Pendleton area and served as Round-Up Director of Hay & Barns from 12/1/70-12/5/72; and Publicity from 12/5/72 until 12/5/78. Bill invited us out to his ranch to talk over his years as director at the Round-Up.

"This is my place," Bill said, referring to the bunkhouse located behind his home. "This is my home-away-from-home. I fixed up the bunkhouse strictly for myself." Pictures adorn the walls, mostly of himself with Montie Montana and a few old friends. Bill had a special friendship with Montie Montana over the years. Even though Bill is no longer directly connected with the Round-Up, his younger brother Jack has taken over as a director, and continues with the family tradition of lending a hand at Round-Up time.

Montie Montana...I got him into the Hall of Fame, and I got him to be the Grand Marshal of the Westward Ho Parade here in Pendleton. You know why he wants to come back to Pendleton? It's nostalgia. He's homesick. I was talking to him a year or so ago, and he said: "You gonna get me back there and have me as Grand Marshal again?"

I said, "We already got one picked."

Montie said, "Well, get rid of him, and I'll do it again."

Montie scares these guys. They want to spend it all on themselves and parties and everything.

I did the horse and bank-robber, that was my act in Happy Canyon. Montie always said if we could get a bunch of Indians and that act at Happy Canyon back to Madison Square Garden, we'd never come home again. He thought that was a great act.

Montie Montana (back), Monk Carden (left), Bill Shaw (right)

Montie was just like a door handle, everybody knew him. If you didn't know him, you were a stranger. He married Marilee in 1981. Boy, she's a knockout! She was a trick rider. They live in Agua Dulce, California, Palmdale, out of Edwards Air Force base. He's got his home in the high desert. It sits on a bluff, and the road runs around the house. We drove up there one Sunday, and Marilee had dinner ready. Then Montie said, "Well, let's take a little drive."

Pretty quick we heard the sound of horse hooves and a "Whoa! Come here, get over there!"

I went out there, and there was four spotted horses. Governor and Senator were the wheelers, and I forget what he called the leaders.

The women got into the stagecoach, and I got up with Montie. "Hay!" he yelled, and away we went, downtown Agua Dulce.

People honked their car horns and waved; they'd back into driveways and let him go on by.

"You pack a lot of weight around here," I said.

"This is my town," he said. "They even have Montana Drive."

Anyway, we went along there, and he handed me the reins and told me to drive awhile. "I want to see how tough you are," he said.

"I didn't come in on the last load of turnips," I told him.

"You know how to get through the gate?" he asked me as we arrived back at his place.

"Why don't you get in back with the women!" I said to him.

"Get over Governor!" I yelled, and he started pulling. They just went way over to the side, like that, and all of a sudden they fumigated, and there was just enough clearance on each side.

"You drove a team before, haven't ya?" he said.

"Yeah, I've driven a team before," I said.

We just had more fun. He's just an idol to me. I think he's the greatest thing in the world.

I was on the Round-Up Board for eight years. Yes, sir, it was the best eight years of my life. I served under four Presidents—Bob Hale, Glen Thorne, Frank Tubbs, and Jiggs Fisk. They were the four greatest I ever knew, and I knew a lot of them. I've been around there about sixty years, counting everything; everybody worked together. LaRoy Thurman would say, "I think I'll have a work day on Saturday," and you wouldn't have to send out invitations or anything. On Saturday there would be fifty guys there, ready to go to work. I'd have all the fun in the wagon, and I'd have all the sandwiches made. That was my job.

For two years I was with Hay & Barn and then with Publicity. That was 1970-71. The rest of the time I was the PR man. I had to drink all that whiskey and tell all those lies. They was pouring it faster than I could drink it, but you never wanted to make that statement.

When I got off the Board, I told Don Hawkins, "I want you to do one thing. Every time the phone rings, every time you do anything for the Round-Up, write it down; and then, after you get off the Board, get a ghost writer, or whatever they are...that sounds like a good name—get it all together, and you'll have one of the best books ever."

I remember I got acquainted with Larry Jordan, who was the head of Hoofs and Horns. He said he figured that maybe 15% of the people who came to the Round-Up just came to watch the Round Up; 35% came to see the Indians; 35% came just to get away from home; and 15% came to town to drink. Maybe the percentages aren't exactly right, but there it is. I got people who got up and walked out on the Indians. I got people you couldn't pry out of there; some didn't even watch the show, they just came to watch the Indians.

You can't imagine some of the things that happened. They would almost stop the world.

I'm 72, and Bud Jory was a little older. Bud was born in 1915, and I was born in 1925. Arvene Porter, Vern Terjeson, Delmer Wyatt and a bunch of us went to Halfway, Oregon. They had race horses and calf ropers. J. L. Bartlett pulled his pants up and stuck his boots inside and put his cap on backwards, and he'd be a jockey. It was a homemade deal. We had more fun than a barrel of monkeys. Bud Jory was pretty good with a rope. I was good when I was 22, but from then on...but we had more fun. They'd fight right there on Main Street. It was a tough town.

I get lonesome for old Peanuts Pozegar. I had to go up to Peanuts' house every New Year's morning at 7:30 and have coffee and toast, and we'd sit and watch the Rose Parade. Montie Montana would come on and wave, and Peanuts would say, "Look at that, he's a wavin' at us!" Old Peanuts passed on.

When he was seven years old, Peanuts would be on his unicycle, riding up and down the main streets of Pendleton, yelling, "The Round-Up's comin' to town!"

MONTIE MONTANA

Montie Montana is synonymous with the Pendleton Round-Up. He began his career in trick roping as a fuzz faced kid by the name of Montie Mickel and became one of the most famous personalities in the rodeo world and one of the most photographed figures in the entertainment world. Bill Shaw, his long time friend, also interviewed in this book, says that if you didn't know Montie, you didn't know rodeo. We talked to Montie by phone at his home in Agua Dulce, California, in 1997.

Montie Mickel at 12 years old.

I knew a lot of contestants and worked with them at a lot of the shows—Chester Byers, Buff Brady Sr.; his son works in the movies and lives in the San Fernando Valley; Bonnie Grey, Hugh and Mabel Strickland, Paddy Ryan, Yakima Canutt, and Pinky Gist were some others.

I knew a whole bunch of the cowgirls: McGinnis, Fox Hastings. And an Indian boy by the name of Bobby Burke. He was a trick roper.

I went to Walla Walla, Washington one time and did a show at the State Pen, and, you know, there was more cowboys there than anyone else.

I first met Ben Jory at Gresham at the Fair and Rodeo in 1927. Ben furnished the rodeo stock. He was very nice to me and told me if I came to Pendleton, he would try and get me a job. When I arrived there, he told me to be at the Round-Up track at 6:00 a.m., and he would introduce me to Mr. Collins, the President, and be sure to bring my ropes, which I did.

I did a little roping, and Mr. Collins said, "Kid, you're okay. I'll give you $25.00 a day to work the show."

Ben had a lot of rodeo stock. I knew him well, and he was sure a nice fella. He helped me get a lot of jobs. When I saw him the last time, it was in the '40s. He furnished bucking horses at Gresham and Salem and a lot of different fairs around the country. In later years Ben had a couple of teams of oxen that he drove in the Westward Ho Parade and Happy Canyon.

If you get a chance to talk to that president of the Round-Up, or the one that runs Happy Canyon, tell them that they're missing a bet if they don't get me back to perform there at the Round-Up.

I guess I have worked there for 40 or so years since 1927, also roped at Happy Canyon many times.

I have a real good friend in Pendleton. His name is Bill Shaw. He told me that they had my display in the back room at the Hall of Fame. They just stored it somewhere, so he was gonna get it back out and put it on display.

They're putting a star in the sidewalk at Palm Springs for me on Saturday. I'm gonna fly down to it.

42

MONK CARDEN

*Monk Carden professes to be the oldest rodeo clown in
the business, and there's no-one around to dispute his claim.
Monk is a living institution at the Pendleton Round-Up. When
we began interviewing people, Monk was at the head of the
list. Jack Sweek, director of the Hall of Fame invited us down
for a visit and arranged for Monk to meet us there. For more
than two hours, Monk made the arena outside come alive.
Monk's family were pioneers to the Pendleton area.*

When I was in high school, the football team had to appoint a
yell leader, so they appointed George Moens. I was a grade or two
ahead of him. He came to me and says, "I'm the yell leader. What
am I supposed to do?"

I said, "Have somebody toss you in the air and turn flips like
they lead yells in college."

He said, "Will you come down to the gym and toss me?"

I said sure. I threw him up in the air, and he came down and lit
on his back. He lit every which way, and he kept it up until he
turned a flip. So, I kind of liked this little guy for his nerve, so we
fooled around until we worked up an acrobatic act. We put it on at
halftime at the basketball game, and I went to throw him in the air,
and his knee caught under my chin, and I went back and grabbed
my chin, and he lit on my back. The crowd laughed, and we thought,
well, that's it. We'll do comedy.

So we worked up a burlesque wrestling act, and it was pretty
good. We fought for 20 minutes, just bang, bang, bang. He'd jump
up and straddle my neck and start pounding me on the head, setting back there. I had some teeth out, and he'd get his finger down
in there, and it looked just like I was biting down on his finger.
He'd get off, just like those wrestlers, and there he was, going like

this, then he'd get ahold of my nose, and I'd hit his hand, and he'd go flat on his face. He'd get up and kick me in the shins. Then I'd grab my shins, and he'd get up and kick me in the butt. I'd go on my face. Then he'd take a run to kick when I'd start to get up, and I'd straighten up, and he'd miss and go up in the air and land on my back. We'd get tangled up, and I'd get ahold of my own foot, and he'd lay back and suffer. Pretty soon we pulled loose and here he was, lying there, and I'd have ahold of my own foot.

Well, we put that on as a preliminary at a professional wrestling match. The wrestlers did some of those things, acting like they were suffering, and the crowd laughed. The promoter, Les Gibbs was going to put us on as a main event. He called it a "Return Grudge Match."

Another wrestling promoter by the name of Elton from Walla Walla was going to take us all around the country. We thought we had it made. But the wrestlers said they wouldn't appear at any show that we were on, and they outlawed us. We tried it once at a boxing match, and it didn't go over so good. So that was about the end of our career until Henry Collins saw George Moens on the street and says, "Hey, Tommy Douglas, the clown for the Round-Up wired us that he broke his leg. Get your partner and come on down and clown the Round-Up."

When Moens told me about it, I said, "You are, I'm not. I've been on a saddle horse once in my life, and then the saddle turned."

He said, "I told him we'd be there." So that's how we got started.

We clowned for about ten years. We went from 1929 to 1938.

We clowned other rodeos around this country, but rodeo clowning was different than now. Our instructions were, if there was a delay in the show, do something to keep the crowd entertained until they could get it going again. They didn't stop the show for a specialty act or anything like that. So, that's what we had to do.

We went to Ellensburg, and they had so many delays that we ran out of acts before the show was half over. We had to ad lib a little.

But we had a lot of experiences and had a lot of fun. We went to Ellensburg, the Tacoma Legion Show, Union Stock Show, Heppner, and down here in Pendleton for five years straight. Maybe

I shouldn't give the reasons why we didn't keep on clowning here, but I'll just tell you what really happened.

The first year we didn't have any idea what we were getting paid. We got a check for $150.00. Seventy-five dollars apiece. We thought that was better than working in harvest. We got that for four years. We had a letter-head with our pictures on it. It said, "Address all inquiries in care of the Pendleton Round-Up." They had us put that on it. "That will help you get jobs," they said.

For four years we got $150.00. The fifth year, the director in charge of clowns, Doc Hanavan, came up to us and said, "We're running short of money, we're in the hole. We want you to work for $80.00."

We said, "Well, okay, but if you have a bigger crowd than you had last year, you'll give us a hundred and fifty."

When we were working for eighty dollars, that was ten dollars an afternoon apiece. We were getting fifteen dollars a night at Happy Canyon. Moens was riding the bucking Shetland with the firecrackers on his tail, and they were lassoing me and dragging me out. We were making better money at Happy Canyon. Anyway, they did have a bigger crowd, but our check was only eighty dollars, not a hundred and fifty.

So, the sixth year he came around and said, "We want you to clown the Round-Up for nothing. We're broke. We don't have the money."

We were standing there, and George said, "What if we get hurt, break a leg or something?"

He said, "Heck no, we don't have to pay any clown's expenses."

That ended our deal with the Round-Up.

That same year we were at a party where the livestock director said, "What's the matter with you guys, you don't clown the Round-Up anymore?"

We said, "Well, they won't pay us. We only got eighty dollars last year, and before that we got a hundred and fifty."

"Like H... you haven't been paid. I saw on the books you were getting $300.00 every year." He turned away, and we never heard any more out of him. That was behind our quitting the Pendleton Round-Up.

But it didn't stop us from helping the Round-Up. We both worked on the barrier when they built it, and we worked in the arena, and I worked up in the announcing stand one year.

But here's another thing. We'd get deals from these other shows, and letters came in and they'd offer us a hundred and fifty dollars. The Round-Up was letting the mail come through here, and they'd say, "Don't pay them any more than that." They were covering up.

The only thing I was really happy about was Homer Holcomb, one of the greatest clowns in the world, crawled over the fence and came out and shook hands with me in the center of the arena. He told me, "You guys aren't getting paid enough." Then he turned around and walked off.

Now, I don't know how he meant it, whether we wasn't good enough or what. But that happened to me.

Have you seen that book, "The Fearless Funny Men," put out by Gail Woerner? It takes the history of rodeo clowns right up to recent years. Oh, it's a good book. It says in the early days when there were delays they hired circus clowns. Then pretty soon Red Sublett and a few others came along.

Red Sublett was before us. I remember someone said that he was sure a dirty-mouthed guy, but I loved him. He sure was funny.

I was born in Pendleton in 1909. My grandmother's sister was married to Moses Goodwin. He started the first hotel, and he built a toll bridge across the Umatilla River. The Oregon Trail used to come through here, and they used to ford the river somewhere between Main Street and 10th Street and went right on out what is now Carden Avenue.

My relatives owned the 160 acres here in the flat of Pendleton and part of the hill across the river.

My dad and his folks lived in Wisconsin. Lightning hit their house. They were all in the kitchen, and none of them got hurt. It destroyed the house, so they packed up and came out and joined his mother and her sister. In the meantime, Moses Goodwin died, and she married a guy named H. J. Railey. My dad got here with his folks in '78. He was seven years old. When they arrived, the Indians were gathering in Tutuilla Canyon. They were going to take the town. They told the kids to get under the dining room table and stay there. Half the town was in the hotel, and the other half was at the old Byers Mill. The troops rode in from Walla Walla, and the Indians called it off. That was my dad's first day in Pendleton.

When they changed the names of the streets, they changed them alphabetically. They named them after early settlers. I guess they couldn't find anybody else with "C", so they named one Carden Avenue after my dad. That was quite a famous street. There was a cemetery on one end and a nut house on the other.

The old street names used to be Ora, Cosby, Ann, James, Marie, Calvin...coming down from Main Street. Peanuts Pozegar used to tell me, "I sleep between Ann and Marie every night."

Peanuts Pozegar was a kid raised here. He was quite a dancer. He danced with the dummy at Happy Canyon.

Back in about 1924 and 1925 I was an usher at Happy Canyon. I kept asking Philo Rounds, the director back then, to let me get in the show. Back in those days, they paid you to be in the show, and you had to be good in order to keep your job. In 1926 I asked him, "You gonna get me in your show?"

He said, "I'll tell you what. I've got a high wheel bicycle. It's right around the corner. I bought it for Peanuts Pozegar to ride, and he can't ride it. If you can ride it, you've got the job." That's how I got my start in Happy Canyon.

Moens later bought a trick horse. He rode it in the parade, and I used to ride that bicycle in the Westward Ho Parade. Moens and I were in Happy Canyon before we got the Round-Up job. He did the "Falling Indian off the Cliff." He put on a breech-cloth and fell into the pond and never came up. I was either Lewis or Clark up in the Silhouette with Sacajawea. And then I was in the rescue act, and then we'd change clothes, and I'd become a Chinaman.

Ben Jory was involved with the stock and everything. He seemed to be there doing everything. He'd be closing the chutes, getting the stock, saddling the horses. He was always doing something. I remember the chariot. I don't know where he got it.

Yakima Canutt's sister, Dena Canutt, was my aunt by marriage. My mother's brother married Dena. My aunt and uncle had a ranch up at Diamond, Washington, when I was a kid. I got to go up there one Christmas. Yak was wintering there. He had a steer out there in a corral, and he'd go out there every day and dog that steer, practicing on him.

Then I can remember I lived up there on Calvin Street, about where Big John's Pizza is now. Our house was there. One Sunday after Round-Up, Yak came down by the house and told my dad, Al Carden, to come down to the Round-Up grounds. "We're gonna' win five hundred dollars," Yak said. Dad and I walked down there with him. He bet $500.00 that Bob Askin could ride "No-Name." They got "No-Name" out and saddled him up.

I can remember Yak riding. About the time he thought the gun should be fired, he'd throw his hat in the air. He was quite a showman. I can remember when he was in the Navy. He came here on leave and did everything in his sailor suit. The crowd was patriotic and couldn't see anybody else. It was during the War. Immediately after that, the rule was made that contestants had to wear cowboy outfits.

I was a kid back then. I graduated from high school in 1928.

Turk Greenough was a real close friend. When we first clowned the rodeo here, some of the cowboys were giving us a bad time cause we were local kids and didn't know what we were doing. Old Turk, he kinda stepped in there and told them to lay off. Well, every year that Turk came back to Pendleton after that, five years in a row, when he'd get in town, he'd call us on the phone. "I'm down at the Club Cigar Store on Main Street. Come on down."

We'd go down and set there and visit with him. He'd generally get in there a day or two before the show. We'd go down there and set there and drink milk shakes. Turk didn't drink.

We kept in touch through the years, and maybe six or seven years ago he got here and wanted to call up Ike Hernandez, who used to be a pickup man. He couldn't get ahold of him, but Turk remembered me. So he called me, and I told him to come on up to the house. In the back of my office I had a room where he could sleep. He came back about five years in a row, and he always stayed at my place. He kept in touch, and later I kept in touch with his nephews. They lived back in Colorado someplace. When Turk quit rodeoing, he went to work in Las Vegas. He was a guard in one of the casinos. When he retired down there, he had a stroke, and his nephews moved him back there where they were. He couldn't talk, but a week before he died there was a rodeo, and he wanted to go to it. So they packed him in the car and drove him to the rodeo. Some of the old boys that knew him came out and shook hands with him, and it kind of tickled him. A day or two after that he died.

He was married to Sally Rand. The way he told me the story, his wife didn't want to travel to rodeos. She wanted to settle down on the ranch in Montana. He wouldn't do it, and he wouldn't quit rodeoing, so she divorced him. So when he won at Madison Square Garden, he said he couldn't go to a party without seeing Sally Rand. "The first thing you know we were together all the time and got married."

Evidently, it was a publicity stunt for her to marry the world champion bronc rider at Madison Square Garden that year. Well, they didn't last too long because it wasn't a real marriage. But Turk's original wife and him went back and got married again, and she was with him until she died. That's what he told me about Sally Rand, and I imagine that's about how it happened too.

Deb Greenough, the bareback rider, is some relation of Turk's, a nephew or something.

Bob Crosby, Carl Aronld, and all those guys used to be bank robbers in Happy Canyon. We knew all of them. They rode in and held up the bank. Carl Arnold was the one that roped me and drug me out. I'd run down there towards the pond and I'd hold up my hands in the air and he'd throw that little loop out there. He wouldn't catch me until I hit the sawdust, and off we'd go. But he would never drag me off the sidewalk or down the street.

I did that for several years, and then they hired a guy from Long Creek. They could get him cheaper. He'd throw a loop and catch me, and then he'd kick his horse and I'd go sailing through the air. He'd drag me up the old wooden walk. I had on these blue pants, like a Chinaman would, but underneath it I had a jacket on. He'd drag me right out into the street. I wasn't the kind of guy to go yank him off his horse and take it out on him because he'd probably kill me. He was a big, tough cowboy. I walked right back in the arena, right in front of the director's stand, and told them they could find someone else to do the drag out.

Arnold was a world champion steer roper and a calf roper. He's in the Hall of Fame here in Pendleton. When he came back here to be inducted into the Hall of Fame, I got a call and went up town, and we had breakfast together. I asked him if he remembered me, and he said, "You're the guy I used to drag out of Happy Canyon."

Bob Crosby and Dick Truitt were down by the stands before the show started one time, and there was a kid named Dale Irwin there. Old Crosby said, "That kid doesn't weigh over 145 pounds."

Truitt said, "He must weigh more than that."

Crosby said, "I'll bet you five dollars."

Truitt said, "Let me lift him first."

Truitt took ahold of his arms and bent him over, and old Crosby had a board back there, and ho, he cracked him with the board, and they laughed. He was one of the guys in the show, and they just happened to see him there.

Every time Crosby came here, he'd always go to church on a Sunday morning over at the Christian Church. He was a church man.

Later on I got acquainted with Sherman Crane. He came in here and clowned around. The clowns didn't make it to the Round-Up one year, and they phoned around the country, and there was a little rodeo going on in Klamath Falls, and Sherman was there. They got him to come up here. That year a "Life" magazine photographer was here and covered that. He got a great picture of Sherman Crane dodging a bull, and the bull's horns were just about that far from his tail. They ran that on a full page in "Life" magazine. Sherman got more calls for rodeos. That made him all over the country. And he got paid a heck of a lot more. But all the years he came back, I think he made it seven years in a row, he never charged them any more than he charged them that first year.

I got well acquainted with him. His wife and kids came with him one year, and they stayed with us. I saw Sherman at the reunion before he died in 1980, the year Montie Montana was going to be inducted into the Hall of Fame. Sherman called me and wanted to come up here. He was going to pull some kind of gag on Montie, and he didn't want Montie to know he was coming.

My house was full, so I said I'd try to find him a place to stay. I came down to the Round-Up office and said that Sherman Crane wanted to come down here. "You got someplace he could stay?"

They said, "Yeah, we got some rooms at the motel for some of the celebrities, and Sherman can have one."

This was a week or so before Round-Up, so I called Sherman back and started to give him a bad time.

He said, "Wait a minute. Who do you think you're talking to?"

I said, "Aren't you Sherman?"

He said, "No, I'm his brother."

I said, "Well, let me talk to Sherman."

"I can't," he said. "He just died of a heart attack."

But he was a great one. Down at the clown reunion at Roseburg, Oregon they had us all at one motel. Old Sherman, when he came in there, he got everybody's name that had already come in and their room numbers. When he got to his room, he'd call everyone up and say, "Hey, this is Sherman. Come down to the bus station and pick me up."

Guys would come out and get into their cars. One car would leave, then another. He had them all going down to the bus depot. We had a lot of fun there.

I was the oldest living clown at the Colorado Clown Convention. They gave me a watch. Old Wayne Cornish might have been a few years younger.

I've been the oldest clown since they started having reunions. I was the oldest one at Roseburg, then at Moses Lake, Washington, then at Guthrie, Oklahoma, then Colorado Springs, Colorado, then Santa Fe, New Mexico. They have them every other year or something like that. I just outlived them all.

Old Bill Shaw, he's my roommate. He takes care of me. He's a wonder. We go down to get on a plane to go to a reunion, and old Shaw goes up to get the tickets. He'll say, "I got this old man that I'm taking care of and it's pretty hard on him."

"Okay," they'll say. "We'll put him on first."

Shaw would come back and tell me, "Limp, act old."

When we went back to Guthrie, we had to change at Salt Lake. We had to go clear down to the other end of the airport. Shaw waved down one of these guys in an electric cart and told the driver, "This old man will never make it. He needs help. He can't walk that far."

We rode. We had more fun. I couldn't make it without old Shaw. He's enjoyed the clown reunions. He's never missed a one.

Old Jack Saul, who is the kingpin up at Moses Lake rodeo, was just 91 a couple of months ago. He wasn't a clown, but he went to one of our reunions and enjoyed himself so much that he makes them all.

George Doak and Bobby Roamer was clowning the year that George Moens and I got into the Hall of Fame. We had a banquet and had our pictures taken, and we were given a plaque in the middle of the arena. He's a character, that Doak. He's a great guy. He came up to the Round-Up a few years back, and we had a party out at Shaw's bunkhouse. We had more fun that night. And Wes Curtis, another clown, he lives down in Roseburg now, was there. It was the four of us and our wives. Doak had a girlfriend with a lot of money. Afterwards, we asked him to come back to the Round-Up again sometime, and he said if he could find another girlfriend with a lot of money he would.

I never got to see Homer Holcomb work. The only time was when he came into the arena to congratulate me. I saw Jazzbo Folkerson work over in Ontario. He was a little roly-poly guy.

You want to know, really, why I didn't become a great barrel man? I loaned my barrel to a friend of mine who went over Niagara Falls, and he never got it back to me. That's what I tell everybody who asks if I was a barrel man. But I was a clown long before they had Brahma bull riding. If they had bull riding back then, I'd have been up in the grandstands helping some old lady find her seat.

Wick Peth was a heck of a bullfighter. I knew him real well. He's been banged up a lot.

In the teens and early '20s, I used to go downtown on Saturday night and watch the fights. And there were a lot of them, you bet. The Prohibition days, the people got a little drunker than they do now. I remember being downtown one night at the old Bungalow Pool Hall, where the Temple Hotel is now. I think it was the Yakima Indians that got into a fight. Cue balls were flying, cue sticks, everything. I stood outside, and they packed five of them out. I can remember that when I was a kid.

The town was a little wilder then. That helped build the Round-Up. When they caught a guy drinking, they couldn't throw him in jail. They didn't have a jail to throw him into. It was full. If you got caught, they'd just take the whiskey away from you, no questions. I think that had a lot to do with getting the crowd here.

When I was a kid, they built a big tower in back of the bleachers to shoot pictures from. I crawled up to the top of that tower, but I didn't stand up. I was afraid. It had a little rail around it. Well, the day of the Round-Up they were going to shoot the picture. The cameraman got his camera up there and went back down to get film. While he was down on the ground, the thing blew over. That's a fact. It was one of those early movie films they were going to shoot here.

I'll tell you a story I heard. I heard it from my brother-in-law. When the movie people wanted a cowboy, they offered the job to Lee Caldwell, a good looking local guy. He didn't want it, so they gave it to Hoot Gibson.

I was out in the arena when Bonnie McCarroll got kicked to death. A horse went over on her. She had the hobbled stirrups. I can see her yet. That horse got up, and her hands were up like this, waving. She was gone then. Her hands were straight up in the air when the horse got up.

Since then, they had some women here who did some riding exhibitions, but that was when Pendleton quit cowgirl bucking.

In the old days, they bucked from the snubbing horses, and then when they went to the chutes, they still had the Northwest Bucking Contest from the snubbing horses to give the people a look at the original way.

The World Championships were held from the chutes. The Northwest was for guys from around here. John Hodgen from Adams won it one year. He won the Northwest.

In the old days guys had to come in from the ranch. They had jobs breaking horses. They used to have try-outs here in the early days. But now, these young guys come out of college rodeos, and they're pretty well tuned up. They're awful good rodeo people. They get a pretty good start in college, and it makes a difference.

I've been to plenty of rodeos. One thing Pendleton has is a running start in the bulldogging. It's more thrilling. There are a lot of wrecks in the dogging, and they blame it on the grass. The reason the grass is in the arena is because in the old days, back in my time, a big wind would come up, and people would get covered with dust, and they'd get up and go home. If the cowboys make them take out the grass, they'll hurt themselves because they won't have a crowd. As it is now, they have to water the track to hold down the dust.

I happened to be on the Board when they were talking about putting in grass. The statement was made, "Don't worry about the cowboys not coming. If you pay them enough, they'll perform on broken glass."

JOHN MATLOCK

*John Matlock is a resident of Pendleton. W. F. Matlock,
John's grandfather owned the original 15-acre site where the
Round-Up is located today. He sold it to the Northwestern
Exhibition Association, later to become the Round-Up Asso-
ciation for $5,000.*

Right down there at the Round-Up grounds was where the
wagon trains crossed the river to get on the north side.

I was down there at the Round-Up in the twenties. I can remember 1925-26-27.

One old timer I can remember so well was "Nigger" George
Fletcher. I owned the Rivoli theater, and he used to be a great show
fan. He used to come to the theater in the afternoon, and he'd stop
and talk to us. He was a wonderful guy, he really was.

George always sat back in the back of the theater on the right
side. Anybody on the colored side sat on one side of the floor and
they couldn't sit on the other side. He always sat on the white side.
He was a gentleman, a nice person. I liked him very much. He lived
on the reservation; at that time we could have been arrested for
not segregating.

He was famous for riding a bucking horse backwards. I can
remember I was down at the Round-Up grounds when he rode one
backwards, and he got bucked off, and it hurt him real bad. They

55

took him up to that little fence and laid him down on the ground. He laid there for quite awhile before he got back on his feet, but he finally walked away.

The Rivoli was built for a Vaudeville theater, originally. My dad was alive then. He built the theater. He had a man dressed up in a gorilla suit, and he'd run up and down the aisles and everybody screamed and hollered. They were scared to death. But it was a great attraction.

Vaudeville was tied up with circuits, like Fancho and Marks. These were variety type of vaudeville—singers and dancers, musicians, magicians. They might have a gift for gab. They could get up on stage and answer questions, get involved in some incident, spin a rope, or something. They played here and there. They were great; they were fun. We never played vaudeville during the Round-Up. We had reasons for not playing it. You always played vaudeville on a percentage, and why give them all the money when it wasn't necessary? Usually, we just played Westerns during Round-Up.

When I started getting active in the theater, I booked cowboys over at the Alta theater. I had Roy Rogers over there and Rex Allen. They'd come out on stage and talk, and, sometimes, if they were talented, they'd play or sing something. They usually had a few other actors for back-up. I can remember Roy Rogers...he was packing them in, and I went up in the operating room to pull some shorts, to slow it down so I could get one more vaudeville in. We were just filling them up like mad. I went down in the dressing room to tell Roy instead of being on at a certain time, he was going to be moved up. He didn't object. That was five vaudeville's in one day. Five acts in one day. That was at the Alta.

I took Bill Nichols and his group. They were from Yakima. The first time Bill ever performed on a theater stage was in the Alta theater in Pendleton. He still kids me about it.

That guy is a genius. Nichols has got the greatest gift of memory I've ever heard of. It doesn't have to be a cowboy song. You can mention anything, and he'll know the words and the music. He's really a genius. He's a great man. That's a gift to be like Bill Nichols.

Anyway, Vaudeville was live action. It always drawed well. The Rivoli was built in 1920-21.

My Granddad owned the Cosy theater. All they had in there was folded chairs. It was the Nickelodeon. You paid a nickel and went in and saw what we called a "two reeler." You were lucky to get 20 minutes. We had a projectionist up in the booth, but he ran the same thing over and over again. My granddad started it, and my dad was the projectionist; at one time there were 5 Nickelodeons in Pendleton, and my granddad and my dad owned all five of them.

Hoot Gibson showed up in Pendleton to do a picture once. It was made around Gibbon. I was pretty young back then. I can remember my dad with him. He got drunk at the Elks club one night, and a great big mechanic just knocked the hell out of him.

Rex Allen was with Republic Pictures at that time. Republic had a branch in Portland. At that time they were trying to get him better known, so they wanted to book him out in theaters around the country. The branch salesman would come over and get you to sign 'em up. He'd play here one night and then go to Baker or someplace else the next night. They had him on the circuit. He was a nice guy. I liked him.

I remember Yakima Canutt. Everybody knew him. He was a stuntman in Hollywood for many years. And a good man, too. He was never good for the pictures because of his voice—his voice was bad. I remember one picture with Yakima Canutt, especially. He was chasing a train on horseback. He rode up the tracks to the caboose. It was a tremendous shot because the horse, as it was running up the tracks, the ties were not equally spaced, and the horse would trip, but it never went down. Many times it almost did. It was running wide open. He was quite a stuntman. Anything daring on a horse, he was the man; that was all there was to it.

I knew Frank Cable well. He was a ranch hand out around Pilot Rock. One time we were organizing an elk trip, and we had a cabin up at Lehman Springs. We got Frank and his wife. She was going to do the cooking, and Frank was going to be the guide and show us where to go. We had quite a deal up there for three or four days. He was a noted bootlegger. In fact, there was quite a few of them around. It was during Prohibition.

He was a lovable guy, in my opinion anyway. His wife was a wonderful woman. I can remember getting up in the morning, say 4 o'clock, and sitting down to a breakfast of hot cakes, sausage and eggs and hash-browns. She could turn out a breakfast like nobody I'd ever seen. In fact, when you got finished with one of her breakfasts, all you wanted to do was go back to bed.

BILLY NICHOLS

Billy Nichols and his partner Don Hill, known as Lukey, teamed up as the Punchliners for many years to entertain in Pendleton night clubs. I've never met a man with more enthusiasm for his work or more dedication for his calling. You can hear Bill playing at Stillman Park for the Cowboy Breakfast every morning during Round-Up.

My name is Billy Nicholson. I call myself Billy Nichols because Nicholson is too long a name to put on a sign. Most people wouldn't remember it anyway. I come from Louisville, Kentucky—southern Indiana, actually. I started doing radio programs over in Louisville. I played with all those good bands down there. I got hooked on country music. That was before TV. Both states claim me. Kentucky claims I'm from Indiana, an' Indiana claims I'm from Kentucky.

I was born October 18, 1919. That's going back a lot farther than you thought, probably.

I first was up in Billings, Montana. I was playing part time, and working in a mill. I just got out of the service. I was in the Navy. So I moved out to Billings, and I joined a band. I got me a little radio program goin' along with it. I was kind of a big frog in a little pond. There was a lot of competition back in Louisville, too many guys after any job you get. We had two radio shows goin' on back there; one from a furniture store at noon, a half hour program; and then over to the WAV studios at 5 o'clock. We were ridin' pretty high. A booking now and then, an' we'd get an extra twenty dollars for that. Then Pee Wee King came to town an' got both of our sponsors pretty darn quick.

He had some big hits, like "Slow Poke" an' "Tennessee Waltz." He wanted a place to settle down instead of Nashville. We sang on his program. Red Stewart wrote "Tennessee Waltz."

I got a chance to come out to Billings. A steel-guitar player from Louisville called me, and I got acquainted out there, an' that fall I went back an' got my furniture an' came back to Billings.

I was there in Billings about ten years. I started coming down here to Pendleton in 1956. For about three years I'd come out here for a couple of months and then go back to Billings for a few months. Finally, the winters got longer there, an' the spring came sooner down here; so I told my wife to pack up and we came to Pendleton, and we've been here ever since. At that time there were six or seven night clubs here using live music six nights a week, and you could find plenty of work. Once we got here and got settled, we started booking out of Pendleton.

At that time, people were comin' in who appreciated music an' the old tunes.

On the week of Round-Up, I entertain at the Wally Byam Caravan on Monday, Tuesday, Wednesday, and Thursday. Friday mornings I play for the Cowboy Breakfast at Stillman park at 7 a.m., and then I play at the Elks the same night. I double back at 5 o'clock in the afternoon until about 7:30 when the other band comes on down there. Saturday morning I play the Cowboy Breakfast at Stillman park croaking like an old frog. I come through it all right. About a week after it was all over with, I started to get a hoarseness in my voice, but once I'm away from it, it comes right back. I worked the Fort Henrietta Days over at Echo and then Amber Valley nursing home for some of the programs they put on for the old people.

I met quite a few country stars here in Pendleton. I played in about all those clubs, the Ranch, the Pendleton Hotel, the Temple—those were the good ones. Then we moved uptown to the Temple, an' that was our winter job for about ten years. Sometimes we'd go to Jackson Hole, Wyoming, or Nevada in the summer. It was a good stop for us. We never missed any work. And then we'd be home seven months of the year.

There was a lot of big names who played here. Bob Wills was one of 'em. I'm not sure which club he played at. Me an' Donny Hill, or Lukey, they called him, played with him for a week in Las Vegas at the Golden Nugget. Bill an' Harley, who had a trio, went down there several times, an' Bob Wills was there for a week with his band. Hank Thompson an' Carl Perkins played there too. So I got to know some of those guys through my travels. Talk about those old cowboys, Hoot Gibson was one of the first to ever win a championship here in Pendleton at the Round-Up. He came back after that an' made a lot of movies. He came back to town an' was puttin' on some programs at the schools. Our band appeared with him at some of those schools. Two or three of the grade schools put on assemblies, an' we'd sing some of the Sons of the Pioneers songs. Hoot Gibson twirled some ropes an' told some stories. He'd do the talkin', an' we'd do the playin'. Play a little, talk a little. I wish I had pictures of that, but I didn't hold onto any of that stuff. That was shortly after I got here, around 1957 or 1958. He was left handed, I remember that. He'd rope and draw his guns left handed. Hoot Gibson was a likable, friendly guy. He, being a movie star, I was almost afraid to talk to him.

Rex Allen came to town once for some kind of promotion. They had a parade. He got up an' sang with ol' Donny an' me at the Temple Hotel. What a voice!

Ol' Slim Pickins, the rodeo clown came into the Temple Hotel once. He wasn't a singer, but he asked for a lot of requests that no one knew except us. Boy, he took to us pretty good.

When I was in Billings, we went to Miles City, Montana, an' played some. An' Slim had been there a lot, rodeoin'. I'd met him there at the 17 bar. His partner he used to work with was from Miles City. His name was Scrap Iron Patch, a little, short guy but a heck of a rodeo clown. They talked me into gettin' in a parade with 'em. Gene Autry was a headliner there. He was the Grand Marshal for the spring rodeo at Miles City. Anyway, they talked me into gettin' in the parade with em', I put on some old ragged clothes, an' I had my fiddle. I'd saw off a tune, an' them guys would do a Buck & Wing dance, an' they stopped pretty often. They was crazy. There was a bar on every corner, an' they'd stop an' get em' a shot of something, an' then they'd get back in the parade.

They had so much fun that when it was over, they wanted to do it again. So we took the fiddle with us, an' the first place we hit was Roy Milligan's Silver Dollar Bar. Gene Autry was there with a couple of his musicians that played for Melody Ranch programs. Carl Cotner arranged music for the Melody Ranch program. I'd play a hoe-down, an' them clowns would be doin' their dance. Finally, Gene came over an' asked me if his partner, Carl Cotner, could play a tune on my violin.

Course, I knew who he was, so I said that he could have it if he wanted it.

61

So I went over an' sat with them. Gene asked me if I played bass, an' I said no, I didn't. I only played guitar an' sang. I told him that I played some of his old songs.

Gene said, "Tell you what, one of these guys has a bass fiddle upstairs and my guitar." They went up an' got them. Gene played the bass, an' I played the guitar for about three hours there that afternoon. What a fine player. That's another one I'd give a thousand dollars to have recorded. That Gene Autry was a fine man, a good hand. I learned a lot of his songs way back there.

Then I got playin' Jackson Hole, Wyoming. I played there for about twenty summers. I met a lot of big name performers there. One time they had a fire there in Jackson Hole. The Trading Post was burning down. We was playin' at the Cowboy Bar. Henry Fonda had been comin' in to see us quite a bit. I remember that I went out on our intermission to see what was goin' on. They had a bucket brigade goin'. Here comes Henry Fonda, taking steps like an old farmer. I said, "Why aren't you up on that bucket line?"

"I was," he said. "Then I heard some people talking about when the dynamite was going to go off, so I thought I'd come down here."

We had a lot of good times over there. I met a lot of other movie stars there. I met old Ben Johnson, the cowboy star. I talked to him a little bit, but I didn't get much out of him. He was a true cowboy. Some of those ol' timers were the real stuff in the movies.

Clint Eastwood came over there to make the movie "Every Which Way But Loose" with Clyde the orangutan. They had filmed some of it there in that park, the Elkhorn. I was playin' at the Rancher back then. In between shots they'd come in there an' have a plain Coke or whatever. I got to meet an' talk to those guys a good bit. So one night I was down at the Ward Hotel after I got done with the early show at the Rancher. The Ward Hotel featured Rusty Draper, a fine entertainer. He was really packin' them in. He always got me up to sing one or two of my comedy songs. That night I did, an' boy, it just brought the house down. Ol' Clint Eastwood was sittin' there, laughin'. Later, he came up to me an' asked me where I had learned all those crazy songs. Yep, that ol' music has taken me a lot of places.

Pendleton has always been more or less my favorite. Years ago they'd have "Dignitary Parties" here in Pendleton. Those parties were given for the Round-Up President. Johnny Bauer was there two or three times. Fred Hill was another. Governor Mark Hatfield came a couple of times. Tom McCall also. I got a picture of Tom McCall, the Governor, singing with me. He was a heck of a man.

Then I worked with Bonnie Guitar an' Rusty Draper. Down in Jackpot is where I met a lot of good entertainers. I worked on the same bill with the Sons of the Pioneers an' got to know 'em pretty well. They'd get done with their main show an' come out an' listen to me finish up at the bar. They'd start naming old tunes. They'd ask me where I ever learned those old songs, an' I told 'em "Out in Indiana an' Kentucky."

Dale Warren, one of the Sons of the Pioneers, asked me if I'd ever heard of a group called Uncle Henry's Kentucky Mountaineers.

"You bet," I said. "I won the five dollar prize on their amateur contest once."

"That's my Mom and Dad," he said. They were good country musicians, not corny. It was fine stuff.

Sonny Spencer, another member of the Sons of the Pioneers, was from up in the hills of Kentucky.

Slim Miller was another one I knew in Kentucky. He was on the Renfro Valley Barn Dance that I worked with. A little later I met them out in the state of Washington. I knew Ernest Tubbs from back in Kentucky an' his appearance around Louisville. I got to meet a lot of those old boys.

Tubbs had an old country voice, but it was special. Like a lot of guys, they was in their old age before people really got appreciating them.

Stuart Hamlin was another. He played there in Jackpot, Nevada. He'd come out an' listen to me sing some of his old songs. He couldn't believe anybody knew his songs. He was a fine man. He was a real cowboy too. Stuart Hamlin wrote "Back On The Texas Plains," "Won't Go Hunting With You Jake," "This Old House," "It's No Secret What God Can Do," and "Remember Me, I'm The One Who Loves You." What a fine guy. He'd tell you, "I'm not a singer, I'm just a cowboy who likes these things."

He told me how he came to write "This Old House." He was a good one for hunting mountain lions up in the Sierra Mountains with a pack of hound dogs. He got way back there one time, a place he'd never been before, an' he came upon an old cabin. He went around back, and there was a skeleton lyin' across the doorsteps. No way of knowin' how long he'd been dead. Stuart Hamlin started thinking about the old house and started writin'. He could sure put it together. "Golden River" was another Stuart Hamlin song.

I met Reba McEntire's dad, Clark McEntire. He was a heck of a rodeo hand. I met him years ago. He was the bulldogging champion here in Pendleton.

John Matlock, who used to run the old Rivoli theater on Main Street, used to have me an' the band play during the half hour break between shows in the afternoon. I had cowboy clothes on, an' we sang western songs. John seen a lot of those guys come an' go at the theater. Roy Rogers played in his theater. I never met Roy, but I met his boy, Dusty Rogers. I played golf with him. He was built like a football tackle...a heck of a singer.

My old partner, Lukey, lives in Yakima. Been thinking about recording some more stuff with him. He came down about two months ago and helped me go over three or four tunes. We did a little harmonizin', some ol' cowboy songs.

We've redone one of my old tapes. I've been thinking. I keep getting requests for all them old cowboy things: "Does Your Chewing Gum Lose Its Flavor On the Bedpost Overnight?" "The Preacher And The Bear"; "I'm My Own Grandpa." Nice old tunes that nobody does anymore.

I played mostly a single. Sometimes I'd do a duo or a trio. The bigger the band, the more they expect out of you. One guy, they feel sort of sorry for. Truth doesn't hurt, does it?

I cherish these old songs. The Sons of the Pioneers songs were the best to me.

Billy Armstrong was the fiddle player for the Sons of the Pioneers. He came to Jackpot an' worked awhile when I was there. Then another time he played at Umatilla near Pendleton, and I went down to see him play. He'll do that Orange Blossom Special an' wear out a bow string in the middle of it, an' he'll just grab another bow an' finish. He's a worker.

I was down at the Grand Ole Opry a couple of times to see if I could feed my songs to somebody, but I never had much luck. Some of 'em listened politely, but I never got anything out of it. But I went out to the Grand Ole Opry, an' it was so much different than it was in the old Ryman Auditorium. That was close, just like an old kitchen. Your good old timers were workin' there then. Now, it's too much Country Rock. But later in the evening they'd always bring out Bill Carlisle, Hank Snow, some of the old timers. They'd save 'em for late, an' the roof just raises. Ernie Tubbs was like that. He'd just talk an' smile, an' he'd bring down the house.

Rose Maddox was real down-home. That's the way country music was supposed to be. Them old timers knew how to do it.

I got my first radio job with a band called Cliff Gould's and the Texas Cowboys. They came to Louisville. We had been doing barn dances an' square dances around the country. We'd go over and catch their show. That's where Eddy Arnold formed his first band. He'd been down there by himself. He was with Pee Wee King. He formed his first band with four players out of that little band down there in Louisville. Speedy Knight played fiddle, and Gabe Tucker played bass. That's how I got into radio.

I never heard Cattle Call sung any better than Eddy Arnold, except maybe for Slim Whitman.

My partner, Lukey, an' I played together in Vancouver in Canada an' as far south as Tucson, Arizona. We played Jackson Hole together and West Yellowstone, Montana, an' a lot of clubs in between.

I knew the Linderman family up in Red Lodge, Montana. I knew Doug real well. Doug was one of the younger ones. He was a fine bronc rider, but he didn't make it real big, like Bud an' Bill did. Them guys out there on the ranch was real tough. They'd shoot at each other with .22 rifles instead of BB guns. I went fishin' around there one time, an' Bill's mom asked us to stay the night, an' we had breakfast in the morning. We had breakfast with Bill's mother and old Packsaddle Ben Greenough. The Greenoughs were great rodeo people. I used to sing a song on the radio station there in Billings, Montana, called "Great Granddad: When the West was Young." They'd request that song for Packsaddle Ben for his birthday every year. When he died, they wanted me to sing it at his funeral, but I'm a little leery about singin' at funerals.

One time me an' my partner, Johnny Barrett, were up in Montana playin' in night clubs. We were going to make a trip up on the "Highline." That's what they called the little towns along the Canadian line. We were looking for places to play. Big old dark clouds were rollin' in. We didn't get 15 miles out of Billings when the hail started comin' down. Boy, it was that big around. We'd passed a farm house a few miles back, an' I said, "Let's turn around before the car gets all dented up an' get under that old fir tree a few miles back."

A man was standin' on the porch of that old house, and he motioned us to come on in. He ran a dairy farm, I think. He took us around and showed us some original paintings by Charlie Russell that nobody had ever seen before.

We rode the storm out there. The town was somewhere between Billings an' one of those little towns along the "Highline." I forget the guy's name, but the highway was #2. We called ourselves the Nightriders...me an' Johnny Barrett.

One old boy told me a story about Bud Linderman. He was in the 17 Bar there in Billings where I was playin'. I didn't see this, but the guy who did lives near here in Irrigon, Oregon. He'd been in a movie with Forest Tucker called "War Paint." It was filmed along the Yellowstone River near Billings. He said that he was sitting in the 17 Bar one night, and Bud Linderman was in there. He was broke, and he wanted to buy some more beer. He said, "I'll be right back."

Bud walked out front, just outside the door, an' ripped a pay phone right off the wall. Then he came back with it tucked under his coat with the phone cords hangin' underneath. He tipped it up an' shook out a bunch of quarters an' started buyin' beer.

Another time, down in West Yellowstone, Bud got into a scrape with a guy that owned a bar next to where I was playing. I was playing at the Cowboy Bar. Toward the end of his drunk, he got mean. So he caused a few fights in there. Old Jim somethin' or other, I forget his name, said, "Bud, I can't have you in here anymore. You're causing too much trouble. I ain't gonna serve you anymore. Get out!"

"Whose gonna make me?" Bud said.

"I am," Jim said, an' he pulled a gun.

Bud just walked up to him, jerked the gun outta his hands, an' like to beat him to death with it. He wasn't afraid of nothin'.

Turk Greenough tried to put on some rodeos in Billings. Billings was a real tourist town. Turk put on some Sunday rodeos, an' we went out there an' played. We never got any money out of it, but we went along with it for awhile.

We didn't see Turk again for several years after that. Then one day when we were playin' at the Golden Nugget in Las Vegas, this guy who looked like a sheriff came walkin' up to me. He asked me, "Aren't you Bill Nichols?"

"Oh, oh, what have I done?" I said.

"I'm Turk Greenough," he said. I didn't recognize him. He was a security guard at the Golden Nugget.

Turk married the stripper Sally Rand. He was tough people. Alice an' Marge were his sisters. They were the rodeo Greenoughs. Packsaddle Ben Greenough got his name from carryin' the mail from Red Lodge, Montana, to Cook City in the winter. They close up there. The snow gets 15 feet deep, an' nobody gets through that highway in the winter. But he made the trip once a week, Old Ben Greenough.

When they asked me to sing at his funeral, I'd have loved to have done it, but I just felt a little funny about it.

I just like to travel. I can look at a bunch of cactus an' sagebrush out there an' love it. I wrote a tune called "Ely, Nevada" cause I went through there an' felt sorry for 'em. I thought, a little town this far out, I wondered if anybody ever mentioned it in a song. By the time I got to Las Vegas, I had a pretty good little song about it, an' it's on one of my tapes.

Right now, if I'd do any traveling at all, I'd like to go to someplace like Ely. I'd like to go there in the summertime where you're kind of special. I'd do some songs that I've written about Nevada—some of those little towns where you can really feel appreciated.

REBA PERRY ROBERTS BLAKELY

Reba Perry Roberts Blakely is a resident of Alturas, California. Reba is a member of the Cowgirls' Hall of Fame at Fort Worth, Texas, and has received recognition for her work in rodeo research, especially from the 1920s. Reba was a rodeo performer and in later years a chronicler of her friends from her rodeo days. She is a natural promoter of things Western and an astute observer of a world that she knew thoroughly—rodeo.

———————⊱•◈•⊰———————

"In 1926, when I started rodeo, there was a rodeo every 50 miles."

Mother was a great horsewoman; as soon as she could, she got me on a racehorse. She got me riding in circles, and the circles kept getting bigger and bigger, just like my life. They kept expanding.

My father's name was David Howard Perry, and my mother's was Susan May Drake. My Father was the engineer who was in charge of engineering when the Union Pacific pounded the golden spike at Promontory Point, Utah. My mother was a school teacher. We lived near Puyallup, Washington.

I was born in April 1908. I was ninth of nine children. I was born a cripple. I walked on my ankles. Even though I was tiny, I grew up on horses. I was a trick rider and a trick roper, and I rode bucking horses. I even won a championship relay for C. B. Irwin. You never forget your juicy days.

I had a horse named "Buddie," and what a horse he was. He would lay down on stage, and I'd trick rope off him. Entertaining the public, that was what it was all about.

I had a broken leg with a cast on it, and I still rode racehorses. They'd throw you on a horse and you'd breeze 'em. You'd do that early in the morning. You don't have time to think about yesterday or today. You had to think about now. You really had to concentrate, or you'd fall off. That was my job, to open up a horse's lungs.

C. B. Irwin was a sub contractor for the U. P. Railroad, and he transported his show by train. Five different railroads met at Puyallup-Tacoma. Three rivers flowed through Tacoma. The stands at Puyallup were built into the mountainside overlooking Puget Sound, and they were covered with Red Fir and Cedar.

C. B. Irwin used to whittle and tell anecdotes to relieve tension at rodeos, and he could keep people laughing. He was a darling, a dearly beloved rodeo producer and a great man. He loved us like family. There wasn't anything he wouldn't do for you.

Sam Garrett was an expert in pony express riding, and he also rode relay races for C. B. Irwin. I rode in Union, Oregon, and Grangeville, Idaho, for C. B. Irwin.

In those days, women had to prove themselves to be able to compete in the big rodeos. I couldn't ride at the Western Washington Fairgrounds in Puyallup without having the okay to ride in Pendleton. But once they made it, women were pampered.

We were greatly admired. We had fan clubs, and we were paid extra. We learned to get our checks and leave town, so everyone wouldn't borrow money from us.

One of my favorite rodeos was Packwood, Washington. I would wait tables for an owner of a restaurant there. They wintered racehorses there.

The attitudes changed when Bonnie McCarroll died in the arena in Pendleton in 1929. Women weren't allowed to compete in rodeos after that until recently. Women were reduced to barrel racing, and they were strictly decorative. In the 1940s they relegated the cowgirls to looking pretty. She could dress up in a beautiful costume and drive a $45,000 car. She could barrel race and glamorize parades, and that's all she could do. It took years to get events back for the cowgirl.

I was well acquainted with Ben and Mildred Jory and worked many rodeos that they produced. Mildred was just a darling. She watched over us girls and kept the "townies" from sneaking into our rooms at night. Ben was a capable showman, a jolly person. He always had a smile. The Jorys were well liked by the rodeo world. We were always thrilled when the Jorys came to town.

Mildred and I would room together, and Ben would stay out at the grounds. He was a very busy person. He had to have everything, all the equipment ready for the parade, and he had to have all the hands lined up, who was to do what, in all the varied events. It was a very grueling period for Ben Jory, believe me. He went on two or three hours sleep a night because he stayed out at the rodeo grounds. He had stock to take care of, he had to prepare for the street parades—all the antique wagons and the proper teams of horses that went with them. You could say he was one of the busiest men in rodeo in the years when I first met him. That was when I first started riding at the Pendleton Round-Up from 1926 to 1943.

Hugh Strickland saved my life at a show. I was trick riding and my horse tried to savage me. Hugh yelled at him and he straightened up. Hugh laughed easy and he was a joking man. He could have you laughing. He was #1—the best rodeo manager God ever invented. Mabel and Hugh Strickland went to separate rodeos, both being individual rodeo "Stars." Stars were paid extra just for their quality. Hugo was an all-around cowboy and rodeo manager.

I remember the death of Bonnie McCarroll at Pendleton in 1929. I was there. It was tragic. They had just given Bonnie and Frank McCarroll a big write up in the papers. They had been long-time performers at the Pendleton Round-Up, Cheyenne, Ellensburg. That was a big, powerful, wonderful rodeo. It was so tragic that day, so tragic. I think people just wanted to forget it. But not me, I was there. After she got a big announcement, down went the horse and came back up and kicked her to death. We didn't know that for sure at the time. The ambulance went right out and the show went on. It was an old story in rodeo.

If you had one friend among cowgirls, you were lucky. You competed against them all the time. If you had one to pal around with, you were lucky.

Pat Owens was one of my boyfriends. I remember that I got all gussied up and went dancing. I could have married a lot of cowboys. I was married twice. The first time was to Ike Leo Joseph Roberts. I remember that he was bucking off regularly, and I was making my rides. He finally won the Northwest Bucking Contest in Pendleton in 1934 after we were already separated. My second husband was Bill Blakely. He was a cattleman. I remember he was holding out for higher prices in 1929. He was offered $45 a head, and he was waiting for $50 when the stock market collapsed. It dropped from $45 to $19 and he went to shipping cattle. He died in 1957.

The late Bonnie McCarroll had an omen. She always felt that she would meet her demise in rodeo. In this picture, the stirrups came unhobbled, must have broke, and that made the stirrups fly up, we weren't use to that. Bonnie McCarroll was a "hard luck" girl. I was at the rodeo when Bonnie was killed riding a bronc. I witnessed it. But that's another story.

"Grace Runyon, smiling as she goes down, left her right arm free.
This was pre-1920."

"Bonnie Grey on her horse King Tut."

"Vera before 1920. Here she is still dressed in military patterned attire."

"Mabel, so pretty."

"Fox really enjoying her ride. We were taught to smile. Note the cowboy in the left holding a blindfolded horse."

Vera had a huge amount of fans. She was one of the greatest "stars." She had boosters who traveled all over to watch her. She went to Wembley, England, for 40 days and 40 nights of rodeo. They loved her. She went to Glasgow, Scotland, for 30 days and nights; Paris, France, 30 days and nights. The fans loved her. She raved about Paris as the U. S. was in Prohibition, and in Europe they could have a drink.

1920s there were no chutes. They saddled three horses in the arena, blindfolded. You'd climb on, stirrups hobbled under the horse's belly. When you were ready, you'd nod, and they would let you go.

These were really tough girls, the relay riders. Bonnie Grey was in Wild West movies, very prestigious. She was a little reserved and "picky" when it came to friendships. She was a nurse and from an affluent family.

"Prairie Rose is just getting picked up by the pick-up man...here she grabs the saddle cause she is getting picked up, but look, the rope is behind the pick-up man's rump—oh my! Look at those bloomers she has on!"

"Bertha Blancett was a wonderful rodeo star. She could do it all."

ED DELANEY

In 1996 we interviewed Ed Delaney, brother-in-law of Ben Jory at a nursing home in La Grande, Oregon. Ed is 96 years old and a life-long resident of Union, Oregon. He was still a young man when he helped Ben fashion the yoke for his team of oxen used for many years in the Westward Ho Parade at the Pendleton Round-Up.

———◆———

I remember that Ben Jory wanted me to build three sets of yokes for his six oxen. I drew up a pattern 12 X 12 and took the plans to the Union High School shop teacher; together we built the yokes, using wood from the old Woolen mill, still standing on 5th Street in Union.

When I built the yokes for Ben's oxen, we sent to Missouri for the bows, which held the yokes on. Ben only had six oxen. When he had twelve oxen, he was using the six Pendleton Round-Up oxen.

Ben trained those oxen on the main street in Union. He would talk to them as he walked them up and down the street, getting them used to being around people. The law stated that the animals had to have a rope, so Ben laid a rope across them and talked them into doing whatever he wanted. The townspeople really enjoyed watching Ben and his oxen. I remember three of the oxen's names: Old Red, Brindle, and Pet.

Ben also trained a half cow-half buffalo they called Half Breed, and he broke it to ride. He also had a longhorn steer he put a saddle on and broke to ride. He rode it down the main street of Union and entertained the townspeople.

Ben had a pickup-man who lived on Indian Creek near Elgin. His name was Luke Geiger. He went with Ben to all the rodeos as his right hand man. I took Ben over to Indian Creek many times to pick Luke up to go to a rodeo.

In 1942 or 1943 I rode in the back of the covered wagon in the Pendleton Round-Up Parade. I really had fun.

Ben and Louella had a friend that did rodeos with them. He was a clown, and while he was in Union, at the Eastern Oregon Livestock Show, he painted a big picture of Ben on a bucking horse on Ben's barn at the back of his house on the main street of Union. It has since faded, but you can still barely see it today. It was a landmark in Union.

Ben and Louella did their last rodeo in Payette, Idaho in 1948. I remember this very well as I drove over to see them from Union, Oregon, and on the way home I was in a head on car crash, which left me crippled, and I almost lost my life.

Ben sold his livestock to Harley Tucker.

Ollie Osborne and John Spain took a horse, "Five Minutes to Midnight" to Madison Square Garden.

Ben quit rodeoing and took over managing the city park in Baker, Oregon. One of his jobs at the park, I remember, was rounding up the squirrels in the winter. He'd get them all together in a little shack and feed them out of a hundred pound sack of peanuts. A squirrel roundup.

Ben died in 1954.

JENNALEE SCARBROUGH

Jennalee Scarbrough and her husband Murvin live in Baker, Oregon. Jennalee is Ben Jory's niece. In 1998, Jennalee invited us to the Delaney family reunion at Summerville near La Grande, Oregon. With her help, we pieced together both the Delaney and Jory family histories following Ben's marriage to Louella Delaney.

Ben Jory rode bucking horses, roped calves, and bulldogged in 1908. Ben helped build the rodeo grounds, which is now called the Eastern Oregon Livestock Show and Rodeo. Ben built the bucking horse chutes and calf roping chutes, which have now been rebuilt, but on the same place. He rode many bucking horses and roped many calves at the show, which is still going strong. Union is the oldest show in the Northwest.

I know he would have been so proud if he knew that two of his nephews in later years have been E. O. L. S. Presidents, and five of his nieces have been Eastern Oregon Livestock Show Queens. One niece, Wythel Bronson Delaney, was the founder and organizer of the Blue Mountain "Tac" team, which she took to many rodeos. These twenty girls all dressed alike and rode their horses with no saddle or bridle. They were very popular!

Ben and Louella were in two movies. One was in Lewiston, Idaho. I remember the other one was "Golden Earrings." I remember watching it on t.v. years later. I told my Aunt Louella that I had seen the movie. She laughed and said she remembered it was a "Cold Part." She was a Gypsy, and she was down by the creek washing clothes most of the time, and the water was freezing...cold. Brrr.

THE OMAK CHRONICLE, JULY 6, 1917

The following newspaper clipping was part of the Ben Jory collection. The Omak Chronicle has since been changed to The Omak Okanogan County Chronicle. The Wild West Show that Jory and Somers put on at Omak later became known as the Omak Stampede.

<hr>

The first accident of the celebration happened at the Wild West arena when the bucking mare 'Red Pepper' threw "Sonny" Palmateer of Tunc-Creek Monday morning when he attempted to win the $50 purse for riding. The lad was badly jarred.

A very regrettable accident marred the fun on Tuesday morning and while a number of broken bones was the result thereof the wonder is that more were not seriously or perhaps fatally injured when the large grand stand of the Wild West arena collapsed with something over four hundred persons on it. When we say collapsed we mean just that in the broadest sense of the word as the entire structure gave way and was a complete mass of kindling wood after the crash.

The cause of the accident was a simple case of overestimating the carrying strength of native Bull pine. Manager Jury (Jory) of this concession, had prided himself upon his foresight and caution by procuring new lumber of heavy dimensions from the Indian saw mill on the reservation east of town and had the seats firmly and properly made but failed to count on the natural brittleness of this native timber. While there could be no real charge of carelessness or criminal neglect on the part of anyone connected with the attraction, Mr. Jury (Jory) came forward with a voluntary offer to stand, so far as it was within his financial ability, the doctor bills of the injured persons and thereby do everything within his power to make good the accidental damage.

The grand stand was immediately reconstructed of much heavier timbers and the show continued very successfully throughout the remainder of the celebration, giving ample satisfaction to the large crowds attending every performance.

ROBERTA CROSBY BURKSTALLER

Roberta Crosby Burkstaller is the daughter of Bob Crosby, world champion steer roper and winner of the Roosevelt trophy at Pendleton. She and her husband live in Roswell, New Mexico.

Bob Crosby
as told by
Roberta Crosby Burkstaller

My father was born in Midland, Texas on Feb. 27, 1897, but he was raised at Fort Stockton, a little ways from Midland until he was about 13. He lived on the NA Ranch. It's very famous. They were very well to-do, the Crosby's were. They moved to Oklahoma City, and Mr. Crosby, my grandfather, bought a ranch right near Will Rogers' ranch. Will Rogers had a nephew, Herb McSpadden who ran his ranch for him, and at that time he was performing on the New York stage. On the weekends, Will would come home. He was a little older than Dad. He and Herb and my daddy would ride all day long and rope. Will could rope anything, you know. He and Daddy were reared together. The three of them would rope all day, and then they would come back and, this was unusual, they would write poetry all night. Mr. Rogers loved poetry. Everything they did, he wrote a poem about it. Herb McSpadden had a son who still lives in Oklahoma. I talk to him quite often. His name is Trent. Clem McSpadden is an announcer for the National Finals Rodeo in Las Vegas.

I have a lot of poetry they wrote.

Will Rogers never drank. He was a very clean-minded man. My father was raised with people like that. Herb was that way, too. Richard Merchant was my father's very best friend. He went every-where with him. He went with us in a Buick coupe and held me on his lap hour after hour. One time we were going to a rodeo, I don't remember where it was, and we were taking the horse Daddy won just about all those trophies with called Comet. He had him in a trailer on behind. There was Mother and Richard and Daddy and me in the front seat of the Buick coupe. It started raining, raining, raining, and the road was getting so flooded that we couldn't hardly see anything. We came to a bridge. Daddy said, "Well, Rich, what are we gonna do about this bridge? Should we just go on over it?"

Richard was a very quiet man. He never opposed Bob. He was a very fine man.

Rich said, "No Bob, I don't think you ought to do that. Why don't you just get out and ride old Comet over there and see what happens?"

Well, Daddy got out of the car and rode Comet across the bridge and back, and just as Comet reached the side where we were on, the bridge went out. So, we were very lucky.

He has trophies in four museums, so that shows that he won more than any other cowboy. The cowboy that got the most points in three consecutive years, in Cheyenne and Pendleton, would win the Roosevelt trophy. They had three trophies before that, like if one cowboy won one year, he kept that trophy, and then, maybe another cowboy would win the next year. The one that had the most points for three years won the big trophy. For three consecutive years he won the most points and won the Roosevelt trophy. It's in the National Cowboy Hall of Fame in Oklahoma City. No one else has ever done that. Not even the young ones have done that. He's still the world's champion, even though he's dead.

I knew Ruth Roach real well.

I was the littlest cowgirl when we went to England with the Tex Austin Rodeo. I did a lot of trick riding in little jodhpurs. I was three and a half years old. I have some pictures of our trip to London. Some were taken on the boat on the way over there. I went again when I was 13. The second trip was a failure because the humane society said we were being cruel to the animals, and they made a big mess over there at the time. Ruth Roach took care of me on the trip, but I was a little girl, and I wouldn't know too much about her as an adult. I have a picture of her when we sailed for London.

Wembley Sports Stadium   Copyright K. Reitz

Breezy Cox. When he got out of line with his language and drinking, Dad popped him in the nose. But he was a good friend.

Daddy was a moralist, and he was always trying to keep Breezy Cox from getting drunk. Breezy was quite a funny guy. He wasn't just what you'd call dependable, but you know, everybody liked him. My father didn't think much of him as far as his character was concerned, but he was a good friend. He was loyal to his friends. But that day in time the people, the really fine cowboys, didn't do a lot of drinking or cursing or things like that. They were pretty high class guys. They called Daddy the Preacher. He kind of made his own rules.

If anybody stayed around him, they had to quit smoking. He was overly dominant about it all. He didn't ever drink. The reason he didn't was because his reactions were faster if he didn't drink. If he'd had a beer, he didn't have as fast of reaction. He could always beat anyone who had a beer. I never drank in my life. I wouldn't have done anything like that because I loved him so.

He went to rodeo after rodeo, and sometimes he'd go to two rodeos to other cowboy's one. He'd drive all night long. If he won anything, they'd have to send him the money. Then he'd take off and go to another one. He'd pick up hitchhikers to help him drive while he got some sleep. He picked up this guy this time, he was on his way to Cheyenne, actually, and it was in the daytime. He picked this guy up, and the guy pulled out a cigarette. Daddy looked at him with steel gray eyes and knocked the cigarette out of his hand. "You can just get out, young man. I'm not taking you."

The man said, "Well, Mister Crosby, I won't smoke anymore if it upsets you that much." Daddy said, "Well, all right, we'll try it again."

He got back in the pickup, and they went on tootin' along, and in a little while he started telling a story with a lot of four letter words in it, and Father said, "If you can't clean up your mouth, you're just not going with me. Just get out."

So the kid said, "Well, Mister Crosby, what can I do? I'm sorry."

He just wanted them to act right, especially around me. He told me, "Ro, if you ever smoke or drink, go ahead and do it, but don't ever do it around me. I don't want to see you."

My father never did believe in cursing, and he never said anything but, "Oh, gosh." I've seen him change fifteen flats, and he never said a single curse word.

He was an Englishman, and he couldn't stand bad English. His mother was from Canada. She was English, and she was a very formal person. She brought her piano out west when she married this Texas Ranger. His name was Richard Henry Crosby. That was my grandfather's name. She taught all eight children how to play the piano and took them to beautiful...every little bit of culture she could in the west. And so his family upbringing was with a great deal of formality. When they went to Oklahoma and bought the ranch near Will Rogers, they went to watermelon feasts and all kinds of rodeo get-togethers. He went to his first rodeo when he was thirteen. He won everything, and they were all adults.

Mother and I traveled with him constantly. He loved Pendleton. In 1926 he traveled all over the United States to one rodeo right after the other so he could practice and be in good shape to win the trophies in '27. All that summer, all that whole year, we didn't go with him. He traveled night and day, and Richard traveled with him. He was practicing and training. Rodeo was our living, and he was trying to be the best.

He never wore satin shirts or fancy hats. He just wore Levi's and cotton shirts. And he had a big smile. He was the most conspicuous man in the parade. He didn't wear fancy clothes, and he was the only one who didn't. That made him pretty conspicuous.

My father was a quiet man until he got older. He was humble. He didn't want to show off. He just wanted to do his job good, and he loved people. Unconsciously, he was outstanding because he did everything so differently from the others. He didn't follow what they did. He just wore his ranch clothes. He went there to make money. It was a business to my Daddy. He was a business cowboy. He was very, very strong. He could lift the back of a car.

We were with him when he was working for that Roosevelt trophy.

A few years ago somebody came to my brother and me and wanted to make a movie about Bob. We gave everything—reminiscences, stories. It was changed. Everything was changed and twisted, and it wasn't about my dad at all. They even changed his name.

BILL HANSELL

Bill Hansell lives on a ranch near Athena, Oregon. He has been Commissioner for the Port of Umatilla and President of the Umatilla County Cattlemen's Association. He graduated from Washington State University as a veterinarian and worked in that capacity with the Round-Up for many years.

My father ran horses south of Arlington, Oregon. We lived near 5 and 8 Mile Canyon. My mother was a school teacher, and she taught in a little country school. My mother didn't want to be a "Gypsy horse-trader's wife," so we moved to Athena and rented some property before World War II. I was born in 1921.

My dad helped at the Round-Up from the start. He helped separate steers and calves when they started numbering them. He worked behind the scenes when Herb Thompson was livestock director. Herb was director for a zillion years.

I helped him some. He conscripted me from the Athena High School Band in the 1930s. He took me around back and put me in the corrals. I wore white duck pants and shirt, which was usually mud covered by the end of the day. They paid me a dollar or two a day to help. I cut calves and steers out in the pens and separated the roping and dogging steers out in the east end of the grounds.

Dad finally retired. I wasn't selected to follow Dad after that, and that sort of burned me up, and I quit helping for years. Eventually, I was asked to take over Dad's old spot.

When I took over for Dad, they had three corrals. It was an awkward setup. It was really a pain in the neck. I fixed up the chutes and speeded things up.

My dad was critical of early directors, and he didn't like the politics. Fred Hill took ten years to put an end to the abuses of past Round-Up presidents. I turned down the directorship four times.

My son, Tyler, played football for Washington State, and he also wrestled. When Jiggs Fisk was president of the Round-Up, he put Tyler on the Board. He gave him the same job that my dad and myself had.

One year Danny Torricellas parked his camper on the grounds, and he plugged it into electricity. Tyler came along and unplugged it. Tyler told Danny, "You know you weren't supposed to park there." Torricellas got some of his buddies and went back to talk to Tyler. There weren't any blows, but Tyler told him what was what.

Torricellas won the all-around at Pendleton that year. Since Torricellas won the all-around and almost got into a fight with Tyler, the word got around that if you wanted to win the all-around, you had to have it out with Tyler as a prerequisite for winning.

Ron Anderson told Torricellas the next year, "You're the luckiest guy in the world. Hansell would have tromped your butt in a mudhole."

One high point for me was a signed pass by Shoat Webster. And my dad was a friend of Carl Arnold.

PAUL CIMMIYOTTI

Paul Cimmiyotti was born and raised near Condon, Oregon and moved to Pendleton to open a restaurant in the 1950s. He owned and operated Cimmiyotti's on Main Street for many years, and now is retired and lives on a ranch near Pendleton. He roped steers in both Pendleton and Cheyenne for many years, and his restaurant has been the official watering-hole for cowboys during Round-Up, especially the ropers.

I was born in 1922 on a ranch outside of Condon, Oregon. My dad had 125 head of cattle and a band of sheep and wheatland. That's where I was raised and went to school, all eight grades. The teacher stayed at our home. She used to saddle her horse up, and that's when one teacher taught all eight grades. She did her own janitor work and everything.

I rode horseback to school. Pretty interesting thing in those days. I went to a country school for seven years and never did get a substitute teacher. I know that some days that teacher didn't feel good; nowadays they have substitute teachers all the time.

I knew Glen Cox personally. He was around Condon with the Seale brothers. He was just a cowboy, like the old day cowboys were. I think he was staying with the Seales at that time.

Sid Seale went south and worked on those ranches. Sid and Walt Seale were known for their "drunken ride" at Pendleton. Sid won the wild horse race there one year.

Art Seale was left-handed. That's the brother of Walt and Sid. He chased wild horses. Art used to bring horses from the Steens Mountains clear through John Day, Condon, Arlington and then go out to a ranch by Blalock Canyon. Wouldn't you like to know how they got down there and how they controlled those wild horses?

They tell me one time he tied up the feet on half a dozen of 'em for half a day, just to get their feet a little sore.

In 1935 I rode at a rodeo in Heppner, and Kenneth Depew had some of the stock there. He was roping there. He said, "I'm gonna take you to Ellensburg and enter you in the bull riding."

I was riding bareback horses and roping steers at Heppner. We went to Ellensburg, and I'll be darned if he didn't win the calf roping, and I won the bull riding. I won $47.00.

On June 17, 1939, I got bucked off a bull and kicked in the face, and it broke my jaw. I still have the hospital bill. I was in the hospital for seven days, at $3.50 a day, a total of $24.50. It cost me $5.00 to get my jaw wired. It cost .75¢ for medicine. The lab fees cost $2.50. And the X-rays were $7.50. That was in The Dalles. I've been thinking about asking my doctor if he'd mind if I put this bill up on his wall.

Do you know what the entrance fee at Ellensburg was at that time? Seven dollars and fifty cents. I won $47.00 in the bull riding there, and that was a lot of money back then.

We had a half-mile track at Condon, one of the few in the state, and Lorena Trickey used to go there. I had a bar in Condon, the Round-Up Room, in the '40s. The bar itself was about 30 feet long, and the ceiling was 10 feet high. I had 8 X 10 pictures clear across it and around the back. I had pictures everywhere. Mabel Strickland came into my restaurant and Yakima Canutt. I had a picture of Mabel Strickland when she was Queen of the Round-Up in 1927. I didn't have her sign her picture either. Why do people think they're going to live forever? I'd have had to take it out of the frame to have her sign it.

Course you know I've got a trick horse? He does 16 different things. That's his picture right there. His name is Barney. I'll tell you what he'll do. He'll shake your hand, he'll give you a hug, and he'll give you a kiss. He'll kneel, he'll bow, he'll lay down, and he'll count his age. He'll smile, and if you ask him if he likes Veterinarians, he'll shake his head. He'll get up on a pedestal and, there's the best one of all...I'm standing right alongside of him, and I'll say "Cross and Pray." He'll cross his legs and put his head down.

Do you know this year, 1997 at the Pendleton Round-Up, they didn't even have an act. A lot of kids go to the show. Little dog and cat tricks, they love 'em. That's why I like to go to Joseph. Every year they have an act. I like Joseph. That's such a lovely area. You've got a front row seat everywhere you go.

Cimmiyotti's here in Pendleton was headquarters for ropers. It started in 1959. During Round-Up we got to feed 'em all. I didn't really get interested in roping until the early '70s. I roped in Cheyenne three years in a row.

The story about Larry Mahan and the girl riding into my restaurant horseback one year at Round-Up time gets better all the time. The horse gets bigger each time someone tells the story. It was really a Shetland pony. A girl rode it into the front door of Cimmiyotti's, right here on Main Street. Larry Mahan was with her. The pony walked over to one of the tables and ate the butter right off the dish of a couple from back East who were sitting at a table having dinner. They laughed and laughed over that pony. It was really funny.

The place was loaded. Can you imagine what those people had to say when they got back home? They never got mad, they just laughed.

As the story went on, the horse got bigger, and pretty soon Larry Mahan was riding him. Everybody said, "You gotta get that horse out of here."

I said, "No use getting excited." Larry Mahan was a nice person but full of the devil.

I was arena director here in Pendleton for eight years. Stagecoaches are too heavy to race right. They had them down here, but they finally quit racing them. They're too big and heavy to race. When I was director, in order to make it a decent race, I made the second stagecoach that came into the arena go to the rail. If the first one went to the rail, it got strung out for a mile. So that's the first time they had a decent start and a decent race. The last guy went to the rail and that gave him a chance.

Billy Hindman from Elgin worked with the stagecoaches. Billy is one of the nicest people in the world. I've been to his ranch out at Imbler.

There was a guy by the name of Punch Guyette who went with Tex Austin to the rodeo in England. Every year near the end of Round-Up, they'd say, "The show is about over, there's one more horse to ride. Punch Guyette drew him. I bet he disqualified."

91

ANN CIMMIYOTTI

Ann Cimmiyotti is married to Paul Cimmiyotti. Three daughters, Shannon, Cyd, and Gregory, have been on the Round-Up Court. Each year, the Queen and her court practice for the Grand Entry at the Cimmiyotti ranch south of Pendleton.

We met Jim Shoulders at the Governor's mansion in Wyoming when Cyd, our daughter was Round-Up Princess.

Our daughter, Shannon, was the first one on the Court in 1973. Then Cyd was Princess in 1981, I think it was, and Queen in 1983. And then Gregory was Princess in 1986. You get so many kids on the Court, you forget when they were on it. But it was fun.

We went to Cheyenne when Shannon was Princess. They took the Court to the rodeo in Salinas, California. When Cyd was Princess, they went to Cheyenne both times.

When Gregory was on the Court, they went to the World's Fair in Vancouver. The girls got to do a "Pendleton Day" at the Oregon Exhibition there.

It's changed a lot since Shannon was Princess. They went to Salinas by car and stopped off at Reno and saw Englebert Humperdink. When Cyd was on it, we flew to Cheyenne both times.

When Shannon was Princess, the only thing they gave them was one good suit and one good dress. Everything else we bought. They gave Cyd a good suit with a couple of jackets but no leathers or anything like that. They gave the Court some Pendleton coordinates; by the time Gregory became Princess, they gave them a set of leathers, a Pendleton suit, and all of the coordinating clothes. I mean, they had outfits worth hundreds of dollars—whole outfits.

Now it doesn't cost the kids hardly anything. It was expensive to have your kid on the Court when Shannon was on it. Mrs. Folsom was telling me that when her daughter was on the Court the first time, they changed clothes in a horse trailer. I think she had more than one girl on the Court.

Now the Court travels in a motor home.

The Round-Up Court usually has their first practice out here at our ranch. Paul measures the arena out, just like the Round-Up grounds—the same distance between the jumps and the fence, you know, and stuff like that so they can practice.

DUFF SEVERE

Duff Severe has received national publicity for his leather work and saddle making. He is a long-time resident of Pendleton, Oregon. He has shown his work at the Smithsonian Institution in Washington D.C. and more recently appeared in the Sept./Oct. 2000 issue of "American Cowboy."

I was raised on a ranch in Idaho. It really gets wintry over there. I mean, tough winters. All of us that lived there we just thought it was that way everywhere in the world. When I joined the service and got away, I found out what kind of weather they have in other parts of the country, and I left there.

My dad used to like to braid rawhide. He did hair ropes, like the hair ropes there on the wall. He did that mostly in the winter time. I was really fascinated with the rawhide work. I kick myself because I didn't learn more about the hair work, but I got to foolin' around with the leather and braiding, and I really liked it.

After I got out of the service, I was in the Marine Corps for five years in WWII, I decided to serve an apprenticeship. I had a chance to go to work with Hamley's in Pendleton. I was stationed down at Klamath Falls. There was a Marine base there. I'd braid my stuff at home at night, and then I'd take it down to an old saddle maker and he'd sell it for me. He was really impressed with my work, so he says why don't you learn to be a saddle maker?

I said I wouldn't know where to go to learn. He said Hamley's in Pendleton was a good outfit, and he said he'd write 'em a letter an' tell 'em about me.

So he wrote to Hamley's himself, an' they wrote back an' told him to tell me when I got discharged to send me up there. So when I got discharged, I went up there, and they put me on as an apprentice. That's how I got started. I worked for 'em for about 10 years.

Lester Hamley, his dad was the original. His dad's name was John. Lester's dad started the business.

At the head of the stairs is a picture that will give you an idea of how many people worked there when I was there. It's a big, long picture. They worked about twenty people upstairs. A lot of local people didn't even know that. I never did count the people, but there were quite a few of them. That picture was taken in 1947.

I went to work for 'em in '45. Then my brother Bill come along about a year later. He was getting discharged out of the Navy. He got discharged in Portland and come through on his way home to Idaho. They offered him an apprenticeship in making saddle trees. He went on home to Idaho and was there for awhile, and then he come on back and decided to go to work for Hamley's.

The farthest I go back is Casey Tibbs, Bill Linderman, Deb Copenhaver, and that bunch. Casey used to stay with us up at the Hotel de Cowpunch, just like the cowboys do now. Bill Linderman was married at the time. He usually had his wife. I don't remember Bill ever staying up there, but Casey used to always stay.

I was just up there last week at the Hotel de Cowpunch. I worked all week up there, mopping the floors and everything. I made up thirty bunks. We can handle thirty cowboys at a time. One bunch will be there on Wednesday. Maybe just a few of them will mark high enough that they can stay over for the finals. So the rest leave, and another wave will come in and take their bunks. By the time Round-Up is over, we put up purt'near a hundred cowboys.

The way the Hotel de Cowpunch got started is Alvin Nelson and Bill Martinelli used to travel together. They'd come to Pendleton the day before the Round-Up. They didn't have any idea of where they was gonna stay. It seemed like they had sleeping bags. I had a couple of leather tables there with leather laid out. I told 'em that they could roll their sleeping bags out on these leather tables and stay if they wanted to.

Then there used to be some cowboys from Montana, Ray Hannon, Tex Crawley, they used to come down when they saddled the buckin' horses in the arena. That was the second year. In the meantime I'd rounded up two or three bunks. If I remember right, they come up an' they were helping my wife. She was canning fruit, so they was peeling apples. I fixed 'em up a bunk. There was three of 'em—Eddy Duffy, he was the other one. And Bill Martinelli

95

and Nelson come back. In the meantime, I started gathering up these old army bunks. This was up at the airport. I lived downstairs, but upstairs where the saddle shop was there was a lot of room. It just kept building up and building up, and I kept picking up a few more bunks. This started, I'd say, about 1948-50.

Randy Severe still keeps the Hotel de Cowpunch goin'. There's a big sign. You go in the lower gate at the airport, an' you can't hardly miss it.

For a long time there was six or eight cowboys who were good guitar players. One of them was Reba McEntire's brother, Pate. He was real good. Then there was Monty Hanson, Hawkeye. Bruce Ford was pretty good, and the two Highland boys were real good. And Ivan Daines. But there don't seem to be a single cowboy that plays the guitar now. But the guitar is really the most popular instrument. Any of those well-known bands have two or three guitars. But the younger cowboys haven't taken it up like the older ones.

It happens every year, I'll meet somebody downtown an' they'll say, "Any cowboys staying up there this year?"

And I'll say, "Yeah, they's a bunch of 'em."

"Boy, I'll bet that's a drunken mess!" they'll say.

I'll say, "Why don't you go up there an' visit an' see the drunken mess for yourself?"

But they won't go up there cause they'd have to change their story. They like to be able to say that that's a drunken outfit up there.

Then I'll tell 'em, "Those are businessmen; they didn't come here to get drunk."

I watch pro bull ridin', especially if it's somebody I know, like those Carillo brothers, Adam an' Gilbert. They're twins, you can't tell 'em apart.

They was at the airport, an' they come in. I said, "Gosh, I'm sorry, but I can't tell you guys apart a-tall."

One of 'em said, "Don't feel bad. Our mother can't either."

Every time I see one of them little buggers get on a bull, I just have to look the other way for fear I'll watch 'em get killed right in front of my eyes.

It's real popular, the Bull-A-Ramas. It's really hurt the PRCA cause they kinda pulled out of the PRCA, an' they got their own organization. They can go to one rodeo an' make as much as they would in ten other, smaller rodeos. I've seen little Gilbert win three different times. I've seen him win the $16,000.00. I did see Adam win one. I don't know if he got hurt or somethin', but you don't see him much.

Do you remember the old rodeo photographer De Vere Helfrich? We got quite a lot of his pictures. He was kind of cross-eyed, and they figure that it had something to do with his eyes. It just fit the action. He could get a picture of a guy...when a bronc rider collects pictures, he collects the kind where he really makes a pretty ride, but a contractor collects the ones where they really get flattened. De Vere could get 'em pretty near the way anybody wanted 'em.

I knew Bill Linderman, but I didn't know Bud at all.

I remember one time behind the chutes some cowboy got mad at Bill. Bill was kinda teasin' him. He told Bill, "I'm gonna whip you."

The old chutes down there was built different than now, but anyway, Bill, he jumped up an' grabbed an' overhead beam with his right hand, and he chinned himself three times with one hand, an' then he dropped back down an' jumped back up with his left hand an' chinned himself three times with his left hand. Then he turned around to the guy an' said, "You still want to whip me?"

Did you ever try to chin yourself with one hand?

Jerry Ambler was a real nervous guy, just extremely nervous. He wouldn't even go near his bronc in the chute; he'd get somebody else to saddle it. When it was all ready to go, he'd hang back. Then he'd run up, an' on that bronc an' out he'd go. He didn't want to fool around. He didn't even like to be around when they was saddling or anything.

Casey Tibbs used to do quite a bit the same. Bill Martinelli used to check his saddle an' everything for him.

Casey used to stay with us up there at the Hotel de Cowpunch, just like the cowboys do now.

Casey, he was quite a prankster. I remember one time he used to drive a big Cadillac with a big, silver "CT" on the door. The big quonset building just inside the gate down there at the Round-Up grounds, they usually had some benches along there in the shade. I was sittin' there, talkin' to somebody one day, an' I heard a kind of a commotion, an' here comes the Cadillac in the front gate. I couldn't tell whose it was, but when it got a little farther, I recognized it. It was Casey's.

Casey Tibbs on "Banjo"

He drove in, an' he was dragging his bronc saddle. He pulled up along the corrals where they keep the bulls an' pulled over along the side; by that time people was starting to gather around to see what was going on. So he pulled up there and stopped. He got out and walked up along the corral fence. Finally, he found a rock about so big around. He picked the rock up...by that time there was quite a group. Everybody was circled around his Cadillac.

Casey, with his old bronc saddle on the ground, acted like he didn't know there was a soul around for a hundred miles. He started beating his old bronc saddle all over with this big rock, just whanging away on it. He did that for awhile, and pretty soon he threw the rock down an' got up an' opened his trunk an' threw the saddle in the trunk, slammed it, an' walked off up towards the Indian Tepees. He never did act like there was a soul around. He just got a kick out of pulling that kind of stuff. A lot of those people are probably still scratching their heads right to this day wondering why he did that. He never said a word to anybody. He didn't even look back at 'em. I knew what he was up to. I seen him pull stuff like that before.

He headed toward the Indian village, an' I thought, God bless them poor Indians. He was gonna go an' terrorize them.

He kinda got involved with one of the Indian girls one time, an' the next year or so after that happened, he was up there at the Hotel de Cowpunch, and somebody sent him a package in care of the Round-Up. Some cowboy had picked it up down at the Round-Up office an' brought it up. Casey opened it up, an' it was a little toy bow and arrow.

One time, it was the first day of Round-Up, the cops come up to the Hotel de Cowpunch an' asked if I'd seen Mac Griffith. I figured if the cops was looking for him, that wasn't such a good deal, so I told 'em no, I hadn't seen him. I told them that I didn't think he'd even entered here in Pendleton, so they left. I knew Mac was downtown at the Round-Up office. They were drawing stock. So I run right down there. Mac was a pretty tough guy hisself. I went in...they was about a dozen cowboys around there, an' I said, "Mac come outside, I'm gonna beat the hell out of you."

I turned around an' just started walking out, an' he started followin' me. All them other cowboys run out the side doors, runnin' to get a ringside seat. They wanted to watch the fight.

Anyway, I got Mac out by hisself where nobody else could hear, an' I said, "Mac, the cops are lookin' for you." An' I don't to this day know why they were lookin' for him. I think he went ahead an' worked the Round-Up. I don't know how he managed to stay clear of 'em, but I don't think they got their hands on him.

Another time a guy came up to me in back of the chutes an' asked if I was Duff Severe. I said yeah. He said, "Well, I'm Turk Greenough." I couldn't hardly believe it. He was there watching Deb Greenough, his grandson. That was within the last three or four years. He was a real old guy. I couldn't believe it when he told me he was Turk Greenough.

Eddy Akridge was dealin' cards down at Benny Binion's in Vegas for a long time. Benny loved cowboys. He hired a lot of them retired cowboys—he took care of 'em. If they couldn't work, he took care of 'em anyway.

I knew Sid Seale. His wife, Doris is still alive. She lives on a ranch at Condon. Sid used to have the "Drunken' Ride" in his trick riding. He used to stand up on the horse an' weave all over like he'd been drinking.

My brother, Bill an' I were partners in the saddle business. I don't know how to start to tell you about Bill. He was my brother. I loved him. We got along real good. All Bill's friends were cowboys. He was a pretty good roper. For awhile he had the fastest time in the bulldoggin' of any Oregon cowboy at the Round-Up. I don't know if it still stands.

When we decided to go on our own making saddles, we left Hamley's. We worked there for ten years, an' I finally got up to $1.78 an hour. Anyway, we decided to leave an' go on our own. We had that big old building at the airport, but we really wasn't plannin' to stay here in Pendleton. We went down to Heppner an' looked at Noble's...it was for sale. Anyway, Tim Bernard from up around Omak, Washington, got wind we were gonna move, an' he said, "If you guys would move up here to Omak, I'll put you up a building, any kind of building you want. You just draw up the plans, an' I'll have it built for you."

Tim Bernard was a rancher an' stock contractor at Omak.

Then some local guys, Vern Terjeson, Arvene Porter, an' Tony Vey, they all came to us an said, "Don't leave here. If you stay here, we'll guarantee you that we'll keep you so busy that you can't leave."

So we thought, well, we'll give it a try. Sure enough, Tony Vey he come up an' orders two saddles that I know he didn't need a-tall. The other guys did the same. They did keep us busy. We never did get caught up. Never to this day. An' we never run a single ad. We never spent five cents for advertising. Randy only takes orders in the month of January, an' he gets enough to last him a year.

I remember one time Joe Malloy an' I were together, an' Joe said, "Let's go see Bud Jory."

So, we went down to the Round-Up grounds. Me an' Joe was walkin' along there, an' there was a guy breaking horses. He saw us comin', an' Joe was a little closer to him than I was. This guy says, "Watch out for that horse tied up there, he's a kicking son-of-a-gun. Don't walk too close; he'll kick you."

Joe said, "I'll show you how to handle them kickin' horses."

He walked right up behind that old horse an' give him a thump on the rump. Then he got him by the tail. When he grabbed a-holt of that horse, that old horse just almost squatted down. That cotton pickin' Joe got that horse by the tail, an' he put one foot up on one of his hocks, an' pretty soon he had the other foot up there, an' he's standin' on that horse's hocks, pullin' on his tail. The horse

100

was just shakin' all over, tremblin' like that. Pretty soon Joe stepped down an' steps back, an' he told that guy, "That's how you handle them kickin' kind."

I never saw anything like that in my life. Never. That was the craziest thing I ever saw anybody do. I'll never forget that.

There's been so many people visit me here at my home I've lost track. One time a couple of ladies come out, an' they said, "Would you mind if we bring some of our club members out to see your place on the river?"

I said, "No, I don't mind."

I'm not kidding you a bit, pretty soon a string of people come stringin' in here, an' they was three buses parked out there in front. They was about 200 people come through my house.

I still do a lot of work in my shop upstairs. I couldn't get any work done with a phone in the house, so I had it taken out. I didn't have the time to talk for an hour on the phone. The only way I could get rid of 'em was to say the doorbell was ringing.

I gotta go.

Eddy Akridge on Whirlaway. Yuma. '50

NORM CONNER

Norm Conner is a member of the Umatilla Confederated Tribes, and lives at Mission, Oregon. Norm is an avid collector of western tack and historical artifacts, and has been active in Indian rodeos throughout the Northwest.

Jim White raised racehorses. They used to run horses up to Cayuse and then down here at the Round-Up.

Edith Johnson used to win the Squaw Race all the time, back in the early teens. Used to be quite a horsewoman. Ruth Johnson is related to her, I think. She loaned me a couple of horses to parade on. That was in the '50s.

Tom Johnson and his wife were the last ones to go up and down the mountains here horseback. That was clear into the '50s. They used to camp up there at Telephone Ridge out there on the point. They used to have a horse corral there. They did root digging and berry picking and stuff like that. Just camping out.

You used to have people that had game hides yet. Clarence Burke was one of the last ones. They had one Happy Canyon Princess here a few years ago that had a cougar pelt behind the saddle. You don't see that stuff anymore.

Alex Saluskin had racehorses here in Pendleton. He was from Toppenish, Washington. There was more people from Toppenish over here. I see their grandchildren now still have horses. I'd like to look at a program and think of the names again.

We've got a picture of Richard and Bob Burke around here somewhere taken in 1925. They were both involved in racing.

Charley Wocatsie used to rope calves here at the Round-Up in the late '40s and through the '50s.

When I was still riding quite a bit, my mother went to the Country Club rummage sale, and she came back and threw me an old

Stetson like you see in the old rodeo pictures. A big Stetson. "I bought you a good hat," she told me.

I asked her how much she paid for it. She said, "a quarter." I wore that old hat 'till it fell apart. The bands on those old hats were hard. You could hit something with it.

I go to Western auctions. I went to Arlington to help a guy brand some calves about seven or eight years ago, and the guy had a barn full of old tack. I asked him what he was gonna do with it, and he said, "I live here, an' I'm just gonna keep it here." He had old chaps that thick. If they'd drop on you, you'd knock yourself out, they were that heavy. I had a quirt made out of Elkhorn. I used to make a lot of them. I have an old Hamley 'Potlatch' saddle, too. From my aunt's dad.

I used to feed cattle for old Ralph Tachella. He had a silver-mounted saddle. You had to be a man to pick that thing up and throw it on a horse.

You don't hardly ever see the old silver mounted saddles anymore.

Art Parr, he's 90 something. I was showing him some of the old pictures of the school out here at Mission. He inherited Til Taylor's Martingale. I'm gonna go out and get a picture of it. Nobody makes those any more.

It took a lot of work to make those. It goes down through a ring along the chest and up under the jaw.

When I was rodeoing, I was up in Dayton, Washington, and one of the guys up there used to shoot pictures like Doubleday with the big camera with a harness on his chest. For some reason, he didn't get out of the arena during the bull riding, an' the bull throwed the guy off and then took after the guy with the camera. He grabbed the fence, and that bull hit him and throwed him up in the air, but he had a death grip on that fence. His feet would go way up in the air when the bull hit him, but he wouldn't let go of that fence. Guys were layin' down an' rollin' around on the ground laughin' so hard. One of the clowns had a dog that went in an' saved him. A little, small dog run up an' got the bull right by the nose.

They had a rodeo up at Herman Rosenberg's in 1948. My uncle had a horse there. They called him Dewey like the guy that was running for President. Everyone was scared of him, so they'd "cinch bind" him. He'd go like a quarter horse, but he had feet like a workhorse, and boy could he clear the ground.

103

You hardly see a horse get off the ground anymore. They can't buck a foot off the ground. Horses used to buck with all four feet in the air.

Did you ever see pictures of where the bowl was in the Indian Village where they used to do their celebrations? That only lasted until up in the '40s; then they filled it in.

Up at the airport they used to have Indians simulate setting fire to covered wagons to start out the Round-Up. Some of those guys would be on green horses. Round-Up would be over before they got back to the campgrounds.

Guy Cash used to ride down here. He was a good rider. He went up to Calgary and Cheyenne. He was a little guy, but he could ride like mad.

The Snake River country is really steep. In fact, Duff Severe, before they moved down from up on the hill, after they had bought that place across the river, he got an order for eight modified, Association roughout trees. He called the guy back and said, "Is this order right? Do you want eight saddles?"

The guy said, "That's right."

Duff asked why so many saddles.

"I'm getting sick and tired of losing my cowboys up here in this Snake River country. They try to ride in and out of these canyons and fall off their horses and roll down the hills."

So that's what he got. The saddles got a high back on 'em, you know. The Snake River comes around between Idaho and Oregon and then on over into Washington. That's awful steep country over there. Those guys stayed in the saddle all day, and they really knew how to ride.

BOB CHAMBERS

*Bob Chambers is a two-time National Finals Rodeo an-
nouncer who hails from Portland, Oregon. Bob has announced rodeos all over the western part of the country. He
was the voice of the Pendleton Round-Up for twenty-two years
from 1967 to 1989. He currently lives with his wife Phyllis in
Sun City, Arizona.*

I've spent my life pretty much in the rodeo game and around
it. I don't know when I fell in love with the cowboy legend. I wasn't
a country boy to start with; I was born in Portland in 1923. Somewhere along the line the cowboy bug bit me pretty hard, and I've
never recovered. It led to trying to cowboy. I rodeoed on a very
slim shoestring of a budget from the time I was 15 until I went into
the army. Most of us in those days rodeoed when we could and
worked when we had it. We rodeoed for the fun of it because there
wasn't any money in it for anybody, really. You could win first and
go home with $35. I loved the life.

I rode my first bull out of the chute about 1939 at Sedro
Woolley, Washington, and I got to the whistle. Nobody was as surprised as I was. I'll tell you what, it did something to my mind, and
the fever developed from there. I couldn't wait to get on the next
one. I had 'em step on me and kick me and mash me; one lay on my
leg one time, and it broke my spur. I had one hook me right in the
face when I was sittin' right in the middle of him at Fort Riley, Kansas, but as far as being badly hurt by a bull, I never was. And that's
rare. I wasn't riding them as often or of the caliber they have nowadays. When I was ridin', the Brahma was just becoming a starring
role in rodeo you might say. The producers wanted the hump-back,
silver-tipped bull. That was what the public expected. Head for
head, these bulls they're riding now in the PBR and the PRCA are

far ahead of what we got on in those days. A Brahma in the Northwest was a rarity in the first place. He didn't come from this type of country. Howard Merrin, who was an old friend of mine in Seattle, was one of the early bull riders, and he says the same thing.

It started about 1929. But look what it did...bull riding stands on its own now. This PBR thing is tremendously popular and doing well. But you'll also notice the riders continually change. They either get weeded out by injury or common sense takes over, and they say, "Hey, I'm gonna get killed doin' this," and go home. Thankfully, these kids have the courage to develop and go to these schools and learn, and then they get into the PBR and go for that big money. You give a kid from a little punkin roller town in Texas a check for $22,000, and what's he gonna do? He's gonna be there again next week. It takes a lot of guts to rodeo on that basis.

My rodeo winnings were very limited, and I'm the first one to admit it.

I was drafted right out of high school. It was January of '42, I guess. Two weeks later, after I graduated from high school I was in the army. I was at Fort Lewis, Washington, and it wasn't even a week before I was at Fort Riley. They shipped us on a train. My buddy Ed Hepfer and I got off the train in the middle of the night, colder than blazes in January in Kansas; out there on the plains it gets a little crisp. They picked us up in a horse-drawn buggy and hauled us out to Camp Funston, which was a Cavalry training center. We just grabbed an empty bunk and unrolled a mattress and went to bed. We didn't even have a proper uniform or bedding or anything. We just kept our overcoats on and went to bed.

So we took our basic there. We were exposed pretty heartily to the Army way. What I remember most is hard work. If you were on stable police, you got up at 3:30 a.m., and you might still be there at 9 o'clock that night. There was no mercy. But I'll tell you what, you got exposed to horses in every way you could be exposed to 'em. It was a great experience.

When we finished basic, they put me to driving a team. I'd drive a team and load hay, anything that was done with horses and wagons. It was in the dying days of the cavalry. There was such an effort on to retain the cavalry, but I think everybody really knew the end of the line was really coming, and a year later it did. But, it was a great experience, and in those big mounted reviews we had lots of fun. Full uniforms, everything spit and polish; eight hundred horses on the parade grounds with pack horses; it was something that people nowadays never had a chance to experience or to be a part of. When that Saturday once a month came, you were mighty proud to be a part of that. You couldn't help it. If you loved to be on a horse, and you were an American, you had to be proud; I'll put it that way. There was just something about the spirit the old horse outfits had.

We had cross country runs that they made movies of...I got to see one of 'em. That's one of the biggest reservations in the country. They worked those horses and then turned a bunch of 'em out to rest and rehabilitate themselves out in the open country. We processed new horses in from Fort Reno, Oklahoma and Virginia. Right off the trains. This lasted about a year and a half, and then the bugle blew and we went across.

July 4th, 1943, we had a rodeo at Fort Riley. It was at Camp Funston at the end of our basic training. We had a poppin' good rodeo there. We had a lot of the wild west boys from Colonel Eskew's outfit back in New Jersey. They'd rodeoed with him, and they just were naturals for the cavalry; they all had horse experience. They were boys that we met as a result of this rodeo. There was a lot of California boys in our outfit. It was quite a gathering, and we had 13,000 people at that rodeo. They'd never heard of an army rodeo. People sat on a grassy hillside; as I remember, we had bleachers on one side.

I got lucky. I was 19 years old and drew a bull called Fiddle Face. Jimmy Howe, representing the Sidney, Iowa, Rodeo Committee who came with the stock, told me that this bull hadn't been qualified on in four years. Well, here's a little 19-year-old kid just doing basic in the army. I put my bull rope on him and rode him and won the bull riding. Pure, straight luck. This bull hooked me right in the face while I was sittin' in the middle of him after the whistle blew and broke my nose. I've got a picture of this to show you what the result was. It was just pure luck because I couldn't ride that bull...I knew I couldn't, but I did get to the dinger, and they let me win it. A lot of other guys got bucked off, and I'd ridden a "reputation" bull. One of the judges was a fine old saddle maker who lives in California. I got a $50 War Bond, $45.00 in cash and a home-made buckle made by Bill Wyche, a little Texas cowboy who volunteered to make these trophy buckles. In addition, my name even made "Hoofs & Horns" magazine.

I've still got that buckle. It would cost a maximum of 40¢, but it's a treasure to me. And then it didn't go on my belt right. He put the loop on the wrong end, and it wouldn't go on your belt right. If you put it on right, the engraving was upside down. Bill Wyche could play the fiddle. He lived near Midland, Texas. He was a ranch cowboy. He'd get about five bottles of beer in him, and he could literally eat a fiddle alive; sober, he couldn't play a note. He was a great little guy.

We wore Levi's and Levi jackets at Fort Riley quite often. As long as they was blue denim, nobody cared. They fit, they didn't hang on you like a blanket.

The Fort Riley days were somethin'. It was just Army duty, but the horses added a lot of spice. You lived with 'em. I mean you lived with 'em; all day, thirty-five or forty miles on horseback across country on maneuvers and boy, when you got in the picket line your horse was watered, tied up, fed, groomed, and his feet and back were checked. Then you took care of yourself. It might be dark before you got to do that. You rode for fifty minutes, and you led for ten.

We stopped at a little village one time—a little rock building—a store, way out in the country someplace near Fort Riley. I couldn't tell you where it was. We pulled up there and we were resting the horses; everybody was on the ground, holding their horses, and I saw this cooler outside this old store. They didn't have room for it inside. It said Dr. Pepper on the side of it. That was the first time I ever saw the name Dr. Pepper. I thought, what is Dr. Pepper? It was 1942 or '43. So they sent one guy out of every troop to go to that store and get everybody a candy bar or something; and I'll never forget, there was a bunch of city boys in our outfit, and this little Texan, Billy Jones, he's a dear friend of mine; he lives in Ellensburg, Washington now, I see him every Round-Up time—and he was as Texas as it gets. When the boy from his troop started back to the store, Billy stood up in his stirrups and said, "Hey, bring back right smart!" Everybody said, "What did he say?"

What he meant was "bring back a bunch."

I kid him about that every time I see him. I say "Hey, bring back right smart."

He'll say, "Ah, shut up."

In 1943, following basic training, I was stationed in Fort Riley, Kansas. I was with the 129th Cavalry Regiment. I got a letter from

Lynn Beutler in Oklahoma, and they let me off to go to a rodeo in Dodge City. They were having a hard time getting enough cowboys because everybody was in the army.

I got on the bus first and got way off out there someplace, and they had a lot of high water, and the bus got stopped. I had my riggin' bag and my bull rope, so I jumped off the bus and here was a train. I asked that bus driver where the train was going. He said it had to go through Dodge City. The rodeo was the next day, so I waded through that water and got on the train and wound up in Dodge City. Ernie Barnett was competing at that rodeo. I admired him. I watched him ride broncs there. Former world all-around champion Louis Brooks was also there.

Freckles Brown and Ernie Mutch from Montana were at Fort Riley. Mostly cowboys. The rest of 'em were weeded out pretty fast. Two clowns were there that worked for Colonel Jim Eskew out of New Jersey. They were known as the "Brahma Twins," Clyde and Claude Rogers. He put on the first building rodeo back before there were any. Fort Worth was the first, they said.

A friend from Turkey, Texas, his name is Morris Stevens, put on a rodeo a year after we had ours at Fort Riley in 1943. He put on one right there in Junction City, which is just outside the gate at Fort Riley.

Turk Greenough was in the 129th, but what troop I don't know. He was only there a short time. But during that time, he had Sally Rand, who he was married to at that time, come down, and they promoted a rodeo at Junction City, just right outside the gates of Fort Riley. They had Sally Rand there as a guest draw. She ran up a phone bill that nobody could see over and then left town.

We made a river crossing out of Fort Riley on the Smokey Hill River one time when I was in the Cavalry. We crawled out on the sand, and they called a halt. It was a real warm day, and I had a little blood-bay gelding I rode most of the time on troop duty. He laid down on that warm sand, and I just laid down and put my head down on his neck and went to sleep, and they took our picture, and I've been told the picture is still in the commanding officer's home at Fort Riley.

They slapped us in an infantry outfit, and we went through two campaigns in Burma with Merrill's Marauders. That was a whole different chapter in my life. There was never anything funny or pleasurable about it from the time we landed in India until I came home. It's nothing but a black memory. I don't like to recall it because it brings back a lot of bad days.

The environment alone over there could kill you. It was a sorry place. They nearly starved us to death because of the supply situation. The only way they could get supplies to us was in airplanes. There were no helicopters. They'd come over at a great altitude and drop those big sacks of food out, and we'd wait at the edge of the jungle and pop out into an open place and pick up these cargo sacks; and do you know what we found? Most of the time it was mule feed. Nothing there for the G. I.'s. It was for the mules. We wouldn't see those planes again for weeks. So we took this stuff as kind of a cereal and made a mush out of it and tried to eat that stuff. We had to have something to eat. We killed the little native Brahmas that run around wild; they wasn't as big as a police dog, little inbred mountain cattle. We'd knock one of those down once in awhile with a carbine and hang him up in a tree. The climate wasn't conducive to cooling one out, so we spent a lot of time recovering from eating raw meat. It was a pretty tough time. It's just a nightmare. I don't like to look back on it.

We had another little impromptu rodeo in Burma. We were laid over there, resting our mules. We had to get our health back. Morris Stevens and I and two of the other boys built these chutes. We had four buckin' chutes and the big main posts were sitting on flat rock. We'd cut that big bamboo at the joints so we had a good solid base to come down on that rock. By the time the rodeo was over, there was one chute that was standing. We'd gathered a bunch of wild Brahmas and got 'em within a mile and a half of the arena, and we lost 'em, and everybody was too tired to go get 'em. We just never got 'em gathered back again. Bill Wyche, as I remember, won the bronc riding, riding a mule with a saddle, and I won the bareback riding. They said that I was the only one that really got aggressive and was spurrin' my mule. So I got lucky again. We had Chinamen there. I know we had some Japs. I know it as well as I'm sittin' here.

We didn't have any whistle. We'd just fire a carbine when the ride was over. We were ridin' ten seconds, I think.

We had another little jackpot rodeo one time, and my mule stayed in one place and bucked and the other kids' run off in the jungle and scraped him off on the tree limbs. We were always doing that though, just matchin' somebody. We had a home-made riggin' and we'd make home-made spurs, anything that looked like home. I had an old pair of Levi's that I wore until they were just shreds. They finally went the way of all flesh. We had a little ceremony, and I buried 'em, said a few words and put up a little cross over 'em. Cause they looked like home. My mother and dad would send me Levi's in a sealed can along with some food, cookies, whatever.

Joe Pedro gave me my first chance on a mike. He had a little ranch rodeo near Echo, Oregon, like they had around here in the '40s and '50s. His announcer didn't show up, and he asked me to do it. He asked me to get on the back of this flat bed truck with their little Mickey Mouse sound outfit and announce his show. Well, somebody had to do it, so I said "I'll help you Joe." I got up there and did the best I could. Next week I did another one. Then I had another one. There was no money involved. They were just picnic deals. Everybody brought food, and we'd ride a few steers and rope some calves and wild cow milking. One thing led to another, and people would stop by and say, "Hey, that sounds good. You did a good job."

Well, that made me think about it. I was making saddles for next to nothing every week, taking home about $75.00 a week trying to feed my family. So I wrote a letter to John Ratteray in Condon, Oregon. This was in 1950 or 1951. I waited and waited—this was in the off season, of course. No answer. Finally, in early spring, I think it was March or April, here come a letter from John, and he hired me. I nearly died of a heart attack. The rodeo was on the 4th of July and had two performances.

I got $25.00 a day, and I furnished the sound. I thought I'd never see another poor day. I was on my way.

There was a guy up on the Umatilla River out at Cayuse who had a Dude Ranch, and he put on some little Sunday rodeos for his guests. He went broke. He had this sound system, and he offered it to me. I had just made myself a nice rough-out saddle. So Dale Mercer, who worked with me at Hamley's at that time, he was the head salesman, sold this saddle for me, and I took the money and bought this sound system. I took it to Condon to work the rodeo. Several years later I sold that same system to the committee at Newport, Washington, for more than I gave for it. But that's the way I got my start.

111

My first professional show was at Union, Oregon. It was 1958. I was there 36 straight years. That show is older than Pendleton by two years. I did the races and the rodeo and everything at that time. I never claimed to be a race announcer. I told 'em from day one that I wasn't a race announcer, but they said, "You can do it."

In 1958 I had Union, Halfway, and Moro. Those were my first three RCA rodeos. I started in Pendleton in 1967. That's the first time they had me here at home. I got Portland P. I. (Pacific International Livestock Show); and Lewiston, Walla Walla and Pendleton in a two week period, and I thought I'd died and gone to heaven.

1973 was my first year at the National Finals. I worked with Tom Hadley from Brady, Texas. He and I got along great. I enjoyed Tom very much. The next time was '81; they picked me again. I guess that year the cowboys had a good deal to do with who they wanted or had a say in it. Bob Ragsdale let me know that, and it made me feel real good. I did it with Chuck Parkinson that year. He was a real "pro" and a fine man.

Bob Ragsdale was President of the PRCA at that time. Karl Doering called me from Roseburg before I ever knew I'd been selected, and he said, "Hey, you got the National Finals."

I said, "Well, why didn't they tell me? How come you know?"

"Oh, it's in the woodwork. Bobby Christensen told me."

Finally, they got around to letting me know. So it was a real thrill, and I had a shot at some real money. It was quite an experience. In those days, Clem McSpadden did the opening. He was General Manager. They couldn't have picked a better man to do that opening. He had the culture, he had feel of that thing from day one. Boy, when he'd do that opening everybody was ready to rodeo. He announced the opening, Tom would take the bareback riding, and then I would go with the next event and do the calf roping. We just traded off like that through the program. That's where Reba McEntire was discovered. They give Clem credit for discovering her. He had her singing the National Anthem at the National Finals. Boy, it got her a lot of recognition. It was nice to be there, and Clem made you feel appreciated. He called me at the office and said, "I want you to know how glad I am to see you finally get a chance. You've had it coming for a long time." He made me feel good and put me at ease.

Freckles Brown was another soother. He was one of the greatest little cowboys in the world, one of the most dedicated little rodeo cowboys. Freckles never had an enemy in the world. He was a bull rider and a great one, and he rode saddle broncs. I've got a picture of him gettin' the bad end of the deal with 5 Minutes To Midnight. A lot of people got the bad end of that old pony. Anyway, Freckles was the go-between on the phone between the roping chutes and the announcer's booth. He could see I was stall walkin', and Tom was working, and I was sweating it out—the first shot—twelve to fourteen thousand of the most knowledgeable rodeo fans in the world, and they're waiting for you to say something right. Boy, I was sweating it out, pacing back and forth, just waitin' my turn. Freckles walked up and grabbed me by the arm. "Now look here," he says. "This is just another rodeo. It's a little bigger, sure, more people. It's just another rodeo. Do what you do anyplace else. That's why you're here."

You know, that helped me. He was the greatest little guy. He loved everybody. He had a kind word for everybody. He'd do anything for anybody. He could have the worst bull in the herd drawn anyplace and be asleep on the hood of a car waiting his turn. He just had no nerves. When Freckles was in trouble, when he was feeling the pressure from a rank bull, you'd see those knees come up, and he'd hump up a little bit. You'd see the lower part of his legs curve in behind those big old shoulders, and boy when that whistle blew, he'd be there. He was one great little bull rider.

That night that he rode that bad bull of Jim Shoulders', Tornado, they said that he could have been elected the Governor of Oklahoma. The ovation he got hasn't been seen in that building since. An Okie, and everybody loved him.

They picked me again in '81. This is the Buckle they give me. It's got both years on it. It's a very special buckle to me. Pendleton gave me one. I've got twelve that I was awarded through the years. My son, Jim wears one of 'em that was given to me by the Cree Indians. For several years I did that Cowboy-Christmas rodeo at Hobbema, Alberta. It's out of Edmonton. You fly to Calgary and then to Edmonton. I'd leave Arizona Christmas evening and fly into there that night and arrive about 1 o'clock in the morning. They'd send an Indian over to get me, and it would be 30 below. This Indian couldn't get the door unlocked on the car, and I thought I was gonna freeze flat to death cause I had on all the clothes I owned. I'd come out of that heat in Arizona. That was fun, and it was one of the nicest jobs I had. I think I did that six times for 'em, and then the oil money kinda petered out. It was all built with oil money. It was a fantastic complex up there. It was all indoors. I was employed by the Ermineskin Band of the Cree tribe. Their Chief was Lawrence Wildcat, and he paid me with an honorarium.

The opening of the Hobbema rodeo with the Cree Indians was something that was a little different, and I felt was very impressive. At a certain time, usually 8 o'clock in the evening...even Indian time comes at 8 o'clock...this building was very, very nice. It seated about 6,000 as I remember. At 8 o'clock I'd be in the announcer's stand behind the chutes on a wrought iron podium. A fanfare would go up, a spotlight would hit me, and I had to be ready. I'd greet the crowd and go into my normal routine, getting a little enthusiasm going about a rodeo at Christmas time. I'd go right to the bucking chutes. The first thing out was the bareback riding, but before that ever started, here came Santa Claus on a bucking horse.

I would be willing to bet that the costume on this long, lanky, Indian boy wearing it would have cost several thousand dollars. It had ermine skin trim on the jacket and around the tops of the boots and on the tassel on his cap. This boy would try to make it to the end of the arena on a bucking horse. It was called The Cowboy Christmas Rodeo. That's why they wanted to start it that way. It was a very colorful opening with lots of flags and lots of color, and I always enjoyed having a part in it.

One time I walked into the old Pendleton Hotel, and Mac Barbour was getting off the elevator. I walked over and shook hands with him, and we visited a little bit and I said, "What kind of a year did you have, Mac?"

He thought a minute, and he said, "I think I'm two halters to the good." He had great stock and put on many good rodeos in his day.

He went out to feed his bulls one morning, and this old bull took a run at him and knocked him down. He says, "I just couldn't figure it out. He didn't use to treat me like that." He says, "I got up, and I got a stick and got after him, and he knocked me down again." He said, "That did it."

He and Harley Tucker would get behind the chutes the first day in Pendleton and they'd trade hats. Mac would say, "Well, Harley, what are we gonna do with this feller? Are we gonna let him ride or are we gonna stick him in the ground?" And Harley would laugh, "hee hee hee," that cacklin' laugh he had.

"Well, I don't know," Harley would say, and they'd go back and forth, and all this time they were wearin' each other's hats. They did have a time together.

I had the job at Halfway at the Pine Valley Fair in 1958, and Harley came in and didn't have a place to stay. There was a little tiny motel there with about four units in those days, and I happened to have one of 'em. I had brains enough to call up and reserve one. Harley came in and needed a place to clean up, so we were chattin' away there—he was just out on his feet. He'd go three or four days and never lay down, and that's what killed him. If he didn't have time to do something, he'd just make time and go ahead and do it. He died of a heart attack behind the chutes at Vancouver. He stepped down off the back of the chute and dropped dead.

I worshiped Montie Montana. One of my great friends. I worked with him all over the country. I never knew anybody who could pick up rapport with that audience like Montie as soon as he came through that gate. They didn't care what he could do, they just wanted to see Montie Montana. Oh, that color and that flash...there were a lot of better trick ropers than he was, but I'll tell you what, he had the audience, and he had the adoration of the people everywhere he went.

We pulled into Mobridge, South Dakota, one time, and Montie was there. He pulled in after we got there. We pulled into the grounds, and my wife and I hooked our trailer up. Then, here came Montie with that big van. He was haulin' six head. I went out and helped him unload. We put the tarp over the horses to keep them out of the sun and bedded 'em down and watered 'em and fed 'em. I told Montie, "My wife just baked a Bundt cake, you better come over."

We spent the rest of the afternoon together, and that Bundt cake disappeared while we read his scrapbook until 7 o'clock that night.

He lived a great life. He got a standing ovation here in Pendleton the last year he was here. He spun the big loop around and dropped it and backed his horse away, and that crowd came up as one. I sat there with tears running down my face. His wife told me later that was the last time she saw him on horseback. He had that stroke and passed away.

24—Dick Griffith, Famous Rodeo Star, in Wild Brahma Bull Riding Contest

"Stryker's Rodeo Gloss Series"

Twelve years ago, I'm behind the chutes at Pendleton getting ready for the show, and here's Dick Griffith with his rope, and in the program he's in the bull riding. He hadn't been on a bull, how long? He jumped out and won the first go-round. I mean, he rode that bull. He was 20 years older than anybody there, maybe 30 years older.

He was in his early 60s, Dick Griffith, four time World Champion. He was the greatest male trick rider that ever existed, rode all over the world...England, France, South America. I walked up, and I said, "Dick, aren't you stretching things a little bit?"

He looked around and said, "Well, for godsake, you're the first guy that even recognized me.

I said, "Well shoot yes," and we shook hands. I said, "Are you sure you're doing the right thing?"

He said, "If I didn't think I was doing the right thing, I wouldn't be doin' it," and he looked me right in the eye.

Some of the guys had never heard of him. Here he come on Saturday with his second bull, and he was gonna win it all and his wrist broke. His dad was Curley Griffith, who started out in the wild west days around Fort Worth, and he could do it all. I mean, this Curley Griffith could ride bulls and broncs, he was a trick roper...just a real old Wild Westerner. Dick was a super guy. He was one of those people who could not stand getting older. He just couldn't understand why he couldn't go right on being Dick Griffith. He won four world titles. He made a bet in Arizona that he'd ride their best bull with a glass of water in his free hand. When the ride was over, he still had water in the glass. The bull belonged to Otho Kinsey.

One time I wrote a letter to Bill Linderman; he had just won the bulldogging here in Pendleton. When I closed the letter, I said, "I just want to send my congratulations for winning the bulldogging there at home."

He wrote back and said, "I really enjoyed winning the bulldogging at Pendleton. I'm not that good anymore, but I got lucky. I told those other guys that if they couldn't bulldog anymore they could always join the army."

My dad took me to this Wild West Show that followed the Al G. Barnes Circus. I think it cost 25¢ to see the circus...that's how thin things were; it was during the depression. I was about eight. It was in Portland, Oregon. With the show was what they called a Wild West Concert, and you had to pay 25¢ more to see the Wild West Show. Well, Dad was driving a cookie truck in Portland for about $25 a month. He let me have the last quarter to go to that Wild West Show, and he stood outside and waited. That's the kind of a dad I had. Anyway, Ken Maynard, the movie star, was the star of the show. So I took in this show, and they rode bucking horses on the end of a string in a little circle, and they had all kinds of trick shooting; they came in with what looked like a rifle, but it was full of bird shot, and they'd throw something up to the top of the canvas, and this old guy would ride by and shoot it. If he got a shot within three feet of it, he was gonna hit it. But, anyway, to a little kid this was a living dream. So I was hanging around after the show, and here comes Ken Maynard leading this white horse. He had a trunk there for his saddle. He says, "Hey, partner, would you hold the lid back on that thing so I can put my saddle away?" This was like having God speak to me, only better. This guy was really right there in my eye. So I stood there and held that trunk, and I don't remember what he said or even if he did say anything. He grinned at me, and he was a fine looking, big man. I just stood around holding the lid of the trunk so he could put his silver-mounted saddle away. There was a place for the tapaderas and a place for the bridle. He just had this white horse on a halter, and he was through for the night. When he got done, he reached over and ruffled my head and said, "Thanks curly." I had real curly hair back then. I never quit dreaming about that night at the Wild West Show.

Forty-five or fifty years later I was at North Platte, Nebraska, and I had no further contact with Wild West Shows whatsoever until the Buffalo Bill Show hired me to do the first opening two performances when they revived the show under Montie Montana Jr. Well, Montie told me he wanted me to do this thing when it was ready. So he called me in Canada and had me rush down there. We drove all night as I remember. The next day I was with George Taylor who was appearing with the show. He was a trick rider and trick roper, clown—this guy could do anything. He had trained Brahmas; he had all kinds of good acts. He was a terrific showman. We walked around there together. He said, "Let's go over to the horse tent."

We walked into this gigantic horse tent, and I'll tell ya, you saw horses of every color that you can imagine. Everything showy that they could have to add to that show was there. They had the original format for the Buffalo Bill Show. They even got a gatlin' gun out of the South someplace from an old boy to use in the show. They had all kinds of feature acts there for the first two weeks. I had the privilege of introducing all these acts. Working between these segments of the show, we'd bring in these top acts like George Taylor and other people, and I would work those acts and then I would turn 'em over to the show announcer. It just went like silk. My job was to introduce some of the big county officials who were there for the opening of the show. It was for two days; that's all I could stay. I had other shows. But the night I stepped into that horse tent, that night with Ken Maynard came back to me just like it was five minutes ago. I've never had anything hit me so hard. That tent and all of those fabulous horses and all that color...so much Old West atmosphere. It wasn't cowboy. It was a show world. But I think to this day that that night at the circus had a lot to do with the way I felt about that show.

Homer Holcomb, world famous rodeo clown, showed up one night at the rodeo years and years ago at Newport, Washington. He was livin' up in that north country between Newport and Sand Point, Idaho, a little tiny town. I guess I'm the only one that recognized him and realized who he was. He had a little dog with him. Somethin' told me that this has got to be Homer Holcomb in the grandstand. So I waited for the right moment, and I said, "Ladies and Gentlemen, we've got a man here tonight that is synonymous with the great days of rodeo." I said, "A man who has entertained thousands and thousands of people all over the United States, and I think we should take time to honor his presence here tonight." And I said, "Homer Holcomb, will you please stand up."

He stood up, and they just tore that place down. So I had him come out in the arena, and this little dog did tricks. He showed that little dog and took off his hat and went back to his seat. I'll never forget that night if I live to be a thousand. Homer was wearing an old pinstripe blue suit.

It was the first time I ever had the privilege of introducing him, and I thought, "I'm gonna do this if they fire me." I'd been there 25 years. They didn't fire me.

It was quite a hit. People came around afterwards asking for his autograph and spent time with him. He had to be, I'm just guessin', in his early 80s.

I used to love to call a good trick ridin' because I took an interest in it and studied it and found out the names of the various things they were doin', so I could identify 'em over the mike. I've had the girls come and thank me for doing the kind of job I do for em. I really did my best to sell 'em because even then you could see it slipping. The committees and the demands from the cowboys for more prize money just made it impossible to hire those good acts. It's a sad deal.

Muggs Bentley. He's a grand old gentleman. Five or six years ago he took me on a trip back into the Joseph Plains where he was raised. Can you imagine going around the side of one of those canyons on a bare-footed horse? We stopped at a little graveyard up there. It was still surrounded by a little wrought iron fence. The trip took us, shoot, four or five hours. He was either the first or second Turtle in the state of Idaho. I think Guy Cash was the first one. I think I remember Muggs telling me that he and Guy Cash were the first two Turtles.

It's a pleasure just to know Muggs Bentley. That's the way I feel about it. It's a privilege. He rode saddle broncs and bulldogged in his younger days.

The "Turtles" was the first organization of rodeo contestants. It was formed in 1936 at Boston, Massachusetts. Their goal was improving rodeo, qualified cowboy judges, adding the entry fee to the purse, and regulating stock.

119

Mel Lambert and I were good friends. He was part Indian. He was raised over around Richland, Oregon in the Halfway country. He grew up with Indians, and he knew a lot of 'em. They'd swarm his house there about once a year. One time they had a Salmonella outbreak over at the Warm Springs Reservation, and they all went to Mel's house 'till it was over. He knew all those Indians. He was an honorary Indian in every tribe up here, I think. He said he woke up one morning and there was Indians parked in the irrigation ditch and every place around his house. They told him, "We got sickness over there. We come to be with you for a few days."

A couple of years after I replaced him at Pendleton, he came up in the booth following the show. He was doing some radio work for somebody out of Portland, and he'd been around all week. I said, "Well, Pard, what do you think, am I gonna live or die?"

He took both of my shoulders in his hands and said, "I want you to hear somethin'. I've never heard it done any better." He had been there eight years. That meant an awful lot to me. Mel was a fine announcer with a great mellow voice and was a favorite across the country.

Before Karl Doering died (he had cancer), they had a big gathering for him over at the fairgrounds in Roseburg, and they had me come over and Emcee it. Well, Mel was there. Karl was dying and we all knew it. I had a lot of introductions. It was that old gang that was around Christensen Brothers, and we had a lot of stories to tell. He was one of my favorite people to travel and rodeo with. Karl was one of the most creative clowns that I was ever around. He could take a local situation and build an act into it before he ever got into the arena. Local people just loved it; they could relate to it. He would ride bucking horses with a suitcase full of chickens and laundry and stuff, and he'd go out of there and about halfway through the ride, he'd just unlatch that suitcase and throw it up in the air, and chickens and laundry would go everywhere. He rode backwards on a bucking horse. When he came as a clown to a rodeo, he was in it clear up to here. He gave it all he had.

I bumped into Ben Johnson at the convention in Vegas the only year I went there. Dwayne Madsen introduced me to him. Ben was just exactly the same kind of a guy in person that you saw in the movies. He was just a cowboy. He said the only reason he ever got in the movies was because he could ride a horse. And you know how he could ride a horse. He was a super guy and a total gentle-

man. His Dad was a great steer roper. Ben was World Champion team roper in '47. He just took a year off from the movies and took a car and went after it to see if he could win the title. He was roping with some of those good old hands, you know, and he could sure do the job. And he won the World Title. He said, "The only thing I had left when I got through was a mad wife and a broke down car."

Bobby Burke could rope pretty skookum. I'll tell you, he could trick rope pretty good. Bobby got so deaf he couldn't hear you talking to him. He always had his pants stuck in his boots. When Montie Montana was here, he'd get him down out of the grandstand and rope with him down on the track. People just loved it. I never talked to Montie away from Pendleton that he didn't mention Bobby Burke. He thought a lot of Bobby Burke.

My little wife and I have been married fifty-four years next month. She jumped in and got a Timer's card. Plains, Montana was the first place she ever timed a rodeo. Her name is Phyllis. I'll be 77 in December, and I have no fear of dying. My fear is being without her. She didn't know straight up about a rodeo or cowboyin' or anything when we met. There were 300 people at our wedding in Seattle. Bryce Baker, the old pickup man from Athena, and a bunch of those old hands, rodeo people, and her folks were all from St. Louis—one of the strangest mixes for a wedding there ever was.

The first week I knew her, I took her to a rodeo. They were gonna have a Scramble, which was real popular up in that country, like Puyallup, Washington, did in those days. They put me in charge of putting these bulls together for this Scramble. They'd open the rodeo and just blow all the chutes all at once, and away we'd go.

I looked up, and there's one of these little pair of Levi's that I'd loaned her, a little wider than the others, and sure enough, she was up there puttin' a flank on this bull. The last thing I ever expected. She's come a long way in rodeo since then.

The road is part of your life. If you can't take that highway, you'd better just forget about it. Because you've got to get out and hit that road. That's what drove us out after 36 years. I looked at Phyllis...we had a producer in Colorado that said, "Well, let's go again, Bob." He gave me all his rodeos. Well, I'd been with him for two years and done all their rodeos. We were just like a big family; we just got along great. We knew what they wanted and what they liked and how to do it, and they knew I was willing to give 'em my best every day. I looked at "Phyl," and I never do anything without her approval, I don't care what it is. I said, "What do you think, Honey?"

She looked at me for a minute, and she said, "Bobby, I've had all the white line I want."

I said, "Well, that's it then."

So we worked Union the next spring. Well, I had two that spring that I'd committed to. We had The Copperdust Stampede at Globe, Arizona. I'd been there 19 years with them. I just said, "Okay, when we get to Union, we'll hang it up."

We wrote to 'em and said, "This will be my last year, boys, you'd better get somebody else." So they got Steve Kenyon to replace me. He went in right after I did. The hardest thing I ever had to do was to walk away from Union. I walked out to the end of that arena and looked back at that old announcer's stand. That's the prettiest setting for a rodeo in the country, I think. Those hills go right back right in behind the chutes. It just looks like cow country in every direction.

It's just like a big family. Once you've been a part of this family, you're always a part of this family.

DOWN THE ROAD

In the 1940s the phrase "Down the road" had a definite meaning to cowboys. The horse trailer hitched to a pickup truck, no longer a novelty, was the most common form of transportation, and most of the highways were narrow, twisting two-lane strips of asphalt that tied the little black dots of a road-map together. According to my folks, on "get-away day", the last day of a show, if you asked someone where they were heading, they'd just tell you, "Down the road."

The following section contains several interviews from cowboys who traveled down the road for a living. Their lives and stories are not connected to any particular locale or rodeo, and they are scattered throughout the country from Trenton, New Jersey, to White Swan, Washington.

WAYNE DAVIS

Wayne Davis lives in Joseph, Oregon. Wayne is well known as a world-class bronc rider, and he has spent most of his life in the Enterprise-Joseph area. Wayne won The "World" at Pendleton in 1938 in saddle bronc riding.

In 1925 I started ridin'. I was only 15 years old then. I never competed in Pendleton until 1932. I won the bronc ridin' in 1938 in Pendleton.

Ben Jory and Andy Hefferin saddled my first horse at Pendleton. When they saddled a horse, they rode up to see if everything was all right. Ben and Andy tried to buck me off. I was just a kid, 22 years old, and that was the first time I rode in Pendleton. Ben Jory liked to buck everybody off that he could. So they set the saddle way back here, behind the withers, so it was quite a rough ride that way. So I said, "I ain't gonna get on that horse unless you change that saddle to the way I want it." So they did.

I never went to the World's until 1937. I rode in the Northwest in 1932. Then I missed 1933 then rode through 1936. There was 87 bronc riders one year in the Northwest bucking contest in Pendleton.

The next year I thought, "I'll go to the World's; there's only 15 entered in that." I won fourth that year. If I knew then what I know now, I could have won the Northwest. I was up in the finals, and one of the judges, he was a roper, said, "Wayne, how much would you take for that saddle if you win it?"

I said, "I want to keep it if I win it."

He rode off. That's how crooked those judges was. The boy that won it...I don't really know if he won it or not. Hugh Strickland. I think he was the one that wanted to buy my saddle if I'd have

124

won. He was one of the judges. Him an' one of the Bowmans. That was in 1934. That year they all bucked off in the World's.

They had the World's and the Northwest bucking contests in Pendleton at the same time. When you rode in the Northwest's, they announced the Northwest's; then they'd say the rest was ridin' in the World's.

You drew horses just like you did in the World's. You drew in the Northwest's bucking, and you rode in the Northwest's.

But you had the same judges as you had in the World's. But you didn't have quite as hard a horses. Five Minutes to Midnight was in the Northwest once. Cody Dodson drew him, an' he bucked off.

The Northwest was Idaho, Oregon, and Washington—three states. You had to be from them states before you could ride in it. A lot of California boys slipped in an' said they was from Oregon, but I don't think any of 'em ever won it.

The World's competition was from outside the Northwest, anybody from Canada or Australia. It was open to the World. That's why they called it the World's.

Pendleton was one of the biggest in the country. It was equal to Cheyenne, Salinas, and Calgary. You had to get there the day before Round-Up to sign up. Local boys are kind of remembered more than outside boys, naturally. Pendleton didn't have big money. When I won the World's, it was only $460.00. I won the finals and a fourth in the day-money and a first in the day-money. All together it was $460.00. Fourth in day-money was around $5.00. First in day-money was around $50.00.

But, anyway, the Round-Up people kept all the money. That's the reason the cowboys struck. They had a big strike in 1937. Cowboys wouldn't ride in Pendleton and they wouldn't ride in New York. Noah Johnson or Colonel Johnson from Texas said, "I don't need them cowboys. We can do without the regular cowboys." They didn't have no crowd or anything in Madison Square Garden.

Colonel Johnson had all them buckin' horses in New York at Madison Square Garden an' no cowboys. He found out that he did need 'em before the rodeo was over.

So we started makin' more money for the cowboys. They started giving them a percentage of the gate. The Pendleton Round-Up was robbin' the cowboys too, you know. You'd put up a fifteen dollar entry fee, an' you'd ride against your own money. It's bigger money now, of course. In 1937 the Turtles Association came into law.

The way you judge a good ride—they're supposed to go over the shoulders with the spurs, up an' back. The more you spur, the more points you get. You notice the boys nowadays. If they don't have 'em up on the shoulders, they goose egg 'em.

They didn't play music between rides in Pendleton. They always had something else going on—an Indian race, or relay race, or a pack-saddle race, or an Indian girl's race. You could always bet on an Indian girl fallin' off before the race was over. Eddy Woods, he says, "I'll bet you a dollar an' Indian girl falls off before the race is over." He'd win every time.

Fancy ropin', pony races. That's what was going on during the rodeo. They didn't have bull riding. They didn't have team roping. They did have steer roping.

I knew George Fletcher personally. He was quite a cowboy. A Negro. They wouldn't give him the championship. And Jesse Stahl, another Negro cowboy. My wife and I would meet him on the street, an' he would get off in the street an' bow an' tip his hat. I told Jesse he didn't have to do that. He thought that was what a Negro was supposed to do.

I guess Pete Knight an' Eddy Woods were the ones I remember best when I was rodeoin'. I can't think of all their names.

Pete Knight was a quiet guy. I never seen him bucked off but twice. Once was down in California. He was riding a horse in 1934. He bucked off in Pendleton. Everybody bucked off in Pendleton in 1934. "Ham-What-Am" bucked Pete off in Pendleton.

Pete drank quite a little bit. He carried a pint with him pretty much all of the time. He'd take a big shot before he rode.

Pete had a different way of ridin'. He never spurred behind the cinch much. He always spurred up in the shoulders. He could always see a horse when he was buckin'. When I got on a horse, I was totally blind. I couldn't see anything until I was back on the ground. But it seemed like he could see. If he figured he was about to buck off, he'd reach out an' throw his rein around the saddle horn. He could do that while his horse was still a buckin'.

When he bucked off down in California, he started to buck off on one side, an' he jerked himself back into the saddle. He threw his rein around the saddle horn, an' then he bucked off on his head on the other side. It mashed his hat down.

It made him mad. The next day he drew another horse. I remember these horses because he was such an outstanding rider.

He didn't talk much. He didn't laugh out loud much. I don't remember his wife. He didn't get married 'till late, a year or two before he got killed. He had a daughter. She wasn't very big when he was killed. He had a brother. He was quite a rider too. He was different.

Who was my best competition? They all were.

I had my home base in Enterprise, Oregon. Cody Dodson lived there too. That's about all that was into rodeoin' much. Cody Dodson won the Northwest in Pendleton in 1937, the last year they had it. He rode there several times; I don't know how many. He always bucked off in the finals, except for the year he won it.

One time Cody drove a car into Wallowa Lake. He lost his brand new hat. They pulled him out, an' he said, "My hat's in there," an' he dived back in an' got it. I think it was a sedan.

Do you remember the old Long Creek Basco, Tony Vey? He owned the place at Starkey, an' then he owned a ranch out of Pendleton. He trailed 1000 head of cattle from Butter Creek to Starkey. That's where he had his summer range. Cody Dodson helped him one year. He trailed 'em up through there from Long Creek to Starkey. Butter Creek was where his ranch was. He had a big wheat ranch. Butter Creek was between Long Creek an' Echo.

You purt'near have to go to Echo to get to Tony's place. I never was there but once. He had a rodeo there. Cody went there. Gosh, he was makin' a big ride. He had his feet clear up to the top of the cantle board, an' the horse bucked him off.

You remember Homer Holcomb? He was quite a clown. Me an' Smoky Moran come out of Sonora, California one time. They had a four county contest there in Sonora. I won that in the bronc ridin'. Perry Ivory asked why I didn't enter the other event, an' I said, "I can't ride against Pete Knight." That was where Pete Knight bucked off, come to think about it. The horse's name was "Billy The Kid." He was a hard horse.

In those days they had horses that weighed 1400 to 1500 pounds. Big old draft horses. They'd just kill ya, shock ya. They wasn't so fast an' crooked like they are now, but they hit the ground awful hard, an' they kicked high. Some had quite a roll, an' some were head fighters. They'd shake their heads like that, an' you'd lose it. They'd take the rein right out of your hand.

We did 'er.

Anyway, I was gonna say, Homer Holcomb had a tourin' car, a big Hudson I believe. An' we come out of Sonora, an' Homer gave us a ride. He was alone. He had a lot of suitcases, for his clown act stuff. I an' Smoky Moran, my travelin' partner, had our suitcases tied to the side of the car.

We was goin' down the road, must have been 50 miles an hour on a good road. There was a guy ahead of us, an' he pulled way over in front of us, an' Homer thought he was gonna go through some mail boxes along the side of the road. He didn't. He pulled right in front of Holcomb. Homer turned the wheel an' took down all those mail boxes, about ten of 'em. We went the length of a field in a ditch along the road. When we backtracked, picking up the things from our suitcases that had been scattered along the road, we found out that we had gone along the edge of a canal, which was about twenty feet deep and filled with water. The grass was high, and you couldn't see it. Didn't hurt nobody, but it sure did scatter our clothes around. I never will forget that barb wire fence beside the ditch either.

A feller from Stockton called me outside of Sacramento, an' I an' Smoky Moran went to work on a ranch out there. We worked five days for five dollars apiece. We entered a rodeo, an' we both won $25.00. I thought I was rich.

I knew Buster Ivory when he was just a kid. Perry Ivory was Buster's Uncle. I knew Buster well. I broke some of his horses an' seen him ride several too. There was a slew of them boys down there. Ed Ivory was their Dad. Perry Ivory was quite a bit older than Buster. He was a little older than I am. We kind of rodeoed together. He furnished stock. Perry and I rode in Portland, Oregon. We rode in Pendleton, and we rode together in Burns, Oregon, one time.

Lary Daniels and I traveled together for awhile. Him an' I were at Union one time. I wanted to go to another rodeo. I just won at Enterprise down here at the fair, and Lary said, "I'll go with you."

He had a brand new Chevrolet coupe. He was drivin' loggin' truck. He told his wife he was goin' rodeoin' with me. We was goin' to Wolf Point, Montana. That's a long ways from here. Anyway, we went. He drove all that day, an' when we got into Missoula, it was pouring down rain goin' down that canyon over the mountains by that minin' town over in Idaho. The Sunshine Mine. We got to Missoula around two o'clock in the mornin'. We picked up a boy goin' up the mountainside there. He was wet! He got into the back. A little bakery was open, an' they gave us some doughnuts an' coffee. We filled up on that.

Lary Daniels bulldogging at Lewiston, Idaho.

129

When we got to Great Falls, we was up the Missouri River. I was drivin'. I was goin' 60 miles an hour, an' the first thing you knowed, there was two antelope travelin' right along with us. One of 'em even got a little ahead of us. One of 'em jumped over a bank, an' Lary said, "Catch him, I'll bulldog him!" He would have too. He was standin' out there on the runnin' board.

It wasn't ten minutes after we got to Wolf Point before the rodeo started. We passed a cop, an' I was doin' 80 just out of Havre, Montana. It was a 41 mile straight shot of road. He never even looked at me; he just turned his head. Of course, Montana in them days there wasn't any speed limit.

I remember I was makin' a real nice ride on one of those brand new Association saddles. I was in the finals, makin' a real nice ride, an' spurrin' him good. I thought I'd spur him once more, an' the whistle would blow. I pulled my feet back an' stepped off alongside of him with my buck-rein in my hand. I just handed it up to the pickup-man, just like that.

I thought the whistle had blown, but it hadn't. I know I'd have won the bronc ridin' because I was makin' the best ride. I rode with my left hand, see?

Then we went to Canada. We rode in two or three rodeos up there. We rode at Lethbridge and some of the big ones with a couple of little rodeos in between. We were winnin' some. I wasn't winnin' a great lot. There wasn't much money in them days.

Daniels told me how he won the cow-milking. He did it with a balloon. That was old Homer Holcomb's old trick. When he quit the cow-milking, he gave me his balloon. It was a little squirt thing with a nozzle on it. Stick it in your pocket. It didn't matter if they didn't catch you doin' it. You'd squat, an' squirt this little thing into a bottle, an' then you'd run up to the judges. You didn't have to muzzle a cow. Homer won all them milking contests. Until Daniels showed up with his balloon. He got his share.

I traveled with Lary Daniels in the summer of 1936. He was 21, and I was 26. We won about the same. He got to winnin' more later on cause he entered about all the events, an' he was an announcer. I used to visit him in Lewiston, Idaho. He had a rodeo grounds there once too. Lary liked to fight a little.

I knew Phil Armstrong. He was a Turtle. I knew him well. He was a bronc rider, but he wasn't a rider so much as he was a gambler. Phil flew his airplane up to Joseph one time with another guy, and the other guy didn't want to go back home, so Phil flew off an' left him. Phil was crippled. He had a bad leg.

Hippy Burmeister traded horses with me one time, a balky mare. Somebody gave me a four or five year old colt, an' I took him down to Hippy's corrals on his ranch just below Alturas, California. I didn't know Hippy 'till then. I had the colt saddled an' rode him around the corral. Hippy said, "I've got a black mare. She's broke. I'll trade her for that horse of yours."

So rather than break one, I thought I'd just trade with him an' get a broke horse. Well, he cheated me. That mare was balky. I rode her out of there an' was clear downtown Alturas before she balked. She wouldn't go anyplace. So I unsaddled her an' kicked her in the hind end an' sent her home. I never saw her again. I seen Hippy a time or two after that, an' I told him he cheated me, an' he just laughed. He thought that was pretty funny.

Hippy turned into a movie actor. He was down there with old Yakima Canutt.

I didn't do much after I quit rodeoin'. I lived on a ranch for 11 years. Then I sold that out an' went to Wallowa an' bought a ranch down there. It was only 60 some acres. I couldn't make a livin' off of it. I sold it an' some milk cows an' bought a tavern. I made money in the tavern. It was in Enterprise. Then I sold that out an' moved to Joseph. I worked in the lumber yard back in the sixties. Then I worked on the Gumboat Road until they got it finished. Then I helped with the railing around Wallowa Lake. Then I got another tavern and made more money at that. Then I was a ditch walker. That's where I retired in 1980. I worked for the farmers, not the Government.

I'm not very navigable anymore. I kinda don't get around too fast. They sure make some nice rides nowadays. I don't see how they can stay on there. You see those feet up there in the shoulders. That's the way they're supposed to be goin'. But further up nowadays; close up to the point as far as they can reach.

Did you watch the Calgary show on t.v.? That Billy Etbauer had his hands full with that bronc. He purt'near lost him, but he didn't give up. He kept on spurrin'. That's the way Billy is; he don't give up. I don't know him, but I get that sports magazine, an' I know who's ahead an' who makes the rides.

LARY DANIELS

Lary Daniels spent his early years around rodeo and when he retired from active competition became involved in training racehorses. Throughout the interviews people would suggest that if we really wanted to know something about rodeo that we should contact Lary. One even called Lary the toughest man he had ever known, and others readily agreed.

"My name is Lary Daniels. I hope you remember me."

Lary started out as a cowboy and worked the rodeos as a contestant and an announcer before training racehorses for a living.

His front room is decorated with mementos from his years in rodeo as well as his racing days. The walls are decorated with photos and trophies. He won the all-around at Joseph, Oregon, near where he was born and raised; a pair of spurs adorn a trophy case, commemorating his second all-around win at Joseph. Lary rodeoed all over the U.S. and Canada. He's won a roomful of trophy saddles that he's given away and can't recall just how many or to whom they were given. There are photos of himself, horses and racehorse owners on the walls. Most are success stories. "I bought this one for $800.00," he says as we study the pictures. "I got this one for $5,000.00" he says, pointing to another. "I only paid $150.00 for that one."

Lary walks out to pasture and puts a halter rope on one of the racehorses. While he does this, he explains the pertinent information about each of them, their record, history, and lineage. "This horse is flat fast," he says. Or, "This horse starts dead last in every race. You couldn't hit the front end of the pack with a shotgun, but by the time they hit the finish line, he's that far ahead."

HOME TOWN CHAMP. Lary Daniels, veteran Lewiston rodeo performer and announcer, was declared all-around champion cowboy of the 16th annual Lewiston roundup when final standings were recorded by the judges yesterday. He accepted the silver belt buckle emblematic of the championship while his talented young daughter, Monte, looked on. Art Barnes of Erb Hardware Co., which donated the buckle, made the presentation. Barnes is a director of the Lewiston Roundup Association. Lary wanted Monte in the picture "just to make the day complete." Monte performed at the rodeo as a trick rider, her sixth show in her first year of professional riding in a manner that made her father beam as brightly as when he learned he was the champ. (Munson photo.)

Another horse he characterizes as worthless; another has bleeding lungs. He sold the horse to his ex-wife and bought it back from her when they found out he was a bleeder. Lary will keep him along with the others that he's training for other people.

He has a sixteen-year-old saddle horse that he bought at the age of four from a family with two little girls. He told the little girl who owned it that he would buy it for $400.00, and she agreed. Then he told the family they could have the horse back any time for the price they sold it for, and they could ride it any time they wanted to. They couldn't afford to keep him. On the bill of sale, the little girl said, "This horse is sold to Lary Daniels. Since I have to sell him, I am glad Lary bought him because I know he has a good home."

"Isn't that precious?" Lary says. "I wouldn't sell that horse for a million dollars."

Lary handles all of the horses, high-strung and bred for speed, like gentle saddle horses. They all run to meet him in the pasture. Not one is hard to catch. He leads one, and the rest follow. He talks to them, pats them on the back, puts his arms around them and whispers in their ears.

One, a sorrel, acts like it might be a little ringy, but since the others are not, it doesn't act that way. He says that it does have a tendency to be that way. He constantly talks to them when he goes out to work with them each morning.

Lary feeds the neighbor's horses along with his own. He stopped at Wallowa Lake once, and they had a concession that rented horses for trail rides. The horses were in pitiful condition. Lary took out his Polaroid camera and took their picture and told the owners that he was going to turn them in to the Humane Society. He turned some people in near where he lives. The police and the Humane Society came out but didn't do anything, so Lary fed them himself.

One time his love for animals didn't work out exactly for the best. A woman gave him a goat that followed him around like a dog and butted him every time he stopped to do the chores.

Lary trains horses through the winter months, and turns them back over to their owners in the spring. The owners send trailers and haul them home, and then Lary concentrates on his own horses for the coming race season.

Lary has a picture of a woman jockey. He had given her her first chance to ride, and she had won her first race.

I asked him if any good horses ever got to run at the little tracks like Union.

"Hell yes, some of the best. You never know where you're gonna run across talent. It could show up anywhere. Until you run 'em, you don't know what you've got. You might run into a horse like John Henry at Union. You just never know."

Lary's favorite horse is a gray. He pointed to a picture on the wall. It looked black, but another picture showed gray in the mane and tail. Once, at a claiming race, one of his horses ran so well that he had to buy him back himself after the race.

One time an owner asked Lary's honest opinion about a horse that he'd just bought. He paid $3,000.00 for it.

"You might not like to hear my honest opinion," he told the owner.

But the owner insisted, and Lary walked to the stable with him to look the horse over.

"I wouldn't give that horse to my worst enemy," Lary told him. "And Lord only knows I've got a lot of those."

The owner asked him why he felt that way. Lary pointed to the swollen front knee. "Do you have any idea of the strain racing puts on a horse's legs? They might weigh 1500 pounds, and they can break a leg anytime."

The condition had been known by the owner. The colt had been deformed at birth. The vet had put pins in the leg to straighten the joint. It had grown straight, but it was still bigger by half than the other.

"The only thing the mare is good for," Lary told him, "is breeding, and then there's a good possibility her colt will have the same defect. It would cost big money to breed her to a top stud horse. That could be expensive. And you can't really start training a horse until it's three or four years old. There's no return on your money. Then after all the time and expense, you probably wouldn't have anything. Every horse isn't a racehorse."

"I just told him it was a poor deal. You take enough chances with healthy animals. A good horse could go out there and break a leg in his first race."

"Why start out on the minus side? A healthy horse well cared for is a long shot. Everyone in the business has known of the long shot. That's the ideal thing, buying something for peanuts and getting rich."

"A lot of trainers wouldn't point out defects like that. They would figure if the owner couldn't see what he was getting himself into, why should the trainer say anything. Trainers are in the business of training horses, period. They could make money off gullible owners with sick horses, sort of string 'em along and milk 'em for all they're worth."

135

Lary talked about his childhood and earlier rodeo days:

I was born in bed somewhere out in the country around Wallowa Lake. Most of us kids were born there—Bert, Virgil, Phil, Me, Danny, Forest, and sister Ruth. We were all born in Wallowa County.

Lew Minor, who won the bronc riding at Pendleton in 1912, came from that part of the country.

You'll hardly know of a man who can say he didn't know me. It's the truth. I worked all timed events, every one of 'em, an done pretty well with all of 'em.

I could ride bulls better than ninety-nine percent that ever tied a rope on one. I could really ride them bulls, and I announced rodeos. When I was announcing, they'd save my bull 'till last, an' just before I'd get on, I'd say over the P.A. system, "Folks, I gotta go. They got my bull in the chute, and I want to ride."

I was one guy who was never afraid. I wanted my bull. I wanted him because I knew I could ride him. I looked forward to riding him. Absolutely. I seen guys who'd forget who they was when they walked up to that chute. Not me, I was rarin' to go. So many guys...they like to never got goin' on a bull. They put their ropes on a bull, tighten it, turn it loose, do it some more, do it some more, scared to death. Say, I couldn't wait to unbar the door. I'd say somethin' unspectacular, like "Okay," or "Open the door an' let him have me." But I could ride those bulls. Getting on a bull is easy; getting off is the hard part.

I never did see Casey Tibbs on a bull. As far as I know, he never rode one. But I'll tell you what, he sure could ride saddle broncs.

SNUBBING SNAKE

136

I rode saddle broncs that nobody else could ride. I rode Miss Klamath. Everyone told me I was crazy to get on her. Also Snake owned by Ben Jory. I don't believe that I ever did get on Steamboat, but I saw him buck. I rode Five Minutes To Midnight. I sure did. I didn't make the whistle, but I knew the horse real well. He was a gelding.

I've rodeoed at Grangeville, Idaho, many, many years ago and at Weiser. Tonasket was my favorite show. Omak, not so good. I rode against all of 'em. Freckles Brown, Slim Pickens. I know more cowboys than anybody in the business. I remember Slim Pickens so well. He was a real good friend. He was one of the best. Slim was a bull fighter too.

If I hadn't of had bars an' worked the all-around bulldoggin' an' ropin', I could have been world's champion, no doubt in my mind whatsoever. I could ride bulls as good or better than any man that ever got on one; but it was my problem, I could bulldog with any man, but I was too little.

When I was a junior in high-school, a professional wrestler by the name of Jake Woods taught me how to win a fight an' hurt a man. He wrestled at the AT Shows before the rodeos. He lined me up so many times. I'd get two or three fights before the rodeo an' afterwards too.

One time some of cowboys come down to watch me wrestle, an' we was going through some contortions, an' it looked like he was really giving me a beatin'. They started getting on the other guy about his tactics. I was underneath there, an I was tryin' to tell my friends that I was all right; everything was under control. But they wouldn't listen, and pretty soon they stormed the ring. It didn't do any good to tell 'em that we was just fakin' it. They thought it was on the level.

I can see Jake like he was settin' right here, an' I lived in his house. Ol' Jake!

I was one of the first to fly an airplane to rodeos. I could fly good, but I was very careful. I was equipped, and I learned how to fly. I had a little beer parlor down in Eastern Oregon. I'd go to Baker, an' I had a good friend there who was a pilot. He taught me how to fly. He taught me different things that I ought to know. He said I was the best pilot he ever taught to fly.

Soon as I got started, I flew everyplace I went. I could fly through that door and out that one over there. I flew under the

Clarkston bridge an' scared those people to death, but it didn't bother me none.

I really enjoyed flyin' airplanes. I never put a scratch on one. I had Casey Tibbs, Bill an' Bud Linderman, all of them guys tell me I was the best pilot they ever rode with. I flew cowboys all over the country. Most of 'em paid up so much so I could buy gas. I can say this in all sincerity—I was one of the best pilots who ever got behind a stick of an airplane.

I got Jim Shoulders an' Casey Tibbs sicker than dogs in my airplane. I remember one time I was in a hospital, an' some cowboys come up to visit me in the room. They dressed me up an' smuggled me out of the hospital an' dragged me down to the airport where my plane was. I offered to take the plane up by myself to see if I could fly it, but they said that if I was willin' to try it, they'd all go along.

I have never, ever wrote a bad check in my life, and on top of that I don't owe a penny to a livin' human. I'm proud of what I done. I've loaned a lot of guys money, an' I usually got it back. One time I didn't. I remember one time I loaned a down-an'-out cowboy a few dollars an didn't see him for months afterward. Finally, I was at the Cow Palace, an' I hit the jackpot. I had a wad of money that would choke a horse. I was standin' outside in the street, an' this same guy come up to me an' asked for a loan. I pulled out the bankroll, counted it slowly, an' then put it back in my pocket. "I've just got enough for the party tonight," I told him. "I need every penny of it." And I walked away.

MONTECRE DANIELS

MonteCre Daniels is the daughter of Lary Daniels. MonteCre and her husband Fab Bennett, live at Finley, Washington. MonteCre was a trick rider as a girl, following in her dad's footsteps in rodeo. The family lived in Arizona as well as the Northwest and traveled throughout the country, living in their trailer when they were on the road. MonteCre has the Daniels' flair for telling a story.

One time we were at Phoenix, Arizona at a rodeo, and these guys were talking real dirty, four letter words and stuff like that. Dad said, "Now, fellas, cool it. We got ladies around here."

These guys just kept on talking, and Dad says, "I'm gonna whip the crap out of you if you don't tone it down."

One of the guys was a rodeo clown. He said, "Well, come right on."

Dad beat him so bad that Dad had to take his place being a clown at the rodeo the next day.

He took a pitchfork to Dad, and the women were all screaming.

Another story about Dad was how he got "Old Roany," his ropin' horse.

This guy got drunk, and he kept his horse in the trailer for three days. Dad was so mad. So they were drawing their livestock for the rodeo, and you had to sign your name and put your number down. Dad just slipped a Bill of Sale under the paper the guy was signing, and the cowboy signed it. The sale was for a dollar. Then Dad went and unloaded the horse and took him to his stall.

There must have been 40 cowboys in there, and not one told on Dad. Not a one of them. They hated the way this guy treated his livestock.

The next morning the guy kept looking for his horse, and they told him that he'd sold it to Lary Daniels.

"I wouldn't sell that horse," he said.

"You sure did," they told him. "Lary's got the bill of sale for him."

Dad had the horse until the horse died.

I remember the time when Dad drove off with the top of a service station on top of his truck. That was funny. He drove into a gas station, and when he pulled out, the top just tore off, and there we were, going down the road, and everyone was hollering at him to stop. I got pictures of it.

Another time, we had a place on the Clearwater River near Lewiston, Idaho. It was really a casino. Grandpa sat under a weeping willow tree, and they had a password. Then, one night we got raided. They hauled everybody off. Then they let them all out cause the sheriff was there.

Dad came upstairs and put $10,000.00 underneath my pillow.

They were asking people who they were. One woman said, Ava Gardner; another guy said Clark Gable. Jerry, my brother and I were watching from the top of the stairs when they hauled everybody off to jail.

They called the road that came to our place, "Daniel's Dead-End Corner." The road went this way and turned, and there was another road that turned towards the gate. Grandpa always had to make new gates because people would get drunk at the bar and run through the gate.

One night, a bunch of Indians got drunk and missed the corner and rolled down into the corral.

Dad and I ran down there, and Mom was calling the police. When we got down there, this Indian woman was standing outside the car with her shoes in her hand, and this big old Brahma Bull was standing there looking right at her.

The woman started screaming, "Oh, my god, I went to hell!"

And I said, "Yeah, and wait 'till my dad sees you ruined his gate, too."

FRANK MARSHALL

Frank Marshall is retired and lives in Trenton, New Jersey. We met Frank in the Banquet room of the Aladdin Hotel & Casino at the National Finals in Las Vegas in 1996. Frank is a Turtle member.

I met Paul Bond for the first time up in Washington. He drew a horse there, and he asked me about him. I told him I had a show on him just the week before, and he was a good horse. He didn't buck at all. He ran off.

When Paul started out, his family had a leather shop. They made anything out of leather. That's where he learned. He does the design work himself. He had a factory in Nogales, south of Tucson. He sends the boots to Mexico. He pays duty on 'em going into Mexico, and he pays duty on 'em coming back. An' he says he can do that cheaper than he can get it done in the States. They do better workmanship, and they do it a lot cheaper. I've been to his factory a couple of times. You ever get a chance, drop in there.

Paul was a trick rider and went wherever he had a contract trick riding; and then he'd ride bulls and bareback horses.

I tried to stay up in the Northwest when I rodeoed. You'd go to a rodeo, and there might only be six or seven bull riders. You'd go to Texas, and there might be fifty of 'em. They are little fuzzy faced kids. They look like they're maybe 13 years old, an' they're riding some rank cattle.

I never went to Cheyenne or Calgary. You'd be better off to go to one of those fifteen, ten an' five shows. That was the smaller shows, the punkin rollers. I even rodeoed in the Dakotas.

Mike Hastings was a bulldogger. He was 'Juicy.' He threw some pretty fast cattle in those days. He was still competing when I started. I was a bull rider. I learned to spur in front of the rope,

141

untrack the bull, wake him up, get with him. I rode a lot more bulls after I learned that.

I remember one time Jake Williams went to see Hoot Gibson. He'd been drinking with him for three days. "I'll be damned. I been drunk for three days with him, an' I didn't even know who he was," he said. Jake very probably didn't have any money.

Jake Williams, I don't know if you ever heard of him or not, was a good hand. Bud Linderman called him Jake the Snake. Bud an' him got drunk one night. They got into a bar, I can't remember which one, an' these guys just beat the hell out of both of 'em. They got kinda mad about that, so they went an' got a five gallon can of gas an' threw it on the door an' then threw a match on it. The cops got there damn near in time to see 'em do it. So, the next morning Bud gets over to the window of the jail an' yells, "Ladies an' gentlemen, we have Jake the Snake here...take a good look at him!"

He was a piece of work, that Bud Linderman.

Bill Linderman married another bronc rider's widow. I can't remember his name. He died in a snowmobile accident. She was a real nice lady. Bill's first wife died, an' his second wife had a kid about the same age as Bill's son, so they were twins. The two of them were the same age.

Bud was the bad one. He would rather steal a dime than earn a dollar.

Bill Linderman on 20 Below. Phoenix, '44.　　　　DeVere

Bill went to Houston once. He was riding two events there. They set his riggin' for him, but the only thing was they set it down along the side about that far. Then they got with the chute boss an' told him to hurry him out. "Don't let him change it," they told him. So he bucked off. Well, Bill got up an' walked over an' he says, "Bud, if you ever come near me again, I'll kill ya."

I guess he did stay away from him for awhile. Bud thought it was a good joke.

In California, Bud an' I were broke, and we were gonna' catch a freight. We had one suitcase between the two of us. Bud said, "You just catch that last boxcar, and I'll toss the suitcase to you."

He tossed the suitcase up and it missed the door, and it came open. We finally got it all together, and Bud cinched it up with his belt. We got to San Berdo. We got a ride on a flatbed truck. We rode into town and found a couple of guys, and they told us to come on over. They had an extra bed. One of 'em was a bronc rider, and the other was a roper.

I bucked off my bull, and Bud won the saddle bronc riding and got us money enough to get down to Tucson.

Bud did some of the damnedest, meanest things. Bill, if you didn't know better, you'd think he was a gentleman.

I was down at Aberdeen, and I placed in the bull riding there. Bud had the stock. A bull jumped the fence, and Bud got an old kewpie doll, a "usin' horse" he had there, an' took after him. He finally run him down out in the country. He herded him over to a telephone pole, and he wound him around that, and then he went and got a truck. I knew he'd be gone for awhile, and I told his wife to get down to the office. She didn't want to go. She said, "If I go, he'll be yelling at me."

I said, "Don't put up with that crap. I'll take you down and come back and get him." So I took his car and drove her to the office and then waited for him to get back. He didn't get back until late, probably 9 or 10 o'clock.

"What the hell are you doing here?" he said.

"You don't quit the cattle on a stormy night, do ya?" I told him.

I was working stock there with him. We got up one morning...we was having a hell of a time—an' when we got all done we were sweated up. We just peeled our shirts off and turned a hose on each other.

If Bud had split a fourth one year, he would have won the all-around championship of the World. All he had to do was split a fourth to do it. He was at the Cow Palace. But he got drunk and never entered. He just stayed drunk. Bill said he followed him around one night and picked up his change. Bill had a sizable wad.

There were some guys, I'm not going to name names, but Bud was one of 'em, at the New York show. Bud proceeded to take money from queers. He took all their rings and money. I knew of one guy who came back and bought his ring back for three hundred dollars.

On June 29, 1942 I went into the U.S. Army. I was in three years, one month, seventeen days, five hours, and some minutes. I was sent to Fort Riley, Kansas. Turk Greenough was there. So was Paul Bond. I went over to visit Turk along with a girl by the name of Roberts and another one named Betty Hagen. We took Turk out to dinner.

Turk went out on the firing range one time, and he was layin' in the prone position when a Lieutenant came up and told him, "You must not have your heels up; your spurs glint in the sun." Turk had a broken leg that healed crooked. The lieutenant stepped on his foot, and Turk got up and decked him.

Turk Greenough was married to Sally Rand, a feather dancer. They called Turk, Mr. Sally Rand. She bankrolled rodeo at Fort Riley with Beutler Brothers stock.

BILL SYLVESTER

Bill Sylvester once served as a model for a poster adver-
tising rodeo at Madison Square Garden in New York City. Bill
was a RCA member and traveled the rodeo circuit often in
the company of Bud Linderman in the 1940s and '50s.
  Bill was born near Pilot Rock in Eastern Oregon and left
before entering high school. In his early years, he worked on
cattle ranches in the Southwest. He worked on the Shirley
ranch in New Mexico with cattle and as a horse wrangler.
After he quit rodeo, he lived in Las Vegas for many years
  Bill has a million stories to tell, and from what we've
heard from people who knew him, most of them are true.

That's where it used to be declared...the National Championships. In San Francisco at the Cow Palace. Then they went to Denver, and now they have the big thing in Las Vegas. They've got the
World's. You've gotta get all these points to go to Vegas to the National Finals.

In those days, it's the same now, a point is a dollar. Now
Marshall might have come to the Cow Palace at that time, so I'm
not calling the man for not telling the story right. I just want to say
I know cause I was there when Bud Linderman wouldn't get on
the horse. All he had to do was to get on the s.o.b., but we were
drunk in that cowboy bar over there, and Bud and I had been runnin'
the roads an' stealin' an' doin' whatever bad boys done at that time.
Bud says, "Who in hell wants to go out there? I been the champion
of the world before. If I go out there now, those detectives'll be
jumpin' out of all sides of the arena. They'll lock me up."

Bud wouldn't get on the horse. He just says, "To hell with it,
I'm not gettin' on." The law was after us. They wanted him in Wyoming, Montana, New York, Chicago.

Bud Linderman on "Red Ryder". Pendleton Round-Up, 1949.

Bud was a strange, strange hombre. Everything was fun. I mean, in those days everything was fun to us. We even laughed about death. But it was fun. I mean, we did the meanest things, an' we thought it was a hell of a joke, but most people thought we was absolutely nuts the things we done.

It's gotta be there. It's just like fallin' in love. It's gotta be the right place at the right time. I got these stories, I can look at pictures, hear some music, and it'll bring back another story. I mean really vividly in my mind. I can't remember which side of the bed I got out of this morning or where my boots were, but I can remember those things so vividly.

146

Elmer Sharp's joint in Fort Worth was one of the toughest joints in the country, right down where old Fort Worth is now. The things that went on at that bar, they used to kill 'em an' throw 'em out in the alley. Elmer used to go around, a great big, huge man, about 6'6" an' weighed 350 pounds, an' he wore shorts; he was the funniest lookin' thing you've ever seen. He'd come around an' say, "Damn, who in the hell killed that s.o.b.? Why didn't they throw 'em someplace else besides behind my bar?"

It was an outlaw bar. In those days they was a lot of those outlaw bars. You knew where they was at when you pulled into town, Billings, Montana, an' Reno, an' Vegas. Bud an' I was more into the hustlin' an' beatin' a poker game or spreadin' dice. You couldn't make any money at a rodeo. If you won the whole thing, you couldn't hardly get out of town. You was still starvin' when you got out of the city limits before you got to the next town, an' then you'd have to promote entry fees. Anything you could do to get into the rodeo. The rodeo was a hell of a stall for us. Hey, Bud was a hell of a cowboy. He was a rodeo cowboy. He wasn't an outside cowboy. He was a natural, like kids are nowadays. He was an athlete, an' he was healthy, an' he was tough, an' that's what it took.

Those old places I tell you about they was open 24 hours a day, an' the girls of the night would be down there. The pimps of the town would be there. An' old piano player would be playin' the old piano, playin' those ol' torch songs. But it was the way it was. It would be hard for anybody to comprehend nowadays unless they seen it in a movie or somethin'. They could really see the way it was at the outlaw bars. They wasn't anybody that was champions. There was a few cowboys. Now Mickey McCory, he was the one that turned Bud Linderman out. Fritz Truan was a tough s. o. b. He whipped a Captain when he was getting discharged out of the service, an' they sent him right back to Iwo Jima, an' he got killed. Bud was supposed to go with him, but they already had him locked up in jail. I said, "Bud, what part of the world did you like best when you went around it?" An' he said, "I looked at it out through a porthole in a ship." He was in the Navy. He was always locked up.

Fritz Truan was a natural cowboy. He was a good hand. Fritz won it here in Pendleton, probably in the '40s—early '40s or the later part of 1938-9. I was tryin' to think. The Turtles came into Pendleton. They had a rodeo, an' then they went to fighting with

147

the RCA. Nineteen thirty-nine was when Lloyd Depew won the ropin' here because they wouldn't let any of the good rodeo hands work because they weren't sanctioned. They was all fighting. It was a mess. I joined it the year it really got started. Cecil Bedford was the spokesman in this part of the country with the RCA. I rode all of these amateur shows an' win the rodeos around here. I was riding bareback horses like a house afire until I got my neck broke. Jack Carson an' I an' Boots MacNamara we was all good hands at the time. They told us we'd have to join, or we couldn't work the Cow Palace. We had nothin' to eat out there. They had little pickles on a toothpick out in the pavilion where the show was goin' on at the stock show at Portland, Oregon, at the P.I., Pacific International.

Anyway, Jack Carson an' I joined, an' Boots says no, he wanted to work Lakeview or some of those amateur rodeos. He joined the next spring. George MacNamara was his name, but they called him "Boots." He was gonna win the Championship of the World, an' he got killed in Prineville, Oregon. He was set to win it an' hit a loggin' truck. There was five of 'em in there, an' it killed them all but Larry Quinland. That's what killed a lot of cowboys, whiskey an' cars. Damn few ever got killed in the arena.

In those days, especially around all the outlaws, you never asked a man what his last name was. They'd say, "This is Tom." All you know is that he was a good guy, an' he was solid, or he was all right. People ask about people now, an' I run into 'em, an' I might have known 'em for 30 years but don't know their last name. I met an old rounder out there at the Casino the other day at the gamblin' joint playin' at the table. He kept lookin' at me, an' I kept lookin' at him. You know the way a man moves his hands on a table, even if he ain't doin' anything. He handles a deck of cards a little different than anybody else. And their lingo, they're quiet. These guys nowadays are screaming an' hollerin'. It drives me nuts to have to play poker with 'em. Used to be we played three days an' three nights, and you'd never hear anything but, "Get another bottle of whiskey," or "deal, cut the cards, or raise." That is as much as went on for three days. If somebody run their mouth off like they do here, they'd have killed 'em. They was quiet an' tough. That's when a dollar was a dollar, an' you was doin' everything you could to win one.

148

Bud Linderman an' I run horses on the Klamath Indian Reservation out of Beaty, Oregon, where there's ten thousand stories to be told.

With Bud an' I, they was always somethin', 24 hours a day, every minute. If we wasn't thinkin' about doin' something wrong, we was doin' it. It was just that simple.

Anyway, it was an Indian outfit, a wild horse outfit at Klamath Falls. Like I say, Bud was a good rodeo hand, but he thought cause he was champion of the world once that you couldn't tell him anything. He didn't know nothin' about cowboyin' an' runnin' those old wild Indian horses, bad horses, all of 'em spoiled. They run about six or seven hundred head there at that time in the '50s. All you gotta do is mention Beaty anywhere within a hundred miles of Klamath Falls, an' people will say "Don't go there." The cops wouldn't even go to Beaty. They killed people out there all the time.

We had two, three hundred head, an' we'd trotted 'em down off a place they called "Tableland." It was terrible country, rough, about 60,000 acres. Those wild horses could go across there like goats. If you were horseback, it was a tough run. But, anyway, we told Bud after we dropped down off this point and into the flatland, all around was marsh around that river, an' we said, "Bud, you stay off this road. We know those trails through there. If you get out there, you'll drown, you an' your horse both."

"Hey, I wouldn't have been champion of the world if I didn't know how to find my way through. Look at it, it's a nice clean creek," Bud said.

I'm goin' along, not payin' any attention, an' Bud let out a war whoop. An old mare went to run back, an' he went over to turn her back. I seen him, an' then I went to look back, an' he was gone. The next thing all I could see was Bud's head an' the horse's head stuck out of the marsh. We had to rope the horse an' Bud an' drag 'em both out. If we hadn't been there, he'd have died. They couldn't have got out of there because that old mud just freezes you all over. That river was the same way. It didn't have no bottom in it. If you didn't know where to cross that river, you'd drown. You an' your horse cause the horse gets floundering. The power of a horse hits you, an' if you're close to him, he's gonna get you underwater. If he goes plumb under in deep water, you're in a world of trouble. Like I see in pictures of a guy jumpin' off a horse an' grabbin' ahold of the tail. You sit straight up on a horse when you're swimming him across a river. A river is dangerous.

We're ropin' these wild horses, an' they've all been spoiled. We'd buck 'em, an' they'd all been spoiled. We buckaroo-ed off 'em, but I mean, boy, you had to buckaroo when you rode 'em. They were all snaffle bit, an' we had a big, round corral there. Miller an' I was in there, ropin', takin' turns. One of us would be on the ground, an' one would be ropin' these wild horses. So Miller was ropin', an' he'd roped this one horse an I was gonna go up to him. I was right up close to his nose. A horse will pull back an' choke down, you know. And I'm back about five or six feet on the rope from him. I was just gonna hold him tight, so the guy could loosen up his dallies an' ride up, but I'd still have enough pressure on the rope so he wouldn't get loose. They'll stand there if you hold the pressure right in there. An' so, here comes that goofy Bud. He done it on me before two or three times. He says, "Let me show you how to handle one of these." And here he come. He ducked under the rope in front of me. Well, he didn't know those horses was all light in the front end, an' they could strike you so fast it would make your head swim. They'd drive you. So, here comes Bud.

"Don't run under that rope," I told him.

"How in the hell did I get to be a world's champion cowboy with you sittin' around here tellin' me somethin', Sylvester? You don't know nothin'," he said.

That old horse...I just give him a little slack, an' he pawed that Bud, he purt'near buried him. Boy, down on the ground he went.

I put him on his last buckin' horse. It was just one of those broncs. I was tryin' to tell him something, an' he was tellin' me how he was a world champion.

Well, you'd better turn that big old horse around because he's walking on his tiptoes, an' you jerk that cinch into him an' step on him without turnin' him around or movin' him, an' you're gonna stick your head in this frozen ground, I told him.

"You've seen a few of the buckin' horses I've rode," he said.

I said, "Yes, be my guest, Bud. Remember the water hole, Bud, remember what I told you."

But he was hard-headed, I'll tell you. A little hard to learn. Thick between the ears. You couldn't teach him nothin'. He was just tough an' mean.

150

So this old horse was walkin' on his tiptoes, an' I'm watchin' him, an' Bud's goin' along too, braggin' about what a great hand he was.

Some cattle seen us an' started to run towards the river. There's only one place they could get across. I said, "We gotta get down there an' turn 'em."

"I'll get 'em," Bud yelled, an' he touched that old horse with a spur an' that old horse farted an' bucked him off. He went up in the air like an arrow. He just turned over an' came back to earth. He ran his head in that ground. He'd broken his neck twice before.

Bud never got on a gentle horse after that. He died in Phoenix. I seen Danny Daniels, an' he said Bud died down there. He said he went to the hospital with him. Bud gagged around, an' said he'd be all right, but he wasn't.

Anyway, Bud probably smoked three packs of cigarettes a day. We drank at least two fifths of whiskey a day, at least, not counting wine. We drank wine by the gallon, an' that's night an' day. We'd go down an' sleep long enough to sober up an' start drinkin' again. We were alcoholics, but we didn't know what the word alcoholic was then. We knew a lot of other people were, but not us. We didn't have no problem. We'd get around an' do anything. Those drunks was all passed out in an alley, an' we was out stealing. That's the way it was.

I was gonna tell you about sleepin' with him in a room. Bill, his brother, wouldn't even come in a room where he was sleepin'. He'd snore so hard he'd blow the covers plumb off the bed snorin'. He was terrible. Nobody could really sleep. I could sleep with him 'cause I'd just pass out an' let him do his thing. This was in his later years. Damn quick he was to die about a year after that. He just gargled; you could hear his old lungs. He'd go to breathe, an' you could just hear that chokin'. Too much smokin', I guess. I smoked all my life. I'll wake up one of these mornings just like him, dead.

But he was a character. Bud, he'd be sober—half sober. We was punchy all the time where you can carry on a decent conversation, but after 5 o'clock in the afternoon, we was loaded an' ready to go again. It's a terrible disease, an' all my friends have died from alcohol.

Bud had a twin brother, Doug. I think he was a twin; they looked exactly alike. Doug had a bar. Imagine a Linderman with a bar...if that wouldn't drive a liquor inspector completely insane.

He had a piano in there. There's stories about every cowboy if they was wild men that are good. But, anyway, Bud was tryin' to get someone to play the piano. He tried to sing, an' he couldn't. What a voice he had. You think I got a whiskey voice, he really had it. He'd get over there an' snap his fingers an' dance. I can see him yet. So Doug said, "I had enough of this."

He knew a trapper there, an' he asked him to get him a bobcat, a big, mean one.

The trapper brought him one, an' he tied it to the piano. An' that kept Bud away. Bud finally got over there an' cut the rope, an' the bobcat got underneath a car an' a guy said, "Bud, you're tough. Get under there an' grab that bobcat."

Like I told you, Bud was a little thick-headed. He got underneath the car, an' that cat scratched the hell out of him.

Breezy Cox was a good friend of mine. Him an' Lonnie Allen. I was livin' in Pilot Rock, an' I run away from home when I was fourteen years old. I went to live with my sister in Portland. Mama said, "I can't keep him in school."

My sister said she'd put me in school in Portland, but I never enrolled there. I said, "Oh no, I gotta go back to Pilot Rock." I had no idea about goin' back to Pilot Rock.

She bought me a bus ticket back to Pilot Rock, an' I just took the bus ticket when she left the bus station an' traded it in. I said I wanted to go as far south as I could go. I got to Shasta, California, an' they dumped me out in the middle of winter. I ended up in Red Bluff. I stayed there with Carrol Owens. He put me at a sheep camp the last of October. It was cold up in those hills where we was lambing. Bob Ward an' Carrol Owens had about ten bands of sheep in there. I let a bunch of lambs die. Carrol put me up on a cow outfit after the sheep died. He liked me, so he didn't fire me. He took me up an' put me with his horses.

When I got enough money, I got into Phoenix. I hadn't ate, never had no place to sleep, nothin'. I was standing outside of Gene Autry's store. I had an old beat up hat on, and a pair of run-over boots too big for me. I must have looked like a waif out of the hills. These cowboys walked up to me, an' it happened to be Breezy Cox an' Lonnie Allen. They was about half full of whiskey. Breezy says, "Kid, you look like you come in off a long haul. Are you hungry?"

I had to show it. I was scanter than a snowbird. I'd put my nose on a window an' watched people eat. In those days, nobody took care of a kid. They'd run you out of town. They'd "float" you just like they would an old man. If you didn't have any support or people or a place to live, they'd just take you to the edge of town an' kick you in the butt an' say don't come back.

I got well acquainted with Bobby McGee an' Lonnie Allen. I think they made that song about Bobby McGee. He was a dandy. Bobby McGee an' Zack McWiggins an' Lonnie Allen an' Breezy Cox. And Breezy's brother "Slugger Sloan." Tommy Parish. These was all the head men at the Adams Hotel. The Adams Hotel at that time was a huge hotel right downtown Phoenix where all the big cow deals were made an' all the cowmen. It had a huge, long bar. It was Western. All of it. Tuscon, when you get down along the border, it was a paradise for a young man. I found just exactly what I wanted. I wanted Indians; I wanted Mexicans. I wanted everybody that was different. I looked for the strange an' the new. I wanted something different, an' I didn't care what it was if it had to do with horses, or stealin', or card games. I loved cards.

Jerry Ambler set the pace for bronc riders. He absolutely did. Casey Tibbs probably watched Ambler an' seen what a bronc rider did. Ambler was completely out of everybody's class. I mean, he was way ahead of 'em all. Dutch Martin an' Sonny Turman was the first guys to jerk their knees on a bareback—I mean a bareback horse, an' fall over backwards. But Ambler...

Jerry Ambler on Which Way. Lewiston '47

He was as crazy as Bud Linderman. He was tight with money. He wasn't a drunk like Bud was, but he was nuts. He would absolutely drive that car a hundred miles an hour. He had an old Buick. He'd cut a corner an' bet somebody five dollars there wasn't anybody coming the other way. Now, that's a hell of a bet. And if you think I'm kidding, I'm not kidding. I've got out of cars an' just hitch-hiked they'd scared me so bad. Now, if I'd done it, it was all right.

If you had scraped as many people off the highways as we did...

That's the way he got killed. He was cutting a corner. I think it was in California. He was living down on the river bottom, Waggs Blessing, an' Ambler had a bar down there. That was the end of Ambler.

He was getting near the end of his day. The last time I seen Jerry, he'd been setting chokers in the woods. I was making a rodeo at Myrtle Point, Oregon, an' I was walkin' by the buckin' chute, an' I seen this guy down there. I looked under his hat that was tipped down over his eyes. He was leaned up against an old saddle, an' he was about half asleep.

He got on a buckin' horse, an' he looked terrible. I said, "Ambler, don't ever get on another one." But he was takin' his holts. You get hurt enough you want to loosen up.

I remember Lee Caldwell. The last place he worked was on McKay Creek near Pilot Rock. He had a few race horses. I used to buckaroo up there for the Cunhas, an' Lee Caldwell was at their head-quarters camp right there at the head of McKay creek. I used to love to sit around an' listen, but very little did I get to visit with Lee. Being a young boy an wanting to get out in the brush an' ride, I didn't pay any attention to old men's stories at that time, only a few he told. But he would giggle, an' he was a very good storyteller. And he had a sense of humor that wouldn't quit. He told me about going to Montana one time. A guy took him up there, an' they knew how to make money. Guys all had horses around there. They dressed Lee up in a pair of bib overalls an' high laced shoes, an' they bet any amount of money on horses or a deck of cards in those days.

This guy said, "I got a horse nobody can ride."

The guy with Lee said, "I'll bet that ol' boy standin' over there can ride him for any amount of money. He used to be a cowboy."

The ol' farmer looked at Lee an' laughed, an' Lee got on an' spurred the livin' crap out of him. An' ol' Lee would laugh an' slap his leg when he told the story. I can see him yet.

He told me how he trained his race horses, and he was right, too. He said, "I'd get out there behind 'em with a bullwhip and take 'em around the track about three times, a poppin' that whip. I'd pop that whip when they'd leave the gate, and they're runnin'."

They was so many of them old men. Old Frank Cable, Lee Caldwell. I don't think Frank Cable went with Lee Caldwell to Montana. They were just a different breed of men. Old Frank Rosenberg he bulldogged in those days. Frank Cable, Lee Caldwell. They wasn't too many around this part of the country.

I really started these kids around here roping. They seen how much fun I had. I should have roped all my life, but it took too much time taking care of a horse. I should have been doing that all of my life. I win a lot of these little ropings.

When I was just a little boy growin' up in the town of Pilot Rock, I learned some good lessons the hard way. This old Indian squaw came to town in a buggy. Maude Spino was her name. Old Maude would come in with these old high-laced moccasins an' heavy coat an' gloves. Indian gloves. They'd line 'em with flower sacks. But old Maude would come by, an' I'd hide over behind some tumbleweeds, an' she was drivin' kind of an old broncy horse anyway. By the time he'd get to me, I'd jump up an' let out a war whoop out of me an' throw gravel at the horse. And then I'd run off. I'd done it twice.

She come by the next time, an' she was waitin' for it, so I didn't go out. So she goes downtown an' buys a little sack of candy. When she comes back she says, "Boy, boy, boy."

I went over there, an' she reaches down off that buggy an' grabs me by the back of the neck. There was a holder for the buggy whip, an' she got it out, an' I'll tell you, she educated me. She brought the welts out on me.

I yelled, "No more, no more!"

But, anyway, there's lots of stories, an' they just lead to 10,000 more.

TEX SMITH

Tex Smith lives in Dillon, Montana, and is active in the senior rodeo circuit. Tex was involved in pro rodeo during the forties and fifties, mostly as a roper, and is a Turtle member. During the past two years, we have received inestimable help from Tex in identifying people in our pictures. In a telephone conversation, he asked if we knew anything about Stub Bartlemay, and, if not, why not? Tex pointed us in the right direction, and we truly appreciate it.

I'm well acquainted with all of the Greenough's and Linderman's. Deb Greenough, the world class bareback rider, won the World in 1993, I think. He's in the National Finals now. He won the first go-around. He's a grandson of Bill Greenough which was a brother to Turk and Alice and Marge. He's livin' back in Red Lodge.

There's a new museum, or they moved the old museum to downtown Red Lodge, and they didn't have it done very well when I was there this summer. I'm hopin' they'll get it better. I kinda got on 'em about it. I said, "You've got the two greatest rodeo families in the world come from here. You've got an abundance of stuff around here if you just go and dig it out." There is a pretty good exhibit on Alice Greenough there, and a little on Turk, but hardly anything on the Linderman's.

Another one that rodeoed out of there that was real tough was a guy by the name of Bill Daggert. They've got one pretty good picture of him in that.

I've got a picture of the whole Greenough family—Packsaddle Ben and his wife and all the kids.

Bill and Bud Linderman were practically the same age as I am and, also Gene Rambo. But all those, Turk, Bill, Marge and Alice, was all ridin' when I started, and they stayed with it for several years.

156

The Linderman's were actually raised in Belfree, but they ended up calling Red Lodge their home. There's four of the brothers buried at Belfree. Bill isn't. He died in an airplane crash in Salt Lake City. I think he was buried by his first wife. She was from Livingston, I believe. I've never went and looked it up, but I believe that Bill is buried in Livingston. I've got pictures of all the stones of the other ones, the four Linderman brothers.

I've been working on a "Hell's Angel" story. I've got the documentation on it. In the Hall of Fames of both Oklahoma City and Colorado Springs, they give credit to a guy by the name of Buck Yarborough for owning him, but he never had anything to do with him whatsoever. They've got his breeding wrong.

They bought him here in Dillon in 1933. I was there. I was only twelve, but I remember him pretty well. So that's one thing I'm working on, getting that changed. I went down to see Yarborough's nephew, Owen McGill; he's got a ranch down there between Wheatland and Laramie, Wyoming. He concurs that Buck Yarborough never operated in Montana.

When I get this folio all put together, then I'm gonna go camp on the Hall of Fame steps in Colorado Springs, and then I'm gonna go to Oklahoma City and sit on their steps. I think if you're gonna have history, you ought to get it right. It seems like, to me, that the people that do write, that can write, don't have anything to write about.

Cheyenne is the Daddy of 'em all. And then Calgary, I think, is probably the greatest outdoor rodeo in the world because they have so many different things there. Pendleton would probably be number three in stature if you won it.

I used to go to Denver to rodeo and to Omaha, Nebraska in the Fall. Denver in the winter. After I got to traveling in the senior pro circuit, I contested in Arizona and Nevada. I went to Wickenburg, Arizona and Goodyear. I'd go down there and stay about three weeks in February generally. I went to the Old Timer's National Finals in Reno three years in a row. And then I used to go to Elko, Nevada.

In my hey-day, I used to come out to Oregon and Washington. I went to Spokane, Washington, when they had a good rodeo there. They had the rodeo out at Playfair racetrack. I used to come to Pendleton, Dayton, Washington, and Walla Walla.

Mostly I stayed in Montana, Idaho and Utah. I went up into Canada and stayed three weeks one summer. I went to Calgary, and Lethbridge, Pincher Creek, and Raymond. They were all in the month of July.

Bud Linderman was a fighter. He wasn't a fighter, he liked to fight. He always picked on the toughest guy in town. He's the guy that should be in the Hall of Fame cause he was kind of like cowboys were in them days. He may have been a little extreme. He drank, and he fought, and he gambled. They got Bill in the Hall of Fame and called him the "King," but us guys that rodeoed with both of 'em thought Bud was the best hand of the two.

They always suspected Bud of robbery and safecrackin,' but they never, ever proved anything on him. He did kill a guy in New York City. It took quite a lot of money to keep him from going to jail. This was back at Madison Square Garden. It was at the Velvet Ear hotel. They had a fight in there, and a guy came in and pulled a gun. Bud disarmed him. He kicked him in a bad spot, and the guy died. The guy was a plain clothesman, but they proved he never identified himself as a policeman when he pulled his gun. So Bud got off on self defense.

Bud died of pneumonia. I believe he died in Arizona. He'd quit rodeoin,' an' he was runnin' gambling games. A year or so before he died, he came up through Dillon during the rodeo and rented a table at the Metlan Hotel an' ran the game himself.

I'd been around Bud a lot, and he was always not very serious. But when he was here that night, my wife and I went over there, an' he wasn't busy. We sat there an' visited for quite awhile, an' I had the best visit I'd ever had in all the time I'd known him.

He could do it all. He rode broncs, bulldogged regularly, rode bareback horses, could rope, did rope some, but he was more of a natural. The first rodeo I ever saw him at he could ride. He was tough. But Bill, when he first came out, he couldn't hardly sit on a fence without fallin' off. But he learned fast. He got to be terrible tough.

I liked 'em all. Bill an' I were good friends. We had our differences all right, but we were still friends.

Turk Greenough was a great buckin' horse rider, an' he always claimed he was a world's champion, but it don't show in the records. Nineteen twenty-nine was the first Rodeo Association of America, an association of committees and stock contractors; they kept the point award system, an' they kept records from 1929 on. Before that, if you was declared, like Denver, the World's Champion Buckin' Contest winner...if you won that you was world champion. If you went on to Cheyenne, they declared that the World's Champion Buckin' Contest. If you won that, you was the world's champion. That's how Turk was declared world's champion. He was in one of those top buckin' horse ridin' contests.

He was capable. In all the years I was around Turk, I can't ever remember seein' him on the ground. He was as hard a horse rider; he could ride most of 'em. But Turk kind of lived off his reputation. He borrowed a lot of money an' never paid anybody back. But he never hurt rodeo any. He was a kind of ambassador. He was from a famous family. All them, Turk, Bill, Marge, and Alice, could all ride buckin' horses.

I knew Deb Copenhaver real well. He lives up in Washington at Creston. Did he preach you a sermon?

His son was a world champion calf roper. He's also a preacher now, he don't do anything, I don't think, but go around putting on services.

It's hard to overcome all of us outlaws.

Deb was a great guy an' had more good ideas than anybody you ever saw. Like, he made that racetrack out at Green Acres where he lives. He leased a bunch of ground an' run cattle on it, and after

Turk Greenough off Which Way, Pendleton, 1944. Photo by Devere.

he'd get things goin' in pretty good shape, then it was kind of a passin' fancy with him, an' he'd drop it an' go on to somethin' else.

I knew Lary Daniels real well. Lary an' I rodeoed together a lot. He was an all-around cowboy. He went the rounds from the top to the bottom. Lary, when I first knew him, was really serious about rodeoin'. He worked out and lived pretty clean; that's when he was married to his first wife. When they split up, he drank an' did everything wrong. I knew him, probably, other than being a really personal friend about as good as any casual friends did. He was a tough cowboy when I first knew him. He wasn't very big, but he could do about anything that needed to be done.

I came out there to Oregon and Washington a year ago last spring to the Old Timers' rodeos. I suppose you've heard of Stub Bartlemay? I was interested in getting some dope on Stub. I'm tryin' to put together a little writing too.

That was what I was out there for, the old timer's rodeo at Arlington. That's where Stub lived when he was rodeoin'. I got some dope from some of his family. He had since moved to Sisters, and then I guess died down at Sisters.

Tater Decker an' I traveled some together in the forties. I never really traveled a lot with many people. I had a family an' generally hauled horses. I wasn't like the bronc riders where four or five could jump in an outfit an' go down the road. Most of the time I traveled

160

alone. I did have some partners, but not many. I started out ropin' an then bulldoggin'. Bulldoggin' was my best event. I won more bulldogs than anything else. During World War II the ridin' was pretty easy, an' I could ride a little; I got in the riding's for four or five years during the latter part of the War. I rode primarily bareback horses an' bulls, not much saddle broncs. I never did seem to get that right.

Guy Cash...I knew him. He was sheriff down at White Bird, Idaho, for many years.

When I first started rodeoin', there wasn't hardly any contest bareback riding. It was exhibition. It was loose ropes for fifty cents or a dollar a head. Then the first one-handed bareback riding as we know it today that I ever ran into was about 1941. They'd had it other places, but not here. Tim Bernard an' Moomaw out of Omak, Washington, put on some rodeos. They put on one at Missoula, an' they had one-handed riggin' bareback ridin'. About that same year, Leo Cremer had it in Butte.

BARE BACK RIDING? (© R.R. DOUBLEDAY)

I rodeoed with Cremer an' worked for him some. He started about 1930 in the rodeo business. In my estimation, he's the greatest rodeo producer. He was way ahead of his time. He had more color, more heart...he had trick riders and trick ropers; also, he used the big horses. He had horses that would buck you off. It wasn't a matter of drawing something that you could win on; it was drawing something that you could ride.

DENNY JONES

Denny Jones owns and operates a 21,000 acre ranch just outside of Juntura in Eastern Oregon. Since retirement at the age of 62, he has added a second career—13 terms in the Oregon House of Representatives in Salem. At the age of 86, he retired from office due to term limitation and now spends his time at the ranch. While in office, he represented Malheur, Harney, and Lake counties and half of Klamath county.

───◈·◇·◈───

The first Pendleton Round-Up was on the first day of September, 1910, I believe. I may not be really right on this, but I think Bert Kelly won the buckin' that year. I was born on that day. Newt Jones was my uncle. He was one of the judges in the first Pendleton Round-Up. He was a brother to my dad. My dad was Gene. He broke horses for the Boer War, and he went to England with Buffalo Bill.

My dad broke horses in Colorado, probably Denver, but I'm not sure about the exact town. In them days they were picking up horses all over. They had some pretty rough ones at times. He broke horses there for the man that had the contract for the horses for the Boer War; he was there quite awhile. They rode horses every day. The idea was to get 'em gentle enough so the inspector would take 'em. It was all hearsay from him with me cause that was before I was born.

I never rode professionally, but I rode lots of buckin' horses. I've roped at the local rodeos around here.

They created a "Big Loop" contest here, and I won it three times. My partner and I. Team roping. You had to have a loop ten feet in diameter. It's based on the old Mexican Vaquero tradition from California. The Vaqueros came up here with Pete French.

There was eight cowboys. We used rawhide riatas—long rawhide riatas. We did it at Burns and Vale. There was three counties

162

that competed, Malheur, Harney, and Grant. They all competed in the "Big Loop" contest.

The way that got started, old Herman Oliver was a great cattleman over at Grant County where he had a ranch. He said that Harney County was the largest county in the state of Oregon, had the biggest haystacks in the state of Oregon, and throwed the biggest loops of any county in the state of Oregon. So, Art Seale from Jordan Valley said, "Well, it is a big county all right. And the haystacks are pretty big, but I'm not sure about the big loops."

So they said we'll just have a contest and see.

There were three teams from Malheur, three from Harney, and three from Grant. And that fall at the Burns rodeo we all roped over there. My partner was Charlie Chaplin from up at Riverside out of Crane. Him and I won that. And then he wouldn't rope anymore, and I got Buck Miller to rope with me, an old time cowboy from Harney County. And we won it twice. I've got belt buckles to show we won it.

I think there are some interesting tales about Henry Miller. He was a big livestock gatherer. The PLS Co., as we called it. Old Henry Miller could leave Sacramento, California and drive to Vale, Oregon in a team and buggy and stay every night on his own land. Now just stop and think about that. The PLS Co. owned a good part of Harney Valley through Harper, clear down to Vale.

There's lots of history around.

The younger generation is a little different. They rope different now. They use rubber inner-tubes on the saddle horns where we'd run somebody off if they did that here. That's hard on cattle. When you take your turns it don't slip. You're supposed to let your turns slip a little bit, an' smoke comes up off the horn.

You lose your thumb or your fingers. It's kind of unusual to lose your whole hand.

My dad had pictures of the old horses there at the Pendleton Round-Up. And the people that used to ride there, like Yakima Canutt. And, this is a dirty word nowadays, but "Nigger George" Fletcher. They wouldn't call him that now. And "Whistlin' Anne" an' "Midnight," those tough horses they were buckin' then. "Warpaint" was still buckin' when he was 20 years old.

Jess Stahl is one of the first ones to Hoolihan those steers. Fact of the matter, he hoolihaned a steer an' got his finger over the end of his horn, an' when he drove the horn in the ground, it cut his finger off. The hoolihan is where you run a horn in the ground. It's agin' the law now.

Tony Vey, who used to live down by Pilot Rock, was kind of crippled in one leg. He had a good ranch. He tried to win the steer-roping many times, but, of course, he was a little bit handicapped. I saw him rope in Pendleton, and he done all right, but it's hard to compete against those boys who do it every day.

I picked up buckin' horses for Harley Tucker for three years, over at Weiser, Idaho. I had a good horse, one of the best pickup horses around. Harley got me to come over and be the pickup man for him at the Weiser rodeo. It had to be 1940-41-42, somewhere along about there.

He was from Joseph, Oregon. That's where he kept his horses, his buckin' string. My horse got out on the highway an' got hit, and it kinda crippled him up. Then I got my leg broke, and I couldn't go back to Weiser the next year.

Harley had a few real tough horses.

I'm 88 years old. When you get this old, you have trouble rememberin'. You're either going to the bathroom or trying to think of somebody's name.

The book "Gold And Cattle Country," by Herman Oliver and retold to Jackman had some pictures in there of people brandin' with a snubbin' post in the middle. I said, "Gee Whiz, Herman, why put pictures like that in when you're close to Harney and Malheur counties?"

He said, "Dang it, if you don't like the picture, why don't you provide me with one?"

So I had a picture that was taken out at the Double "O," out of Harney County years an' years ago. The wagon cook was there with his flour sack apron an' a brandin' fire. So I sent that to him, an' he put that in the second edition.

Old Reub Long from Fort Rock...there was talk that somebody asked him if it had rained lately, an' he said "yeah, it rained, but it was only 30 percent moisture." He run horses with old Bill Brown out on the desert there. That's the way he made his livin' down at Fort Rock. He wintered cattle out down there.

HERMAN VOWELL

Herman Vowell has raised horses all of his life, and he has made a good living at it. As he says, he has made a living at what he loves, and he is a contented man.

Herman invited us into his home, and we sat around the kitchen table talking about his life. Herman is well known in the Klamath Falls area of Southern Oregon, near the California border. Herman and Ray, his brother, were involved in local rodeos but were never professionals although they knew many who were. Alturas native, Hippy Burmeister, Burel Mulkey and Perry Ivory, were well known to the rodeo world and were all personal friends of Herman's.

Stub Bartlemay on Red Pepper. Molalla, Ore. July, 1944.

165

That's ol' Stub Bartlemay, ain't it? I remember he always had that cigarette in his mouth. He got to be one heck of a pickup man with the Christensen Brothers.

Back in the thirties, when we rode barebacks and bulls, all's we had was one rope—it wasn't even a braided rope, and it had a hondo in it. We'd ride the bulls with it for awhile, and then we'd put it on the bareback horses. Same riggin' on both of 'em!

In the modern days now, the spurs would be locked right up there in them shoulders, but in this it comes down. This is the way they rode in the early days. They spurred back as much as they spurred ahead—back to the cantle board. It wasn't necessary to go forward.

Mac Barbour had some of the best buckin' horses in the thirties and forties. He developed em', an' he halter broke em', an' he fed em' grain. They were big stout horses. He had half a dozen there when he went to the Finals, and they just proved their point. They was good horses.

Mac had a horse he called "No Name," a big tall buckin' horse, and somebody rode him and they called it "Shinnin' their shoes." They wouldn't turn their feet out, and that way you could ride him. But Mac said there was no way they could ride him and stick a spur in him. I can't remember if it was Jerry Ambler or Perry Ivory that exhibitioned him...I think it was Ambler. He said, "I'll show you

how to stick a spur in that son-of-a-gun," an' that horse just knocked him higher than a kite. Well, he didn't ride him; he bucked off. That was the only time I can remember Jerry bucking off. Of course he did buck off, but not very often. He was a very, very smart rider. That tickled old Mac Barbour to death. He didn't want anybody to ride him.

Jerry Ambler rode these quite a lot in the late '30s in Klamath Falls. He worked at Montgomery Ward's tack department. He came from Canada. I don't know how long he was getting there to Klamath Falls, but he settled there for quite a long time. He made a lot of friends. He had a spur lick you'd just dream about. He was ahead of his time because he didn't lock down under the fork of that saddle; he just what we called "floated" a horse. It was the beginning of a new era. That guy was just outstanding.

He was a likable man. Montgomery Wards had a store up in the old Medical-Dental building, and he was downstairs. He had pictures on the wall of buckin' horses that he'd ridden. People enjoyed going in and looking at things, and generally they'd buy somethin'. Jerry was a good salesman, a good man. We became pretty well acquainted with him. He said in Canada before he left there, his cabin caught fire and burned all of his saddles and all of his trophies. He had quite a reputation in Canada as a bronc rider.

I knew one day that he'd be champion, but he never traveled enough. He just kind of stayed in this small area here; but when he got out of here and went to travelin', he had a long record to go after he left here. That was in the thirties.

I think he died in Utah. He's buried in a pauper's grave. This friend of mine who wrote some of this stuff in the papers was really interested in Jerry Ambler's grave, and he may have mentioned it in there. They have located the grave and have honored him.

He wasn't a very big man, about my size, but man, he'd just take that old rein...in the old days they'd just lock that hand back and hang on to that nose. Now, he'd just float. He'd reach out with that hand. That was the beginning of an era. Ambler, when he rode, kind of got away from 'em. He got above 'em. Ambler was ahead of his time.

Mac Barbour had some of the toughest horses I think were ever put together. Gosh, he took care of 'em, and they were in shape and ready to go. They were halter broke, and you could handle 'em. You could take care of them, trim their feet. That Ambler, he could just take any of 'em and put on the prettiest ride you ever saw. And they were great big stout horses.

That's how we were taught—to lock that hand. That was how you rode. That was how you stayed on. It didn't make a picture like they make today. In every athletic event they've improved so much.

Old Burel Mulkey came up to this country. He was working for the Bedart Outfit. They bought out a ranch next to Steel Swamp where we were staying, out at the Devil's Garden.

He took over, and they hauled I don't know how many cattle up there on the train. They unloaded 'em over at Hackamore, which was 30-40 miles away. They started to drive 'em, and the cattle weren't broke to drive, and they scattered. They found 'em in Alturas, California, and Klamath Falls, Oregon—everywhere.

The first time I met Burel Mulkey was at Dry Lake. He was in a little Jeep, and we met on a corner, and he was doing about 500 miles an hour. I told him that he ought to learn to drive.

We got acquainted, and he was a great guy. We were sixteen miles away from where he lived. Burel and his wife Myrna got to be real good friends with my wife and I. He'd call me at 3 o'clock in the morning, and I'd just drag myself out to that old country telephone. His wife called me late one afternoon and asked me if I'd like to get even with Burel and put a stop to those 3 a.m. calls. I said, "I'm gettin' tired of it, and I'll do about anything but kill him."

She said, "Call him about 9 o'clock. He goes to bed at 8 p.m." I started doing that, and I lost him after that.

He had an old truck with no bull-board on it at all. He not only was an arena cowboy, but he was a good hand out in the country. He knew cattle. I said, "Burel, for gosh sakes you're gonna cripple something jumping them in and out of that truck."

He said, "Aw, I just back up to a place that's a little lower, and if they can't get out of that truck that's just too bad. I don't want to ride in those rocks."

This was out in the Devil's Garden, halfway between here and Alturas. It's about 60 miles across, and we were out 30 miles, and his ranch was probably 35 miles from Alturas, very Northern California.

We're part of Malin. We were 30 miles out on an old road that finally went to pieces. We finally put in a road that went south of us and it was 50 miles to the ranch, almost 60; I was out there day before yesterday shippin' cattle with 'em. I can't keep my hand out of it. Beautiful country.

When Bedart sold the ranch, Burel and his wife went back to Bakersfield. I hear from Myrna every year, but Burel's been dead for eight or nine years.

Bedart was a man from Bakersfield who raised lots of spuds and grain and stuff, and he bought this northern ranch to run cattle. That's how Burel came up here. Bedart hired him to come up here from Bakersfield.

That ranch sold in 1951, and they got two or three guys to stay on; very early '50s: 1953-54. Burel was an era all his own. He was quite a guy. He was just as good a cowboy as he was a bronc rider. I think he was World Champion in 1937. He was a little, short stocky fella. Don't give him an inch in life 'cause he would take it out on you. He'd pull dirty tricks on you, I'll tell you he would.

I don't think I have a picture of him. We took a lot of 8 mm video pictures at that time, not too much camera pictures. I wish I had.

That ranch had a thousand head of two and three year old steers, and we worked 'em there when we rode over the sixteen miles and stayed overnight. You don't often see that many bunched up any more at that age.

Burel wasn't there at the time. The Archers were there then. They went there in '32, and I think they were there until '50 or '51.

Then Bedart bought it, and some of the Archers stayed awhile to help 'em, and then they hired Ed Ivory. He ran the place for awhile, then Oscar Hayes, and then Burel Mulkey. And then trouble started. Fun trouble. I'll tell ya, it was great fun.

It was impossible to get a pickup in there. Everything you needed you put on your pack horse; sometimes you ran out of razor blades.

I've lived here my whole life. I was born over here about ten miles, and I haven't had but the one job since 1936, although we branched out and have our own place here where we have colts and stud horses and raise quite a few horses. We put on ropin's, and we have a wonderful arena. It's all sand. We're right on the edge of Tule Lake, and you can go 20 feet and it's all sand. For a number of years, Mike Beard and Dee Pickett came up for the roping. We had a lot of kids. Mike is from up at Rufus. He was World Champion in 1984 I believe.

I don't know how my brother Ray and I became so involved in wantin' to be cowboys, but my dad and mom moved from a little town down in Texas up here and homesteaded by Klamath Falls. My dad worked on a wagon hauling lumber. In 1921 he got pneumonia and died, four days after his 37th birthday. I got pictures on the wall of when he was cow boss of the 7F Ranch in Texas. As we grew older, we were fortunate enough to get a job on a ranch in the Poe Valley. In 1934 we worked on a corporate ranch buckarooin' an' movin' cattle. In 1936 I just lucked out an' got on with W. C. Dalton, one of the nicest, greatest guys I've ever known.

I was 20 when I went to work for him, and I just had my 21st birthday when the buckaroo boss quit, and Mr. Dalton said, "Herman, would you like to take over Frank's job?"

"I couldn't do that," I told him. "I've only been across that country once. I wouldn't know enough to work that country."

"If I helped you, would you take the job?"

I said, "Yes, I would!"

"Well, I've got seven or eight guys that want to cowboy, but if I hire 'em they work for me. So, I want you to hire 'em, and they'll work for you," he said.

I said, "Well, how about my brother?"

"All right," he said. So Ray came to work there exactly a year from the day I did. I went to work on my Mom's birthday, and Ray came to work on my Mom's birthday a year later.

I lived on that ranch for 25 years. I got married out there. I got to be foreman, and Ray kept his buckaroo job.

We moved away in 1960 to a little place in the Langell Valley, which had too many mosquitoes to break horses, so we moved here. We call it the Vowell Brothers ranch. We break horses, and we put in a roping arena.

In the Langell Valley, you can hear the horses and cattle just moanin' from the swarms of mosquitoes all night long. You couldn't ride those horses. You had to have a bee mask on to go change the water after dark. The upper end is worse than the lower end. The ranch had some cattle in the pasture up there, and you'd go up there and your horse would back out of the trailer and turn gray from mosquitoes. It's impossible to believe.

We had a chance to buy this little place and it worked out so well. The ground is soft and nice. We've been here for 37 years.

I was born in 1916. One time when Mom was up in her 70's I said, "Mom, can I ask you a question?"

She said, "Well, I guess so."

"How come Ray is more Indian than I am?"

She thought a minute on that, and her little blue eyes just got so doggone bright, I got out of there.

We were livin' in a little one room cabin at the homestead on North Klamath, and Dad and Mom told us all to go outside.

It was November 15, and it was cold and snowin'. We stood outside and liked to froze to death. We whined and whimpered about it, but they wouldn't let us back in. Pretty soon we heard a baby wail, so Dad said, "Well, come on in."

I told my sister about this two years ago. I said, "I'll never forget when we went in there. Mom was cryin', an' Dad said it wasn't his." My sister about had a fit. I didn't dare tell that to my mom.

We had a hard time being raised. Times were tough in the 1920s and '30s. But we had some good neighbors.

I knew Hippy Burmiester. He had a ranch called The Corporation south of Alturas. He made a good business out of it. He was elected Fair Manager at the Modoc County Fair. He sold his ranch, and it was bought up with a whole bunch of other ranches, but it didn't work out, so they finally sold 'em out again. But he had a real nice ranch. He ran cattle on it, raised hay and grain. A likable fella. He was well known throughout this area and throughout the country for riding. But he was beyond that when I knew him. He still reminisced about it.

I didn't know Gene Pruett other than what De Vere Helfrich talked about him. Years before Gene made World, De Vere said, "He's always askin' me about pictures and stuff. He said he's gonna be World Champion, but I really don't think he will."

That's what De Vere told me. Later, De Vere said, "That's one time I had to detract what I said 'cause he did make it."

Gene Pruett on that horse at Prairie City was the most beautiful bucking horse picture I ever saw. His old toes are turned out, and he had a little hump in his back, an' Gene was stickin' on to that ol' horse.

A lot of times they didn't turn their toes out, they'd just polish them boots. And they never had that kick back to the cantle like they do today. It was just a beautiful sight to see Jerry Ambler ride a buckin' horse.

Casey Tibbs rode like Ambler rode above those ol' horses. Casey came to Klamath Falls several times. Another guy that I really enjoyed watching was Gene Rambo. Nice man. Gene was one of those guys that could ride broncs, ride a bareback horse, he could calf rope, he could win a team ropin'; he was just an all-around cowboy. I've got a picture that my wife took of me an' Gene Rambo walking out of the arena at Klamath Falls together.

Perry Ivory lived at the "E" ranch. He had a round barn, and he put a buckin' chute in there. That's how he started all them colts. He'd just mash 'em into them buckin' chutes and spur 'em out. The cowboys hated him with a passion. That's how he'd get his practice. It was like roping the bosses' calves. Every time you went to ride one, it was a bronc ride. I met Perry in 1936. I remember he'd laugh about it. The buckaroos he buckaroo-ed with would tell me, "That's somethin' ol' Perry started." They'd just blow out of the corral with 'em.

He was ridin' a little bay horse called Little Dick, and we met he an' Ernie Archer half way—we had FX cattle strays, an' they had Pitchfork cattle strays. This little bay was a snorty lookin' little booger. I was talkin' with Perry for awhile, and I said, "Gee, Perry, that's a good lookin' horse."

"Yeah," Perry said, "And he bucks about the way he looks. He bucked me off this mornin'."

That just tickled me, oh, gosh, that tickled me. That horse turned out to make the California Reining Champion. That was in the fall of 1936.

Perry Ivory had quite a sense of humor. He started all of those horses out of that buckin' chute. The barn was round like the one they talk about out in Eastern Oregon—Pete French's barn. It's still there. It's a round barn with a hole in the middle and several rings around it.

Most of those old guys in those days were ranch raised guys. Today, they go to college an' go to the rodeo team. They never see a horse, but they can go out of there winnin'.

But Perry and Hippy Burmeister, they was just rough old hands. I can remember when I was a kid they were just tickled to death when the rodeo was over. They had to fix up all the bars. They'd break equipment. They were just raised tough. They're entirely different. It's a money deal today. They lift weights, and they do things that keep 'em healthy and limber. They didn't know what pain was back then.

I remember one time Ray, my brother, an' I loved wild horse racin', and Ray was out in the arena in some event at Klamath Falls, an' this fella, I won't mention his name, he was President of the Association. Anyway, he went out in the arena and told Ray to get out. Ray said, "I'll go when the rest of 'em go. I'm in this event. When it's over, we'll all leave together."

He said, "I said get out!" He grabbed ahold of Ray's bridle reins, an' that didn't go over with Ray.

Ray took his romel, and he said, "I think you'd better turn that loose." And he did.

Well, I won the wild horse race. Mac Barbour supplied the wild horses. He had corralled them north of Steel Swamp. They were 10, 12, 14 year old studs. And they didn't know what a fence was. Well, he had 'em in the wild horse race, and Ray got one of the wildest ones, a big old Indian bay. He eared him down, and Ray was saddling him, and he had a helper with him. This ol' Indian walked out an' said "Hey!" and slapped that ol' horse on the behind, and that horse got that guy down an' wallered all over him. Out of the corral he went with Ray's saddle under his belly. And they had a ditch out there, and he got into that. Ray was quite unhappy.

I happened to have a pretty good crew, an' that son-of-a-gun I got backed out of there and he went the whole length of that race-track an' never looked back and right across that finish line. Obviously, I had won the race.

That night I went to get my money, and this guy that was President he says, "What are you in here for?"

"I'm here to pick up my check," I said.

"You don't have a check comin'," he said. "You didn't win anything."

"I'm quite sure I did," I said.

"Nope, we don't have anything here for you," he said.

So I went out and asked a judge, "Didn't you mark me first?"

"I sure did," he said.

"He's not gonna let me have it," I said.

"Well, I'll fix that," he said. Pretty soon he came out and said, "No, by gosh, you didn't." That's the way they run things. For a few dollars they'd cut your throat. I wouldn't want to mention his name. He's a popular man. It was just a deal where you could get a dollar. You had to have it. It was more important to be dishonest. But I never will forget that.

Anyway, this guy Don Bently was ridin' buckin' horses at this time. He could ride good. And this ol' boy, the same guy, didn't mark him very well. Don was a little drunk. We was standin' out there waitin' for those darn guys to pay off—they never paid off 'till the middle of the night, and everybody was gettin' a little cranky. Ol' Don went up to this guy an said, "You know, you're a sorry so and so of a judge."

"Keep your eyes on this; it's gonna happen quick," some guy said to me. Ol' Don Bently fought in the ring, but he was so drunk. And he just kept tellin' this guy, and the guy looked like he was absorbing it very well, and the next thing you know Don was down on the ground. Boy, I mean he was bleeding, an' that guy just knocked him colder than a wedge. But that's the way the payoffs used to run. Lots of good fights.

But today's world is so different. It's on another level all together. They won't put up with that. That stuff hurts rodeo. In today's world you know the picture. It's so operated I think it's a pretty honest business.

We had rodeos out here. That's the line of trees we planted when we moved here. They were little things about that high. In the afternoon we had all kinds of shade. We just called it Vowell Brothers arena. We had six ropings and one "Ten Steer"; then we had three Benefit ropings for people that were ill or for feeding kids during the year. Nineteen ninety-seven was the last one held here. Ray was just 80, and he won both the saddles we had for prizes. We have in our rules that if you win one saddle, then you can never win another. It would be repetitious. Give somebody else a chance. So, Ray went over to this girl, she's quite a sweetheart, and he says, "Ann, I'd sure like to have that Open saddle. I'd like it best if you don't mind."

And she said, "Ray, if you read the fine print, it says when you win a saddle, you cannot win another. You won the Century saddle first, now you get out of here!"

It tickled him to death. He laughed so hard..."And now get out of here!"

We told people that wanted to fight their horses or use foul language in the arena to just go someplace else. We wouldn't have that in the arena. Everyone was aware that we didn't like that. They can get so foul-mouthed, and there's kids around. One guy was in the box, an' his horse did something. He said a very filthy word, and Ray just went over and jumped on his horse and rode over to where the guy was taking the rope off his steer. Ray told him to cinch up and pull out of there. "We just don't want that language here," he said.

The guy rode straight up to the timin' shed an said, "Boys, I just didn't even think. I apologize. I'm sorry for everything, and I'll never do it again."

We said okay, and we kept right on ropin'. You gotta know the difference. Some people won't regret anything. Some don't know the difference. Like I told one guy, it was in mixed company. I told him, "You know, I don't know whether you know it or not, when you're cussin', you're not sayin' much, and you're not thinking. If you can't tell something that we can all understand, don't talk here."

BARBARA MOREHEAD

Barbara Morehead and her husband Mike live in Pilot Rock, Oregon. Barbara is the great niece of Stub Bartlemay, world renowned saddle bronc riding champion of the world in the 1930s and early '40s. According to Barbara, the semi-official Bartlemay family historian, Stub was always shy and retiring, even at family gatherings, so she decided to write Stub's biography so that the younger generation could know and appreciate having a world champion in their family.

Stub Bartlemay
as told by Barbara Morehead
Pilot Rock, Oregon

Everett Bartlemay, better known as "Stub," spent his boyhood in Arlington, Oregon. A neighbor named him "Stub" because he was such a runt. Stub was always very small for his age until he started to grow when he was about eighteen or nineteen years old.

Stub was a born horseman; the family had a pony, and Stub rode from the time he was able to get on a horse's back. His dad let him ride the work horses when he worked in the fields with him.

Stub was about ten years old when his folks moved to Eastern Oregon; about that age he could already stand on the horse's back and ride at a gallop. This method of riding horses came in handy when he started riding in the Roman races at rodeos; which was riding two horses with one foot on each horse.

Before Stub's folks moved to Eastern Oregon, his dad would send Stub's brother Perry out into the fields with a team to work the fields; Perry would turn the job over to Stub. Stub soon became the best teamster in the country; he was a natural horseman. Stub was shoeing horses at a very early age, around the age of fourteen years old.

His sister Vera recalls that most people think of him as a rodeo bucking horse rider; "I think of him as a natural horseman, and horse lover, trainer. He broke a lot of horses to ride, doctored them." At the age of sixteen or seventeen he rode at county fairs near home. In 1929, at the age of twenty, he won first in bronc riding at Moro, Oregon. He was first again in bronc riding at Prineville in 1930 and at Molalla in 1932. By this time he had gained experience and confidence in his own ability as a bronc rider.

In 1934, he went to Calgary, Alberta, Canada, where he won the North American Championship in bronc riding and was also given the H. B. Bennett trophy, which he treasured. This was a wrist watch with the following inscription on the back:

Calgary Stampede
1934
Champion North American Bucking Horse Rider
presented by Honorable H. B. Bennett,
won by Stub Bartlemay

H. B. Bennett was the Prime Minister of Canada at that time. The Prince of Wales trophy was usually awarded for this championship. Stub also rode in Calgary in 1935, 1936, 1937 and 1941.

In 1935 Stub followed the rodeo circuit to New York, riding in rodeos in Montana, Oklahoma, and Texas on his way. The high point of his career was riding in Madison Square Garden as one of Col. W. T. Johnson's World Championship Rodeo contestants. Here, he won the championship and received a hand-tooled saddle as a trophy. He continued riding in rodeos through 1941, starting from Oregon and traveling east. During these years he rode in rodeos in Oregon, Washington, Wyoming, Arizona, California, Idaho, Montana, Louisiana, Oklahoma, Utah, Texas, Michigan, Colorado, Massachusetts, and New York, ending in Madison Square Garden. His last appearance there was in 1946 when he won fourth place.

While following the rodeo circuit from Oregon to Madison Square Garden during these years, Stub won his share of trophies, belts, etc. For instance, in 1941, he won the first in bronc riding in Cheyenne where he was presented with a saddle.

A great many of the larger rodeos were canceled during the war years of 1942 through 1945, so Stub contented himself with riding in small rodeos. He rode in the Sisters rodeo in 1943 and 1944, winning second in 1943 and first in 1944.

Stub was very superstitious; he was called the "Cigarette Smok-ing Cowboy"; he always rode with an unlit cigarette in his mouth. When he would get a new pair of boots and wear them at a rodeo and didn't win in that show, he'd never wear them again to per-form. He thought it bad luck to put a hat on the bed; he wouldn't allow peanuts in any car he was riding in for fear it would bring him bad luck.

He was a very shy person; when he'd won at his first show he'd hid in the barn, his wife had to go find him. Camel cigarette, Levi Strauss, a gas company wanted to use him and his name to advertise their products, but he declined because of his shyness.

He was one of the tough ol' cowboys; he would doctor himself with his horse's medicine, giving himself shots of penicillin, etc.

To travel from show to show, he would take his trailer home. The last fifteen years he rode for the Christensen Brothers who furnished the stock for western rodeos. During this time he also rode in rodeos in which Christensen Brothers did not furnish the stock. He retired in 1951.

At one time Stub was chosen to represent the bronc riders in a United States sponsored rodeo team to compete in Sydney, Aus-tralia. He was caught in a blizzard in New Mexico while traveling from Denver to Los Angeles to catch the boat. He missed the boat and the chance to compete in this event.

Stub had his ups and downs like other rodeo riders; at one time while in Fort Worth, Texas, in 1937, he was down to 15¢, so he spent it on a hamburger; just then he met a friend who staked him to the entrance fee for the bronc riding event. The tide turned; he won the first event and from there on, good fortune continued to be with him.

He was hurt a number of times, breaking an arm in 1937, in Blythe, California, hurting a knee in Texas, and breaking a leg in Salem, Oregon in 1952. In 1940 he was in a hospital for an injured knee.

While the Bartlemays were living in a trailer house in White Salmon, Washington, they saw a ranch near Sisters, Oregon adver-tised in the newspaper; they liked it, bought it, and retired there.

The Bartlemays had five children: Bonnie Lee, Barbara, Jeannie, Juanita, Charles.

Written by Mike & Barbara Morehead

178

LLOYD BARTLEMAY

Lloyd Bartlemay owns a ranch on the bluffs overlooking
the Columbia River near Arlington, Oregon. Lloyd was a relative of Stub Bartlemay, world champion saddle bronc rider.
Lloyd arranged for us to meet with Tom and Phyllis Sumner,
also relatives of Stub's, at his ranch at Philippi Canyon to talk
about Stub Bartlemay's career in rodeo.

"Ignore the sign and come on up." Lloyd Bartlemay.

Stub was one of Charlie and Millie Bartlemay's kids. He was born in Boring, Oregon; then he moved out here to Rock Creek, just south of Arlington. They lived right there at the junction in the road. He went to a one room school at Round Creek. They had their own school, and it's still there.

He was a bronc rider all of his life. Tommy and Phyllis Sumner were saying the other day that during the winter months Smyth Sheep Company would pasture their horses across from Shutler, and Stub would ride over there and saddle those horses and ride 'em. He had to ride. If he got bucked off, he had to walk home. There used to be some warehouses there. It's on Highway 19 where they turn off to go to Waste Management now.

Stub rode ol' "Philippi" down here once. He was someone's saddle horse that went bad. Stub went down and showed 'em how to ride him. That was just out here by the top of the hill by the mail box. There was a lot of money bet on that. They just knew that horse couldn't be ridden. Stub just kinda had him plumb broke by the time he got through. That had to be in the early '40s. It might have been during the War. I think the Arlington rodeo started in 1946 or 1947.

TOM & PHYLLIS SUMNER

Tom & Phyllis Sumner have a ranch south of Arlington, Oregon. Phyllis is Stub Bartlemay's niece. Tom and Phyllis supplied us with information and pictures of Stub when he won the saddle bronc riding at Madison Square Garden.

Stub Bartlemay made a lot of tracks around this country. Stub won the World's Championship in 1936. We've got a picture taken at Madison Square Garden in 1936 when he won it. It says, "Colonel W. T. Johnson's World Championship Contestants."

We used to have his arm band. They wore arm bands instead of flags. That was kickin' around here for quite awhile. I don't know what ever became of it.

Stub rodeoed everywhere. I don't think he ever rode at Arlington but he won every show in the U. S. and Canada except Pendleton. He had it won one time. He was sittin' there with his legs crossed, and when he went to start his horse, his spur hung up in the mane, an' he was goose-egged. All he had to do was ride that horse. He was showin' off. I don't know if he was doin' that. He was just feelin' comfortable, I think.

The last time he rode up there he got second. That was in 1947. That was when we lived down in Heppner. They stopped in on their way home from Pendleton. That's as close as he ever came to winnin' at Pendleton.

Bob Swaim was a judge at the Pendleton Round-Up for a long time. I remember one time when Deb Copenhaver and another judge at Pendleton rode exhibition rides like it used to be done. All of the Northwest contests used to saddle in the arena. Anyway, Deb and the other judge had to ride the old way.

Deb Copenhaver would be younger than Stub. They probably rodeoed together, but Deb was probably startin' out when Stub was finishin' up. Stub had about twenty years on him.

Pat Fisk and Stub were All-Around Pickup Men at Madison Square Garden one year. They both got belt buckles that I'd sure like to have. It said, "World Champion Pickup Man."

Pat Fisk was a saddle bronc rider and bulldogger. He was a tough one. He was as fine a guy as you'd ever want to meet, but don't cross him. He was tough. He was a big ol' what you'd call lantern-jawed man. He'd grit his teeth and talk, and you could just barely see it. He'd come to Arlington to the rodeos. His mother lives here.

He was going to the dance at Antelope one time, and there was a rowdy guy, I forget his name, they'd just kicked out of the dance. He had a beer in each hand, and he was s.o.b. n' some of these people. Pat told him to quit talkin' like that in front of people. The guy says, "I wasn't callin' you that. I was callin' these other people."

Bang, an' down he sat, and the lights went out.

"I told you to stop talkin' like that. They're friends of mine." Pat told him.

Pat Fisk was in Madras the last time I heard. He worked at the sales yard, but that was ten years ago or longer.

Stub Bartlemay on Red Pepper. Molalla, '44.   DeVere

Stub went to work for the Christensen Brothers from Eugene and traveled all over with them. He was kind of a ramrod. He was a pickup man too. He organized and loaded stock in trucks. He was always the first rider out at all of their shows. Then he'd go back and start pickin' up.

I know he had good friends at White Salmon, Washington. He'd come home an' leave his horses out at Eight Mile. His horses sort of took care of themselves. He'd leave his horses over here an' stay at White Salmon.

When he retired from rodeo, he moved to Sisters, Oregon. He had a dairy herd there. He had a stroke at the barn and nearly froze to death. Anita, his wife found him. Stub died at Sisters.

I knew that rascal Lary Daniels. We were at Hal's tavern in Sisters in 1948. Anyway, Lary Daniels was in there, buyin' drinks for the house. I told someone that he didn't have to do that. It was just beer, and beer was twenty cents back then. Then Lary got up on a card table an' started dancin' with some woman. Maybe it was his wife. Whoever it was talkin' to me said, "He's won more all-around's than any other cowboy walkin', an' he can afford it." That was in 1948 at Sisters.

BOB SWAIM

Bob Swaim - Bob Nordtome Hazing, Pendleton, 1954.

I've lived in White Swan, Washington, for the past ten years. When I was rodeoin' I lived in Arlington, Oregon, and Lewiston, Idaho. I joined the RCA in 1949, and I was really active in rodeo up until 1965. I secretaried or flagged or both from 1963 until 1995 at Pendleton. I started rodeoin' when I was about seventeen, which was in '47.

I ranch now. I raise cows. I have some brood mares and a stud of my own, and I raise quarter horses. My stud horse's name is "Broreba." He's an offspring of Lucky's Last, which goes back...it's kind of a long story. Back in the forties, Lucky Blanton was the blood-line. When you were a calf-roper, if you didn't have a Lucky Blanton horse, they figured you were afoot. That's what all the calf-ropers said back then. I'm sure there's a lot of people today that wouldn't believe that, but I go back to guys like J. B. McMeans and Smoke Kaiser and Buckshot Sorrells, guys that roped. Buckshot Sorrells was from Arizona.

Lucky Blanton was raised in California. I was in Wyoming this Fall at a horse sale and bought a couple of fillies that have his breedin' on the other side. These people back there have five. They're kind of promoting the breed again. Their disposition is exceptional. That's a big part of it, and of course, they have a lot of cow in 'em, and they're just kind of naturally ranch or rodeo horses. The blood line went from Lucky's Last by Lucky Blanton. He was from a horse they just called plain Mark.

Is Muggs Bentley still alive? I had a buckskin horse named Buck that Muggs always rode. Muggs was old even then, but he always rode my bulldoggin' horse. Muggs was a character. We were good friends.

I knew Stub Bartlemay. I lived in the same little town that he did, Arlington, Oregon. His sister was Tommy Sumner's mother-in-law. I knew of him when I was a kid starting out in rodeo in that country. His nephew, Bill Wickland, and I rodeoed together some until he got killed in a car wreck; I think it was 1953 or 1954.

I always admired Stub. He was a true cowboy. He wound up living at Sisters, Oregon. I went over there a time or two. Bill and I stayed out at his place. That was when Stub was a pickup man for Christensen Brothers. He was a good hand and a nice person. He was really quiet, and I never heard of him bad-mouthing anybody, kind of his own person. I think riding broncs or colts and taking care of horses was his forte, and I think he could back anything he wanted to say about that. That's what I know about him.

I'm 70 years old. I joined the RCA in 1949 when I was 19 years old. I knew Buster Ivory pretty well. I met Perry Ivory one time. I think he judged at the Cow Palace when I was down there. I do remember that he ended up in California someplace. And I met Hippy Burmiester. I met Guy Cash through Muggs Bentley at Grangeville, Idaho one year. Also, Burel Mulkey. But they were ten to fifteen years my senior.

I knew Bill Sylvester. He's probably my age. I met him when I was a kid around Arlington. He came down there riding bareback horses, and Dick Thurman, who was a cousin of Sonny, came down to the Arlington and Condon rodeos. Bill Sylvester got his back hurt and quit riding barebacks. He was a character, and he could tell you a lot of stories.

Some of his stories are pretty much the truth from what little I know of him. If you could get them down on paper, I think they'd really sell. I'm sure maybe the cowboys today wouldn't appreciate him, but people from my era and the old timers would. They'd buy a lot of copies. I know I would. It was totally different back then.

I saw Bill the last year I went to slack at Pendleton. I was Secretary, and I flagged at Pendleton for 25 years. I ran into Bill, and we got to exchanging old times. I think he dresses it up a little, but there's still a lot of truth in what he says. I'll tell you a little story about him. When I was Secretary at the Pendleton Round-Up, this is back in the middle '60s, a year or two before the old Ranch Club burned down, and the Round-Up office was right across the street under the grandstands. At that time we had maybe $15,000 to $20,000 cash on us, and Bill came in there. I hadn't seen him for a long time. I knew him pretty well, and he and I was pretty good friends when he was still riding bareback horses.

Bob Swaim on What's My Line. Pendleton, 1962.

I closed up my office that night and went across the street to the Ranch Club to get something to eat. Bill had been in there, and he'd had a nip or two. He came over and sat down.

"You closed up over there?" he asked me.

I said, "yeah."

"How much cash you got?" he asked.

I know what's going through his mind. "Bill," I said, "don't even think about it."

He just looked at me and laughed. But that's the way he was.

He told me one time, I forget which wife it was, number two or three I think, but she demanded that he go to a psychiatrist. He made a deal with the psychiatrist to split the proceeds right down the middle. He was serious when he told me about it. I think the gal he was married to was from down around Roseburg. He said that he went to this guy, and they'd talk and have a good old time, and then they'd split the $50 or $100 a week right down the middle.

Did he ever tell you about Don Bogue? Ask him to tell you about "Booger Bogue" the next time you see him. That's another story.

DARLE RUNNELS

Darle Runnels is the oldest daughter of Rodeo Hall of Fame photographer De Vere Helfrich. Darle and her husband Buff Runnels live "Across the street and up the hill" from where her folks lived in Klamath Falls, Oregon. Buff is a World War II veteran who served as a waist gunner on a B-24 in Bungay, England, just outside of London.

De Vere Helfrich
as told by Darle Runnels

My dad took all the action shots. Mother took all the posed pictures, which were really good shots. When they'd get home from the rodeo at night, they lived in auto camps in those days, they would fix up the bathroom so it was dark and develop the negatives and print the pictures.

In the fifties they bought a trailer and made part of it into a darkroom. They'd come home in the evening after the rodeo, and he would develop the negatives; then he'd go to bed, and she'd sit up all night and print the pictures, and then she'd go to bed. Then he'd get up and put them on the dryer. I don't even know if they do that anymore; then they'd have them back out the next morning before the rodeo started and sell them to the cowboys.

A lot of pictures were sold to stock contractors. They wanted the buck-offs because that showed how tough the stock was; the cowboys wanted the ones that showed how good they rode. They were always happy when a cowboy got a new girlfriend or a new wife because the ex would take off with all the pictures, and then they'd order a whole new set: "Give me everything you ever got of me."

They led a very interesting life. In between, they followed their hobby of following the Oregon Trail. They followed it all the way from St. Louis to the end; of course, they drove as much as they could in a car. They had motor scooters, and they rode those occasionally. They followed the trail around Mt. Hood and the one through central Oregon and then the one through southern Oregon, the Applegate trail.

They edited the diary of a woman named May. That was about half done, and it was finished by a woman named Ackerman, and she published it. They published "The Klamath Echoes," which tells all about the Klamath area, which was not just Klamath County, but mostly around here. They'd go to the little towns around here and interview people who were probably sons and daughters of early settlers.

DELORES SCOTT

Delores Scott lives with her husband John in Jordan Valley, Oregon. They are ranchers and raise cattle and draft horses. John is a Turtle member. Before moving to Jordan Valley two years ago, they lived for many years in Junction City, north of Eugene, Oregon. Delores is the youngest daughter of Rodeo Hall of Fame photographer De Vere Helfrich.

⟫⬦⟪

De Vere Helfrich
as told by Delores Scott

I helped my folks a little bit on the pictures. I got married in 1946, and that was shortly after the war when they really took off and got going. Our oldest girl traveled with them quite a bit and helped sell pictures. They made a living. Because it was the cowboys, they didn't charge them big amounts. The whole time they were going rodeoing after the war they were also doing Oregon Trail history. Daddy did little books they called "Klamath Echoes" that were about Klamath County. What I always liked about those things was he called them "As told to me," and he wrote them in the people's own words instead of dressing it up. To me that's so much more interesting.

Daddy only had one eye. He lost his left eye when he was four years old. I don't think anybody that ever rodeoed with him knew that. He was very private about it. He had better vision than any of the rest of the family with that one eye. The cowboys talked to him too about what the animals would do, so he was better prepared that way. He also had been a rider. He'd never rodeoed, but he had grown up on a ranch. He had his own horse and what-have-you, and they had moved cattle, so he knew how animals thought a little bit better than a lot of people.

Gene Pruett on Colonel Dean.

Another thing, if he didn't like a picture, he wouldn't print it. Nobody ever saw any of the bad ones he took. But the picture that made him famous, really, was Gene Pruett on "Colonel Dean" at Prairie City, Oregon. The horse is more or less standing on one toe. He's straight up and down. The man who supplied the rodeo stock, I can't think of his name right now, he would pick a picture for his advertising for the year, which more or less made it picture of the year. He picked that picture.

My husband, John Scott, was a Turtle. We have his Turtle button and his Turtle card. He was probably only fifteen when he joined the Turtles.

I was traveling with my folks. We were at the Sisters rodeo, and Mother introduced me to this young cowboy from Eugene. Then I wrote to him, and we went onto Montana to five different rodeos, and he was going to go to the Walla Walla rodeo, and I told him, nobody had been at Ellensburg the year before, so he came to Ellensburg, and we got engaged, got married; I only saw him about seven times before we got engaged. We've now been married almost 54 years. In November it will be 54 years.

Herman Vowell was a great friend of my family. He has continued to rope. There was he and his brother. You never saw one but what you didn't see the other.

191

GRANGEVILLE

We traveled to Grangeville, Idaho to interview several people involved with the local Border Days Rodeo. We met one snowy morning in October, 1996, at Sue Kutner's Gallery. There were three men from Grangeville, Kraig Schlottman, Muggs Bentley and Guy Cash Jr.; Gertrude Maxwell was from Elk City. She had driven fifty miles in the snow to be there; and R. E. "Dick" Roberts from Lewiston. He owned Tack-N-More Trailer Sales.

During this trip we interviewed Guy Cash and Muggs Bentley together, and later, Gertrude Maxwell. Guy Cash invited us to his home where we continued the interview. Guy brought out albums of pictures and newspaper clippings to substantiate stories about his father, Guy Cash Sr., and many of the well-known cowboys his father rodeoed with during his career.

The following July we returned to Grangeville to interview Muggs Bentley for the second time. It was on the trip to the Joseph Plains with Muggs that we met Curley Francis.

MUGGS BENTLEY & GUY CASH

Grangeville, Idaho

Guy Cash: I don't think there's a real good rodeo history book out there. There's books like Herman Linder's, but I think you need to reach deeper into rodeo—how it happened, what an impact it had on our entire society. Let me tell you, my original thought was to do an encyclopedia on rodeo. Who knows anything about Jack Wade, for example, or Jackie Cooper? They all had an impact on this rodeo business.

Leo Moomaw, Tim Bernard, Lary Daniels...where's anything written about them? Lary traveled with Jim Bayes for years. Jim ended up as a captain in the highway patrol in Boise, Idaho.

Muggs Bentley: I went to his retirement party.

Guy Cash: And Herman Linder, a few of those guys. Herman liked the glory. I'd like to see Dad's name in print. I don't get to see it as much as I'd like to.

And Stub Bartlemay. He has a niece in Arlington, Oregon. Do you remember Jerry Ambler, Muggs? Jerry was okay. He was a little nervous from the service. He and Dad traveled a lot together.

Muggs Bentley: Did he love the money!

Guy Cash: He sure did. He'd stand outside of that bucking chute like a prize fighter, and when they got his horse saddled, he was up and out of the chute that quick (snapping his fingers).

Another guy, Fritz Truan, from Fresno, California. He was killed on Iwo Jima in WWII. When he went over the top of the hill, he said, "Let 'Er Buck" and died. That was the end of Fritz.

194

Muggs Bentley: Gene Pruett was quite a jokester. Mac Barbour had a tough buckin' horse that bucked with his head right up in your lap. Pruett had been on him, but Fritz never had. Fritz asked Pruett what kind of a head to take on him, and Pruett told him, "Give him a long head." He did, an' he bucked Truan off. He came back, and Pruett was grinning. "You big, dumb s.o.b., get down off of that horse," Truan said. That old horse really bucked Truan off.

Leo Cox. He irrigated his talents instead of cultivating them. Glen Cox was from Boise. There were nineteen kids in the family. His mother was a Scott from Wind River.

Guy Cash: Norman Stewart was the outlaw of outlaws. He was a kind of would-be cowboy, but he was a character, too, wasn't he Muggs?

Muggs Bentley: He was a thief and a gangster. He sold gallons and gallons of moonshine, but he never sampled it. He never took a drink. Or smoked a cigarette.

Guy Cash: Harry Hart was a world champion. Fox Calahan... Irby Munday. You want a colorful cowboy, there was one. He won the world calf-roping championship in 1934.

Muggs Bentley: Hippy Burmeister was a character.

Guy Cash: And Bob Askin. Jack Percifield was a roper. He was a local cowboy who just never went out. Hibbs? He was a cowpuncher, but he rodeoed some.

Muggs Bentley: I still contend, for an all-around, you should work one timed event and one rough stock.

Guy Cash: I agree.

(It was suggested at this point in the interview that Muggs Bentley should be nominated as the whistle blower on the seamy side of rodeo, the crooked judging, the cowboy politics.)

Muggs Bentley: I don't know, I don't think I have the character to be a celebrity.

Guy Cash: I went over to Pendleton and talked to the Round-Up Association about my dad, and they were about as interested in Guy Cash as the Man in the Moon. They did bring out the original record books from 1925.

In contrast, take Calgary. Did you go up the year they honored Dad, Muggs? It was like, after forty or fifty years after he had won the bronc riding, they treated my wife and I like royalty.

My thoughts, in those days, was that Pendleton, Calgary and Cheyenne were the epitome of rodeo. In the '20s. The real epitome of rodeo.

There's bigger rodeos—Las Vegas, Houston, but as far as pure rodeo, it was those three.

Muggs Bentley: I remember when your Dad used to bulldog, rope calves, ride bulls. I don't know as I ever saw him ride a bareback horse. Lary Daniels rode saddle broncs, he bulldogged, he roped calves, he rode bulls and he rode bareback horses.

Guy Cash: Burel Mulkey won the all-around just riding saddle broncs in 1938. After Mulkey, they changed that. Then they had to compete in at least two events.

They have tried to standardize judging and teach judging. In fact, Harry Knight was the first one to create a judging school. Harry was a bronc rider and a stock contractor. And he was a judge. I'm sure he had all the skills. A lot of times a judge was just someone out of the local community.

Muggs Bentley: They used to have farmers judge around here. And everything else.

Guy Cash: Harry Knight was a Canadian, no relation to Pete Knight. Harry should be a character in a book like this. Pete was from Crossfield, Canada.

Remember Tommy Zam? Cody Dodson? Fred and Merle Hunt were Oregon fellas, out of rodeo before your time, Muggs.

And how about Cecil Henley?

Muggs Bentley: Cecil was from Hay, Washington.

Guy Cash: Bill and Sam Edmo were Indian fellas. How about Alvie Green. He was from Fort Hall near Pocatello. And Pete Grubbs? Arnie Will? Floyd Peters was a roper from Browning, Montana.

Muggs Bentley: He had a lot of Blackfoot blood in him.

Guy Cash: And Oral Zumwalt, Dave Campbell, Slats Jacobs. Do you remember Slats, Muggs?

Muggs Bentley: Weiser, Idaho. Frank VanMeter...if that man had good eyesight, he'd a been one of the best bulldoggers around. He wore glasses. I saw him knock a steer down in Lewiston one time, and he knocked his glasses off. He crawled around the arena on his hands and knees looking for 'em.

Guy Cash: Buck Tiffin was from Weiser. Tommy Woods was an Oregon fella.

Muggs Bentley: Tom Bride was from Oregon, and he was hard to put on the ground, too.

Guy Cash: And Stub Bartlemay was from Arlington, Oregon.

Muggs Bentley: We got Jerry Ambler throwed in jail in Union, Oregon one time. He was a great one to chase the women. Kid Roberts and Mac Barbour were there too.

Guy Cash: Irby Munday, a world champion calf roper. Homer Pettigrew was a four or five time bulldogging World Champion. Bill McMackin was a terrific all-round cowboy. I remember Gene Rambo, and Ward Walker; Leonard Ward. Pete and Jack Kirshner from Ogden, Utah. Leo Cremer, the Montana stock contractor. McCarty and Elliot, Bernard and Moomaw, Colburn and Sorrenson. They were the top contractors from this area. Harry Rowell on the west coast, and Mac Barbour up in this area. And the Christensen Brothers. Tim Bernard and Leo Moomaw were from Tonasket, Washington; their top bucking horse was "Badger Mountain," a big gelding that was a challenge for the best of 'em. Badger's trademark was to rare up on his hind feet, and when it appeared he would fall over backwards, he'd throw his head and make a dive for the ground. Many a great bronc rider found himself at the end of his buck rein on the way down. Dad drew him five times and rode him four of the five; the one time he bucked Dad off, he nearly killed him as he whipped him to the ground at the end of his buck rein; Badger was powerful, and he was quick.

Muggs Bentley: Mac Barbour would get a good string of stock together, but he couldn't keep his finances straight, an' he would sell out.

Guy Cash: George Hanna was kinda like Mac Barbour. He couldn't hold an outfit together. Dad had some good bucking stock, but he just couldn't keep them together either.
Pete Welch was another old timer.

Muggs Bentley: Del Blancett, he was the first stock contractor for the first rodeo they had here in Grangeville. 'Course they had a lot of local stock here too. Slim Riley had some wonderful stock if he'd taken care of 'em.

Guy Cash: He was from Homedale or Vale, Oregon. He had Long Tom. He had some good horses. Slim put on the rodeo here when I was a kid. He trailed those horses from South Idaho to Grangeville, and when those horses got here, they were so sore footed they wouldn't buck.
Red Pruett, the father of Gene and Jack, used to ride horseback from the Joseph Plains to the Pendleton Round-Up. Pete Wilson did also.
There are so many people who had an impact on rodeo who will never get any press at all. I'll tell you a picture that I'd like to have, that I've just got in my mind, is that day at Elk City when my dad rode that horse of Tim Taylor's, that Cougar Mountain, and he blew his cork. That was something else.

Muggs Bentley: I was on him once. I got a re-ride. It was the first time I was ever in Elk City in 1940. Your dad won the bronc ridin'.
Well, I'm gonna have to bow out of here. This could go on for years.
I live right next door to the undertaker here in Grangeville. I'm cuttin' down on expenses.

From Pendleton to Calgary

Before Muggs leaves, I ask him about his hat: That's a pretty nice hat you've got there, Muggs. They don't make them like that any more, do they? (It had big stitching around the outside of the brim).

Muggs Bentley: That's a 4 X Beaver Stetson. It was given to me by Mark Taylor. Do you know whose it was? Muggs asks Guy.

Guy Cash: Nope.

Muggs Bentley: It belonged to Dick Combs. It's a seven.

Guy Cash: You and Jack are pinheads. One of the last things my dad said before he died...I can remember, my son, after we brought Dad to the house three days before he died, and Joel stuck a hat on him. Dad said, "7 3/8ths." That's the last thing he ever said.

Muggs Bentley: Mark couldn't wear this, so he gave it to me. I've been doing pretty well. Joe Wilson gave me a hat the other day. It'll cover up that heavy head of hair I've got.
The Spain brothers, John and Fred, were here at the first Border Days in Grangeville in 1912. Later on, John got his hand cut off.

Guy Cash: Mitch Owens was another bronc rider with a hand missing. He was a California fellow. He lost his hand in a dynamite accident. He won the all-around in St. Paul, Oregon. He won the bulldoggin'.

Muggs Bentley: St. Paul and Molalla. St. Paul in the afternoon and Molalla at dark. Molalla laid off for quite awhile, but they're startin' to come back.
Don't forget Harry Rawlins...and Gordon Crabtree (Muggs said as he walked out the door of The Gallery).

Guy Cash: I think I'll call my wife and ask her to water the soup down and have you two come over for lunch.

GUY CASH

Guy Cash Jr. is retired and lives with his wife Maryellen in Grangeville, Idaho. His father, Guy Cash Sr., was a world champion saddle bronc rider in the 1920s. At that time, the family lived at White Bird, Idaho, and owned a restaurant, which Guy Cash Sr. built himself; later he became Sheriff of White Bird. Guy Cash Sr. won many smaller rodeos, but probably his best known victory came at the Calgary Stampede in 1939. He also won the all-around at Pendleton in 1925. He was twenty-three years old.

Guy Cash Jr. remembers vividly being the son of a "world class" bronc rider. He has a knowledge of rodeo and the people who make up the sport that very few possess. He grew up with men like Homer Holcomb and Herman Linder as close personal family friends and enjoys talking about the time spent with his dad around rodeo.

Unfortunately, I'm an old timer now. I really am. How many knew these people we're talking about? Not many. And even though I was a boy, I still knew 'em, and my interests were there, so I really know quite a bit about them. I didn't rodeo much myself, but I announced rodeos for awhile.

As I said earlier, I've considered writing what I would call an encyclopedia of rodeo. My thought was to specifically zero in on Calgary, Cheyenne, and Pendleton, a few of those really big rodeos where all of the real top quality cowboys competed. I'd try to include people like Stub Bartlemay for example. You'll never see or hear of Stub. You'll probably never hear much about my dad, Guy Cash. There's guys like Jack Wade, Jackie Sherman, Jack Cooper—I could name a zillion of 'em that you won't ever see much in print

Guy Cash riding Blucher
Pendleton Round-Up
Dennis Photo

about, but that were a part of rodeo. They are a part of what made rodeo.

At Calgary, the year that Dad won the bronc riding up there, they did a feature article on about half a dozen cowboys. Besides Dad, there was Nick Knight, Burel Mulkey, Herman Linder, and Sykes Robinson, who won the Canadian bronc riding that year. Homer Holcomb is featured in the same article. Homer Holcomb, what a friend he was. We still visit his wife. She lives in Lewiston. She didn't marry Homer until after he was through rodeoing. My dad and Homer started rodeoing together. They were both from Idaho.

I've got more pictures than you'd know what to do with. I've got one with the caption: "Guy Cash on What Do You Think of That?" It was taken at the Round-Up on Joseph Plains, July 14th to 18th. That was the old Fly-Blow Rodeo. It was taken in 1919. In 1921 Dad hadn't started contesting other than just locally.

Here's another picture of Dad winning second place at the Burns, Oregon rodeo. Everett Riggs won it; Dad was second. Jesse Stahl, the Negro cowboy won third place. The photo says, "Winners of the Harney County Rodeo 1924." Everett Riggs was probably just a local fella. He could ride bucking horses, and there was a lot of those guys around.

We had a cafe in White Bird, Idaho, for years. Here's a picture of the cafe when we opened it in 1933. Dad built it himself. He was

201

one of those guys who did everything himself. We had a photo of Don Nesbeth, Homer Holcomb, Perry Ivory, Eddy McCarty, and Everett Bowman at the cafe.

My son has a panorama taken in front of city hall in New York. The cowboys had ridden from Madison Square Garden and paraded up and down the street when they took the picture.

Let me tell you a little story about Eddy Woods. Eddy was a great bronc rider. Back in about 1944 he married a woman in Boston who was in the clothing manufacturing business. Her family was at least. Eddy quit the rodeo business and became an executive in this clothing business. Eventually they got a divorce. We saw him about twenty years ago at the National Finals in Oklahoma City.

Some other guys that come to mind...Pete Wilson, an Idaho County stockman and an old cowboy. He competed in Pendleton. He still rode bucking horses when he was 60 years old. Pete was from over in the Snake River country. Chuck Wilson was another one. He was a professional cowboy.

I remember in 1938 we were at a rodeo in Keller, Washington where Dad was a contestant. We were waiting outside the rodeo office while the cowboys were inside waiting to be paid for their winnings. I was about eight years old at the time, and my brother

Guy Cash on What Do You Think Of That. The Round Up, Joseph Plains. Old Fly-Blow Arena.

Jack was three and a half years older. Two of our friends, Bobby Escew and Dick Slappert, were having a ferocious fist fight. Bobby was one of the judges, and I suppose Dick thought he deserved a better score than he'd received.

I remember that Bobby had always been specially kind to me, and it seemed to me that he was getting the worst of it. Fortunately, about that time, a young Indian came running for his life through the crowd that had gathered to watch the Slappert/Escew fight, and right on his heels was contestant Tommy Woods. Tommy was a little man, probably about 5'6", 150 pounds. The Indian had tried to steal Ruth's (Tommy's wife) purse, and Tommy was in hot pursuit. The Indian was doing real well until he stubbed his toe on the curb, and Tommy was right on top of him. Needless to say, the Slappert/Escew scrap ended and the Indian learned his lesson. And Ruth got her purse back. This was only one of many exciting moments in our lives as the sons of a rodeo cowboy.

There's nothing more exciting and stimulating than a good fist fight or brawl, whether it was a dispute between judges and contestants, cowboys over a woman, or the local tough trying to prove himself by taking on the he-man cowboy.

A couple of fights that I remember, or heard Dad tell about, are worth telling about. The first one, as I heard about it from Dad, was at Nez Perce, Idaho. Earl Thode, the first officially recognized all-around champion of the world had a good scrap with one of the locals, and in the course of the fight, Earl took a pretty good bite out of the local's ear. The law broke up the fight, and Earl had to face the local judge. The judge told Earl that he could pay a fine or spend time in the local jail. Earl replied, "Judge, this is your town; just run it to suit yourself." Not a bad observation from a simple South Dakota cowboy.

The second confrontation I witnessed as a ten year old boy was in New Meadows, Idaho. After the rodeo, Dad and Frank VanMeter, a pretty good world-class cowboy from Weiser, Idaho, and myself were in one of the local bars when a young local fellow stepped up and asked if he was Frank VanMeter, to which Frank answered that he was.

"Then I'm gonna whip you," the young man said.

It seems that Frank had broken up a fight between the local tough guy and another local at the dance the night before, and he had come to pay Frank his dues for sticking his nose in someone else's business.

I remember Frank saying to the young man as he gave a little chuckle, "I guess you'd better get with it."

Frank wore glasses, and as he took them off and turned to lay them on the bar, the young man, whose name incidentally was Yokum, hung one on Frank, and Frank never recovered from that first blow. I guess the lesson from this event was that if you're going to have to defend yourself in a fight, you'd better try to get in a Sunday punch first and take whatever action is necessary after.

The cowboys, who never passed up an opportunity to razz a fellow cowboy, took full advantage of making Frank's whipping at the hands of "Little Abner" Yokum the butt of many jokes.

MUGGS BENTLEY

Muggs Bentley, a 90-year-old retired rodeo cowboy still works with cattle occasionally, helping out friends and neighbors in the Grangeville, Idaho, area. He was a rancher on the Joseph Plains where he was raised as a boy and later worked for years in the woods after retiring from rodeo. "I did everything to make a livin'," Muggs says. "From the time I started 'till I quit, I was in rodeo for 34 years."

The following interview took place July 16, 1997.

The Grangeville Border Days started in 1912. I rode in the first parade. I rode horseback in front of my uncle. I was one year old.

The old arena was up on the south side of town; around 1919 or 1920, it was moved down to where it is now.

I was raised over between the forks of the Salmon River and the Snake. In 1929 I went to the rodeo at Genessee. I just had enough to pay my entrance fee. I had to go without supper to pay it. You had to ride a finals horse back then. There were five of us the final day. The other four bucked off, an' I rode mine. That made me the winner.

205

They had some Hanna Brothers stock there, and there was some good bronc riders there, and I'll be darned if I didn't win the bronc ridin'. Genessee is up on the hills from Lewiston.

I was seventeen years old and that was the farthest I'd ever been away from home. I remember in the seventh grade they were talking about The Great Lakes, and I asked if they were as big as Tolo Lake outside of Grangeville, and everybody laughed. I live within about fifteen miles from where I was born. I was born out here on Gill Point, west of Tolo Lake.

I had a chance to go to Cheyenne right after I won at Genessee. There was a guy there who wanted to take me to Cheyenne. He'd have paid all expenses an' my entrance fees for a quarter of what I won, but I was a green kid, an' I'd never been away from home, an' I didn't go.

I wouldn't say that I'd have been the best, but I might have been one of the best. The Depression came on, an' I went to St. Joe an' went to patchin' up there. I did that for eight years an' rodeoed in my spare time. I only really put in one full season rodeoin'. That was in 1946. That was the only year I didn't do anything else. That was the year I got my neck broke in Susanville, California. I was travelin' with Mac Barbour.

In 1959 I was working in the woods an' rodeoin' on the weekends, an' I made more money that year. I picked up over $6,000.00. I begin to slow down then, but I made some wild runs, I'll tell ya. I was just lucky in 1959. I hung 'em up in '64 in Hamilton, Montana. I decided I couldn't beat that youth.

I rode ten years before I worked timed events. I was getting too old for saddle broncs, an' I needed a second event. I started bulldoggin' in 1938. I won the all-around here in Grangeville in 1959. I won the bulldoggin'. That's the picture there on the wall. There's Red Allen, Francis Turette, Clint Roberts, and me.

My second wife accused me of living in the past, an' I guess I did. I won the all-around here in Grangeville, an' I thought that was something to remember.

Over there where I was raised, there was a lot of wild horses. We kids didn't have any spendin' money. There was a lot of wild horses up there, an' we trapped 'em, an' cut their manes an' tales off an' sold 'em to Sears & Roebuck. I think we got around forty-five cents a pound for the horsehair. That was in the mid-twenties. It's a wonder we didn't get killed. Let a horse buck a kid off today an' they run right to the hospital. We didn't have any money, an' there wasn't any doctor nor any way to get to a doctor. We didn't have any money, but we had plenty of bruises.

We penned 'em up, an' then we rode 'em. Then we cut off their manes and tails. Tails first. You got that first. Course, nobody really claimed 'em; nobody owned the wild horses. Do that now, an' you'd go to jail.

After we cut off their manes an' tails, we turned 'em loose. Next Sunday we'd be up there doin' it all over again. We'd find us another bunch with long manes an' tails an' do it all over again.

Wild horses weren't worth much. I remember this ol' boy Harry Rowell. He had a string of buckin' horse in California. He also had a big ranch, an' he had a slaughter house. He had Callow dog food. You get a good horse crippled, that's all you got is dog food. You get a lot of hard cash tied up in them horses. Golly sakes, buckin' horses used to be just canner prices. Them that bucked, they kept. The ones that didn't, they sold 'em for canners.

The first contractors I remember was Mark an' George Hanna, the Hanna Brothers. Then Leo Moomaw an' Tim Bernard. They were from around Tonasket, Washington. They sold out to the Ring Brothers from west of Spokane, Washington, I think. Then Joe Kelsey from Tonasket. He's dead. Moomaw's dead. Bernard is dead; all the Hannas are dead. Earl Hutcheson is dead. Harley Tucker...dead.

Mac Barbour was from Klamath Falls, Oregon. Hutcheson was from south of Boise, Idaho. He had a lot of those south Idaho shows.

I remember Lary Daniels. That Lary won a lot of money rodeoin'. In 1937, I think, he walked out of Grangeville with everything. In 1938 he got ahold of a jug of spirits, an' he didn't do so well that year.

I believe the last time I saw Lary we both judged at Halfway, Oregon. He was a rodeo announcer along with being a cowboy. He was just an all around hand. If he had really taken care of himself, Lary was kind of a wild character, but if he had taken care of himself and attended to business, I wouldn't say he would have been the champ, exactly, but he'd have made a run at it. He was an all-around cowboy.

Lary Daniels was a funny guy. If he gave you a check for $10,000.00, you could cash it, and it would be good. Otherwise, he'd say, "To hell with you, I ain't got the money, I ain't gonna pay you." That's just the way he was. Regardless, no matter how big the check was, I'd take it. If he gave you that check, it would be good.

I can tell you another thing. I seen him work an old boy over at Moses Lake one time. That's when he owned the bar in Lewiston. This guy gave him a bad check an' Lary run into him at Moses Lake. Lary said to this guy, "Your hide ain't worth very much, an' that check wasn't very big, but I'm gonna get that out of your hide." He did, too. I think it was only ten or fifteen dollars, but that was in 1945.

I remember Yakima Canutt. He was ahead of me, but I seen him a time or two. Over around Nez Perce. Bob Crosby an' Everett Bowman, an' all those guys used to come there. That was quite a rodeo at one time. Bowman was killed in a car wreck, an' Crosby got killed in a jeep wreck.

Ben Jory had stock at Baker, Oregon in 1945. They had a rodeo there before the 4th of July, an' there was quite a bunch of cowboys there. That's when I run into Ben. By golly, I got lucky over there, an' I picked up $800.00. That was a lot of money. That was the only time I met Ben. It was a strange horse to me, an' Ben told me what kind of a head to take on him. We got along fine. He an' Lary Daniels didn't get along. They didn't get along worth a hoot.

I think Lary an' Ben crossed swords several times. I don't think Ben was too happy about Lary marrying his daughter.

I was a Turtle. I don't know what happened to my Turtle button. I got my Gold Card before Lary got his.

The day following the interview with Muggs, he invited us to take a trip with him to the place where he was raised. His lady friend, Lavonne, fixed a lunch to take with us. "If you want anything else, we'll stop somewhere at a store and get it," Muggs offered.

"There isn't a man alive who knows this country better than I do," Muggs explains. "A lot of 'em knew it a lot better, but they ain't around any more. There's a bunch of Johnny-come-latelys who drive through it once an' can tell you all about it. They can probably tell you more than I can."

While we're waiting, the phone rings, and Muggs answers it. When he finishes, he explains that a man wants him to help with a round-up over the weekend, and Muggs agreed. "People who know how to handle cattle are pretty scarce these days. I'm not fast, but I'm at the right place at the right time."

"I agreed to help a guy with his round-up one time. I thought he knew what he was doin'. They were big, black cows. Up in the brush. He just let out a whoop an' charged at the center of the herd, an' they went in every direction. He should have known better, but he didn't."

"Grangeville is a pretty tough place nowadays. After my first wife passed away, I had a guy break into the house one day. I was shavin', an' I didn't have any shirt on when he broke in. I looked around, an' there wasn't a flower vase or anything, just my hands. He was standin' right in front of the t.v. I grabbed him an' pushed him out onto the porch an' then he nailed me. I started one right from my hip pocket, an' he went through the door. He took all the glass out of that door, an' he hit on his back out there on the sidewalk, an' when he did, if I'd of had shoes on, I'd have kicked his ribs in. I grabbed him by the hair an chunked his head on the sidewalk two or three times. It sounded like a ripe watermelon. So I got his attention then. Now I sleep with a gun beside my bed."

When I hit him, he had on big glasses, an' I broke his glasses. I thought they might come back on me with that. I went up to see the chief of police, an' he said, "Why didn't you call me?"

"I'll call you, an' then I'll call the undertaker," I told him."

"Don't do that," he said.

"That's my Wikieup," I told him. "Anybody who comes in there an' starts takin' over...you go into somebody's house an' start a racket, you've pretty well paid for it as far as I'm concerned. I'm not a fightin' man, but when I do, I'm gonna fight to win. Besides that, I'm gettin' too old for that."

With the lunch secured in back and Muggs at the wheel we drove out of Grangeville, heading for the Joseph Plains where Muggs was raised. The day was sunny with a few storm clouds building in the distance. Muggs was talking like a tour guide, pointing out sites of interest as we went along and filling in with bits of information about his life in rodeo. "You don't fool around in the chute," Muggs advised. "It's a mistake. Get on an' get with it."

"You don't see boys riding horses anymore. At the Grangeville Border Days rodeo, you see only girls riding in the parade."

A few miles farther along, the conversation switched to his early married life. "My first wife and I took Les Kamm from around Pilot Rock, Oregon, under our wing. He started out as a bronc rider, an' later he was quite a bulldogger an' roper."

"Bob Chambers was an awful good friend of mine also. He was a fine rodeo announcer, one of the best."

"I used to be a speed demon, but now everybody passes me," Muggs explains as we drive through a small town. "This place used to have a baseball team in the old days. There was a store and a big stockyard here." Muggs points out the radar base on Cottonwood Butte. There's a state prison there now.

"There's a branch of the Bitterroots east of Grangeville," he says, pointing in that direction. "My grandparents came here in 1885 an' farmed 100 acres."

"Back when I was a kid, I had to do everything to make a living. I even herded sheep. I got paid $20.00 a month to herd sheep. I moved up near where Graves Creek runs into Rocky Canyon in 1936 an' had a partner on a ranch. I had $3.50 to get through the winter. For three years, me an' my partner never had a cross word. Then Spencer went to Grangeville and sent a letter an' canned me when I was hurt an' in the hospital. My horse fell with me and I hit my elbow. My tonsils were rotten, and it caused arthritis to set in. I was stuck up there with my wife and daughter. I'm gonna run you up to Pine Bar," Muggs informed us.

The road followed a narrow canyon downwards, and then it leveled out and opened up near the canyon bottom. "There used to be a ferry that crossed the Salmon River. We traveled this country by saddle horse when I was a kid." Muggs said. "There was a WPA road project between Pine Bar and White Bird, but they didn't finish it. It was nothin' but a horseback trail."

"I had a brand new Hamley saddle back then, an' we ran cattle. I tied my horse to some brush an' went lookin' for some cattle an' the horse got loose and swam the river, an' there went my $68.00 Hamley saddle floatin' down the river."

Wispy cotton clouds passed overhead as we arrived at the Geologist's camp. Muggs' aunt and uncle homesteaded the slopes overlooking the camp. Muggs was three years old and lived with them until he was eight, and they moved up onto the Dumaque Plains above. Big Eddy at Pine Bar was the spot where Muggs caught his first fish. There's a grave site there, "Speldon, 1906. Drowning victim."

"Saddlehorse Ridge was the only way in to this country, except ferry," Muggs explains. Sunflowers and blue wildflowers bloomed alongside the road as we headed upward towards the Joseph Plains. There was little cover, a scattering of scrub pine on the slopes and some sumac.

"There's Hogback Ridge," Muggs points out. "It's a long old ridge. The wind's usually blowin' up there. I've rode it a lot of times." The country is an almost continuous series of ridges, bald spots, and timber land. "I worked on this road with the CWA, The Civil Works Administration, one of Roosevelt's programs."

The road climbed up and switched back. From that height, the canyons below looked tiny. There wasn't much clearance between the pickup and the almost perpendicular slopes leading downward, but Muggs gestured unconcerned. Near the top, the vistas were breathtaking. "How do you like it so far?" Muggs asks with a straight face.

"From my side, about the only thing I can see is the bottom of the canyon," I said. Cathy was sitting in the middle and enjoying every minute of the climb.

"I just wanted to see how Cathy would take it," Muggs said with a big grin on his face.

Across from us was the Dumaque Plain. The Canfield Post Office was visible, named after a pioneer family. "Up here is horseback country. A horse an' a good dog. A dog is worth five men, an' they're a lot easier on the cattle."

"Here's where my folks came when they first came here from the old country. The old country for me was Oklahoma. The Lyda Springs homestead. It had five schools on the site, an' there was two more on Dumaque. My first wife was a quarter Cherokee."

"It's all owned by big ranchers now. In the old days, they used to drive cattle from here to Cottonwood an' ship 'em out by rail to Portland, Oregon. You had to weigh the cattle in the stockyards in Portland. After two days on the train, they shrank down. From here to Cottonwood was okay, but it was 26 hours on the railroad, and you had to feed and water cattle. It was Federal law. There was seven different packing houses in Portland. Big stockyards. Heckman, Spencer, Hitchcock, Sawyer an' Robbins own most of this country."

Muggs points out the old site of the Boles Post Office, and a little farther along, the site of the Yellow Pine School.

"There's the old Fly-Blow rodeo arena. The last rodeo was held in 1926. It had a half mile track, lots of moonshine, and no law. It didn't take long to take the fight out of any troublemakers, though. I remember two guys were handcuffed together around a tree for causing trouble.

"Fly-Blow even had a baseball team. They beat Grangeville a time or two. They had a baseball game at 10 o'clock in the morning, a rodeo in the afternoon, and a dance at night. There wasn't any roads in there. It was terrible. By golly, they used to draw a lot of people in there. People came from Oregon on their horses and swam the river and set up their camps at Fly-Blow. There was a big dance hall over by that mud puddle. The cook shack measured 30 X 65. I've seen 2,000 people camped back there in the jack pines."

"The way that Fly-Blow got its name was supposedly from a butchered beef that hung from a log chain. They covered it with canvas, but the flies covered the chain. That's the story I heard about how it come to be named Fly-Blow. When I lived here, they wouldn't eat deer meat when cattle were for sale."

"W. I. Roake was the instigator of the whole thing. He was a stock contractor, an' he run cattle. He reportedly had a "long loop"."

"Now you're looking into the Wallowas," Muggs says, stopping at a viewpoint overlooking the river. "There's Oregon over there, and that's the Seven Devils you're looking at. Over there's

212

the Dumaque Plains. You can see Grangeville from here. We can see where we've been in the distance. We just came around the head of Wolf Creek."

As we continued along the county road, Muggs told us about driving a team from Dumaque Plains in the middle of the winter to Boles, changing to a sled to break through the heavy snow. "The old Sunset School used to set right here," Muggs says, pointing to an open space among the trees. "My dad and mother lived in White Bird when I was little, and I lived with my aunt and uncle."

At the small Joseph School we parked and unpacked our lunch. The wood-framed schoolhouse where Muggs spent his school years was not only standing but looked to be in good condition. It felt like recess time, and soon a bell would ring and children would be returning to classes. "I've got a whole eighth grade education. Thirty-two of us went to school here," Muggs says.

We crossed Rice Creek which separates Joseph from the Dumaque Plains and were able to look down into the Salmon River. "You're looking back at Cottonwood Butte," Muggs explains. "This is where the Twin Rivers Ranch land sales begins."

The old Canfield Post Office is the end of the line. From there we drove uninterruptedly through the land sales with realty signs posted on land that looked almost uninhabitable. Bachelor Buttons and Yellow Star Thistle covered the breaks. Most of the homes that had recently been built looked inaccessible and isolated. The road wound down through tract homes and housing developments ending at Copperfield, a town site existing only on paper. It had never been developed—a ghost town before it began.

From White Bird we traveled up the looping, twisting White Bird Pass with Muggs pointing out high points of interest with the ease of an experienced tour guide. "There's the old highway over there," Muggs said. "They didn't use dump trucks. They used steam shovels, hand drills, horses, and dump carts; they blasted with black powder. There's eight switchbacks, and the elevation is 4245 feet."

As Grangeville came into view, Muggs offered one last observation: "You can tell them you were up here with one of the darndest liars of all time. Not really a liar. Just my kind of truth. I didn't ask the right kinds of questions. I thought the old timers would be here forever to ask questions."

CURLEY FRANCIS

Curley Francis is a working cowboy for the Spencer Company on the Joseph Plains overlooking Hells Canyon and the Snake River. Curley worked as a rodeo clown in his earlier years but now concentrates on working cattle and living the solitary life of a cowboy.

———————◇———————

Muggs Bentley pulled his pickup off to the side of the road to let a herd of cattle pass. Two men were driving the cattle through the timber high above the Snake River near the breaks of the Joseph Plains. The herd passed around the pickup as we sat watching. Following the herd at a short distance, two riders emerged from the trees and stopped at the side of the pickup.

Muggs turned to Cathy and myself and said, "It looks like we're caught on private property, but we'll get away with it this time."

One rider leaned down and poked his hand through the open window and shook hands with Muggs. "I thought I recognized your pickup," he said to Muggs with a big smile which was half hidden behind an enormous twirled mustache that went straight up at the ends.

Muggs introduced us to Curley Francis, buckaroo for the Spencer cattle outfit. He lived nearby in a house built out in the open with connecting corrals. The house had been sprayed with chemicals from a crop duster, and all of the vegetation in a hundred yard radius had been completely denuded. You could look down into the Snake River canyon from a ridge just beyond the ranch house.

Curley patiently explained that there were three kinds of livestock operations. "The first is the single home and farm with five to ten head. This is the biggest today. The second is the family farm. I like this the best, but they can't afford to hire cowboys. They keep people for life and pension them off when they can't work

214

anymore. The third kind is the corporation like the one I work for here at Spencer's."

"Kids don't want to work like this. What's going to happen when guys like me are gone? What's going to happen to me? I don't know. There's no one to take my place."

"My place is clean. I keep things up, I keep up appearances, and that's what counts. That's really what they pay me for."

"I was a rodeo clown for seven or eight years. I worked for Harley Tucker, Christensen Brothers and others. I liked the life."

"I remember once Harley Tucker with his wife and some friends went to a restaurant in Dayton, Washington. Harley broke wind in public, and his wife got on him about it, and another woman took her side. Harley said, "I'll do what I please. In fact, I'll just buy this restaurant." And he did. Harley was a little loud, but that was Harley."

"Tucker died at a rodeo in Vancouver, Washington, doing what he wanted and liked. I hope I do the same, out on the Joseph Plains, doing what I'm good at."

"One time I was out here alone, and my horse fell on me and broke nearly all of my ribs and one leg. The doctor had to completely rebuild the knee. I made it to town by myself and passed out at the hospital."

"I have a deal with the phone company. If they don't hear from me within three days, they send out a plane looking for me. The phone rings most of the time, except maybe in the winter when the lines are down."

"The mail will get to me. I've got a box at the Lemon ranch. People just send mail to Curley at Cottonwood. Once a feller wrote me and addressed the letter c/o Curley, somewhere near Grangeville in the mountains, and I got it."

"I'm even having an article written about me in the Grangeville newspaper."

"I go to town about every three or four months to buy groceries. I haven't watched t.v. in 25 years. I've never watched a VCR. The last movie I saw was a cowboy movie, and the only thing that I remember about it, besides that it was about Australia, was that it had a cowboy riding horseback down a hill."

I asked Curley what he thought about Realtors selling land just a few miles from his ranch at Twin Rivers.

He walked around in circles for several minutes before giving his opinion. "The government wanted an easement or something like that in the past. Anyway, there was a government program to keep this part of the country from being parceled up and sold piecemeal. It was some sort of wildlife program. At first I hated it, but now I'm in favor of it. Anything is better than the Twin River's sell off."

GERTRUDE MAXWELL

Gertrude Maxwell is a member of the Cowgirl Hall of Fame in Fort Worth, Texas. She lives in Elk City, Idaho, in a house that her father built. When she heard that we were going to be in Grangeville to conduct interviews, she drove 50 miles under winter conditions to be there with several others from the local rodeo community.

━━━━━◆━━━━━

I was born in Elk City, Idaho, and taught school for 40 years in Lewiston, Idaho. During that 40 years, I also ran a pack guide outfit. My best friend was Jackson Sundown's brother, Corbet. He would camp out at the ranch at Elk City.

I loved the rodeo world but didn't like the politics in Pendleton, Ellensburg, Cheyenne. I loved Calgary; the politics was nothing like it was here.

I had gone to a rodeo, and some kid came out with a bronc that Prairie Lilly was supposed to ride, but she hadn't made it to the show. He asked me if I wanted to try, and I said yes. I rode and took second place. My parents didn't know I had gone to the rodeo. They saw me ride. My dad whipped me after I got off. My mother didn't say a word. We walked home and my mother kneed me in the butt. My mother made sure her knee connected with my butt every step of the way. Right after the ride, my father grabbed me by the arm and told me, "No daughter of mine is going to be a cowboy."

Ben Jory was standing nearby. He said, "It looks like it's too late."

Ben Jory put on the "Over The Hill" pageant that kicked off the Pendleton Round-Up each year but never got the credit for it he should have. I was glad that Ben and his first wife finally got a divorce. They fought like cats and dogs, and it was ruining their reputations in the rodeo world.

I was Queen of the rodeo in Grangeville in 1937. I rode in Baker, Oregon, and Calgary. I didn't ride the rough ones; I was just in the rodeos.

COLFAX

Bob Hickman is a distant relative of Yakima Canutt. Yakima, who became famous not only as a cowboy during the 1920s but as a stuntman and Hollywood movie director, was born in Penawawa, Washington, not far from Colfax. Bob has had a long-standing ambition to turn the upper two stories of his saddle shop into a museum dedicated to Yakima Canutt. He took us on a tour. Upstairs the walls displayed antique western wear, old photos, posters and tack; on the top floor was a Pendleton Round-Up calendar with the image of the famous bucking horse on a red background with the "Let Er Buck" logo. Antique saddles straddled the railing around the top (mostly Hamley's); he loans them to members of riding clubs for parades.

Early in the summer of 1996 we drove up to Colfax, Washington, and spent the day interviewing Bob, his dad, Larry Hickman, his aunt Wanda Hickman Carter, Oscar Broeckel, Fritz Zuger, and Les and Mildred Riley. Oscar drove in from LaCrosse, and the Riley's arrived later from Centralia. Between interviews, we watched a video featuring Yakima's son Tad. It was filmed at the old home ranch on the Snake River. Tad was horseback, riding the rolling hills of the Palouse, following in his dad's footsteps across the country where he was raised.

Later we received the following announcement:

"Museum Dedication Invitation"

"Yakima Canutt? Who is he? Stop and think who's the most famous person to come out of the Palouse. How many people from this area have been a four time World Champion Cowboy, how many have won an Academy Award, or how many have been a movie star, an actor, or even a director? Just one name comes to mind when you think of it...Yakima (Enos Edward) Canutt."

"Hickman Saddlery has brought undoubtedly the area's most charismatic figure home again. As we put it..., "Yakima's Ride Back Through His Life." With the help of his wife Audrea Canutt, his cousin/close friend John Crawford the museum has been brought to life with a vast array of artifacts, photographs and even movies of his life."

"When you walk into the museum, you enter the life of a man who accomplished unimaginable things. First you will see an eight foot by five foot photograph of Yakima Canutt riding the unridable "Tipperary." Yak was the only man to ever ride this famous horse; they were inducted into the Rodeo Cowboy Hall of Fame together. You will then journey around the gallery gazing upon rodeo pictures, movies, stunt photos, and many articles and letters written about this world-renowned gentleman. Continuing through the museum, you might find his hat, boots, trophies, and many other items that reflect his accomplishments."

"On September 4th, 1997, the museum will be dedicated with a banquet honoring the most famous man to come out of "These Snake River Hills." Audrea Canutt and John Crawford will be on hand for you to rub elbows with and to converse with concerning exactly the kind of man Yakima was. We will be having a prime rib dinner, some good ol' cowboy poetry, and John will talk about the great man Yak. We will then adjourn to visit the museum where you will have the opportunity to ride with Yak back through his life."

"I would like to thank the Palouse Country Cowboy Poetry Association for honoring this great man at their Second Annual Gathering. I would also like to invite each and every one of you to come and enjoy this man's extraordinary life...Cousin Yak, this one's for you!"

Bob Hickman

The sidewalk was lined with straw bales. It was warm and pleasant. Colfax isn't very big; you can see both ends of Main Street from the saddle shop. We went into the Elks' Club where the banquet was being held and took a table near the door. At 5:30 there were only a few people sitting at tables; an hour later, the banquet room set for 180 was filled to capacity.

John Crawford, an actor, friend and cousin of Yakima's was the Emcee, and Yakima's wife, Audrea, was a guest speaker at the banquet. The evening's entertainment featured cowboy poetry and songs by several groups from the area and was followed by an informal gathering next door at the museum. The evening was lively and entertaining.

BOB HICKMAN

Bob Hickman owns Hickman's Saddlery in Colfax, Washington and another in Post Falls, Idaho. Bob is a saddle maker and has been a bit, spur and saddle collector for the past twenty years. He was born in 1961 at Almota, Washington. His great-great grandmother was Yakima Canutt's Aunt. His grandfather was a foundation breeder for Appaloosa's back in the late '20s through '40s. Bob was a calf roper in high school and at Spokane Community College. His business is expanding worldwide. He sells to collectors in France, Italy and Sweden. "There's a big market in Europe," Bob says from the floor of the Sands Convention Center where he's showing his leather work at the National Finals in Las Vegas.

Marlo Ochs was an old bronc rider from way back, probably 1922-23-24 era. He was Yakima Canutt's top competition around Colfax back then. He used to warm up, getting ready for his bronc rides by letting people whap him in the belly with a two by four. Everybody wanted to see how tough Marlo was, and they found out when they hit him with that two by four, and he'd say, "That all you got?" He was just that kind of man. A tough old bronc rider.

Towards the end of his life, he used to just sit out here on Main Street in front of the saddle shop in his pickup and watch people walk by. He just wanted to be part of it, yet. He was a real nice, personable guy. In April of last year (1996), he came in to the saddle shop and started taking pictures with a Polaroid camera someone had given him. And he said, "Here, I want you to remember who took this picture." Most of his words that came out of his mouth were "gosh." "Gosh, look at that!" He'd look around and just say, "Gosh!"

Marlo Ochs.

I made a "horse breaker" for him. He had a design for the horse breaker. He was 88 years old and still breaking horses. He came in here with this design for the breaker. What it was, was kinda like a breast collar dropped a little lower in the front end, kind of like a Britchen, dropped a little lower on the back end, and it was held together with a pulley and a latigo strap on the other side. Marlo was so excited about it. Every other word was Gosh! He said, "This is how it works. Tie about twenty foot of rope between the two pulleys, and when the horse gets to where you're lunging with him, when he gets out of hand, you just pull these ropes together and bind him up. Bring his front legs to the back legs, and the horse will stop."

It was something he was pretty proud of, and it worked. He said he could flop a horse to his knees with it. Just before he did it, he'd yell Whoa! so the horse got to know what that meant. He was a character.

He was just big around Colfax. Ellensburg would have been one of his longest trips.

223

LARRY HICKMAN

Larry Hickman was born and raised in Almota, Washing-
ton. He ran a 250 cow-calf operation and raised Appaloosa's in
the '40s. Larry took his son Bob to rodeos on the weekends.

My dad was a horse trader. Every Sunday was our big day at
home. Mother would start killing chickens. She always wanted to
have company, and Dad didn't want anybody coming. He'd have to
dress up. The cowboys always came riding in.

We had three studs, so we had people there from morning 'till
dark at Colfax. We'd go down into the canyon a few miles and bring
the horses in, and people would start coming in to trade. They'd
bring mares to breed, and come dark we'd maybe take ten different horses back down the canyon.

We had a big, round pole horse corral where the gate would
go together with the fence. It was usually whittled out where you
had to replace it about every month. Guys would get to trading and
get the knife out and start whittling.

*   *   *

We were trailing cattle from Reparia, Washington, to Bolleville,
Idaho, probably 120 miles. It took about 15 days. It was back during the War, so the help you had were guys who were either too
old for the army or too young.

My dad was handicapped. He had a wooden leg. He'd go ahead
in a pickup and set up camp for the night, so there'd be water and
rest when we got there. The last time we done it was 1948 or 1949.
You couldn't do it now. There's too many fences.

Fay Hubbard came through, someplace in Idaho, and he got
to our cook. We had a chuck wagon and the whole darn thing. He

got a quart of wine to our cook, and it put him out of action for days. We'd have killed Fay if we'd gotten hold of him.

Clayton Butcher lived in Grangeville. He was a hard riding, fast living kind of deal. He died three or four years ago. He was 80.

They always said if you wanted to look up the word cowboy in the dictionary, his picture would be there. He worked around the sale yards. He done everything, hauled cattle, traded women pretty often.

Lary Daniels had a practice arena above Lewiston, Idaho on the Clearwater River. Those boys got something like five dollars a head to try out horses, and it cost us several hired men. They'd get bucked off and hurt.

I also remember several years that Lary won the all-around at Lewiston. We'd never really have a horse sale in Lewiston until Lary had a fight. That was the concluding part of every sale. He was right in there. He lived rough; that's the way he was.

There would just be an argument. Horse traders are just that way. One of 'em will say today is Wednesday, and another will say it's Thursday, so they'll have a fight over what day it is. Lary's hammer was always cocked.

I think once you got past Pendleton, you went to Hollywood.

Stub Bartlemay always had a cigarette in his mouth when he rode broncs.

OSCAR BROECKEL

*Oscar Broeckel, at 78, is retired, and his son Brian con-
tinues to work the family farm near Dusty, Washington. Oscar is still active in "The Gentlemen On Horseback" trail ride,
which began in 1949.*

Fay Hubbard came to Dusty one day, and, of course, he always
drove an old Cadillac. It was colder than heck, and all he had on his
feet was a pair of little slippers. I was helping out at the Co-Op. He
said, "Do you know what the Sheriff's number is?"

"I'll look it up," I said.

"Call him," he said.

So I called the Sheriff's office. Well, Fay was wondering who
he could sue. He had a dog that was trained to lead his saddle horse,
and he had a goose that rode the saddle horse. He had an appoint-
ment with "Little House On The Prairie" for an episode. Well, some

dogs got loose and killed his goose, and he was wondering who he could sue.

Hubbard raised a lot of geese, and he rented them to the mint farmers down at Othello at fifty cents apiece for a goose. He had as high as 5,000 geese a year. They would eat the weeds, but they wouldn't eat the mint. They'd eat everything else in the field.

He had something going all the time. He had a bunch of pigeons, and he sold them to some gun club over in Seattle for a dollar a pigeon. They used them for practicing shooting.

There was a guy by the name of Carl Reb over in Endicot who said that if he had to pick anybody that would know somebody from Colfax to New York, he'd pick Fay Hubbard.

He was married to a movie star from New York by the name of Kay Swift. They lived on a big ranch near Bend, Oregon.

I was born and raised in Dusty, Washington. Somebody once asked me where Dusty was, and I told him that if you sneezed, you missed it. They used to have a sign in the old days in the window of the old cafe and service station. It read, "Dusty." But there was so much dust in there, you couldn't barely read it. If you came through Walla Walla to Colfax, you came through Dusty.

I wasn't in rodeo. Old Chuck Glover started a Cattlemen's Ride in 1947, and we used to ride horseback to the Cattlemen's Convention every year. It was located in Spokane, Washington. They met at Colville, Okanogan, Omak, Longview, Centralia. We rode from Spokane every year.

I missed a couple of them. I took the kids to Disneyland, and I missed one other one; otherwise, I went every year.

Old Chuck Glover bought cattle at the stock yards. He and another guy decided to get together in 1947 and ride to the Convention. That was in Okanogan the first year. It ballooned from there. There was forty-seven guys that went that first year. They've had doctors, heart specialists, airline managers, every kind of deal you can think of who liked horses.

The longest trip was to Longview, on the coast, and Centralia. That was another long one. They don't go to the Convention that way anymore because there's too much traffic, so now they just go on a week trail ride every year in June, and they have around fifty guys. I ride a mule.

Denny Stark from Washtucna has mules. He bought a little jackass no taller than that, and then he bought three little miniature mares, and he crossed them with that Jack. One little mule is twenty-one inches tall with a hoof the size of a four-bit piece. That little mule follows him around like a dog—no halter or nothin'. He takes him uptown, into taverns, into the post office; then he turns around and goes the other way. He's not crazy, but he'll just do anything. That mule is the cutest little thing you ever saw.

We have a Threshing Bee and a Plowing Bee at the Fairgrounds in Colfax every year. Everybody says it's a lot of work, but the older guys tell 'em "No, this is fun!"

But it is hard work, too. On the fifteen acres out here, we've had as high as eighty-nine head of horses out there plowing. They come from as far away as Montana, Ellensburg, Pendleton. Jerry Schubert used to come up and plow from Pendleton. We have a Threshing Bee on Labor Day every year.

I remember a long time ago when I was a little kid, Montie Montana asked me to hold his horse. He said, "Don't let him eat any grass." Buster, Buck, Sheik, and Rex was his horses' names. He always had spotted horses. That was in Colfax in the late '30s or early '40s.

I was at the Pendleton Round-Up when Yakima Canutt was the Grand Marshal of the Parade. He was Grand Marshal at Colfax in 1983.

My uncle and I went to the National Finals Rodeo in Oklahoma City, the last one they had there. And we've been going to Las Vegas the last few years. I talked to Les Riley's boy, Sonny Riley. He takes stock down to the National Finals. He's got the "Flying Five". He said, "Shucks, everything down there in Las Vegas is free gratis. The cowboys don't have to pay nothin'."

So they're all for Vegas. And that place is sold out. We talked to a guy, a planner at Las Vegas, that said they're going to raise the roof at Thomas & Mack and put in 8,000 more seats. Now, is that possible? That guy in the last row, what can he see? When we were there, the Etbauer boys, and also Whitfield, the black roper, were just signing autographs as fast as they could, and people were standing in line to get them.

Them two Garrett brothers, they're from South Dakota, but their dad works here in LaCrosse. He's a truck driver. They come out here once in awhile. Marvin has been the bareback champion the last three years. Then, he was leading, way ahead, and his young brother Mark took it.

LES & MILDRED RILEY

Les and Mildred Riley are retired stock contractors from Central Ferry, Washington, where they have spent the past 52 years on the Riley's River Ranch. Their son, Sonny is a stock contractor with the "Flying Five."

Les Riley: I never was a rodeo cowboy. I never did rodeo, but my boy was a pretty good hand. A bull bucked him off up there at Spokane and hurt him pretty bad, and he decided he wasn't gonna ride anymore. We had a few bulls and a few horses.

We used to have rodeos down there on the ranch on Easter Sunday. We'd have a nice crowd. We're set in a valley, and there's a big hill behind us, so we didn't have to have grandstands. They'd just set on the hill and watch. There was room for the kids to run, and we really had a nice rodeo. It was at Central Ferry.

Mildred Riley: I kind of think that's how we got started in the rodeo business. We have two sons. They started roping, and then Dwight Broadhead had a rodeo school out there at the Fairgrounds. They started practicing roping. From there they formed a little group along with a neighbor. Our two sons and three other boys went together and made the "Flying Five." They did real good. Who had "Big Bend," Les?

Les Riley: Big Bend was only dad and another guy. Ralph McRae had it, and we bought it from Ralph. Joe Kelsey had it before that.

We had "Flying Five" and "Big Bend" stock at the National Finals this year (1996). We had Fifteen head—five bulls, five broncs, and five bareback horses this year. Our grandson wore a picture on his shirt of "Dog Face," our number one bull. He's a red bull. "Dog Face" was the number one bull at Yakima, but he slowed up at the

229

finals. "Big Barley" is our top bronc. I bought him in Calgary. I out-bid another guy for him and bought him for $4200.

Stock contractors have to buy so many tickets in advance at the National Finals. And no free tickets. They don't give stock con-tractors much credit. And all they pay 'em is $2,000 apiece for a horse or bull at the NFR. And that's for two times out. Three times, they pay you another thousand.

Mildred Riley: They used to have rodeos over there on Barney Lake, didn't they, Les?

Les Riley: Yes, they did.

Mildred Riley: Who were the stock contractors there?

Les Riley: The Hanna boys.

Mildred Riley: We supply stock for several rodeos. We have all of the Union, Oregon, show; some of the shows we don't have a whole lot. At Yakima, I think there was either four or five contrac-tors. Some of the shows we have exclusively—Union, Moses Lake, Kennewick. We have part of Omak. We do all of Othello.

Les Riley: We do almost all of Omak except for what Calgary sends down. They ain't got no bulls. They send a few saddle broncs and bareback horses. Harry Vold is one of the leading contractors at Calgary.

We have stock in Washington, Idyho, and Oregon. We had a bunch of bulls in Utah last weekend. They go to California. We fed 'em until this year, and we got flooded out with mud. So we moved the bulls to George, Washington. The horses are over by Moses Lake, and we have a bunch of mares in Montana.

Mildred Riley: Our son, Sonny, should have come in because he's really the contractor, but we had a bunch of cattle in Nevada and had to move them home, so he couldn't come today.

FRITZ ZUGER

Fritz Zuger is from Waitsburg, Washington, and currently lives in Colfax. He attended Washington State University and was a member of their first rodeo team. Fritz offered his help and support in a variety of ways, contributing information on many of the people in the book.

———————◆———————

The last time I saw Lary Daniels, he hit me in the belly and my head purt'near hit my feet. I'd just had a back operation. He liked to killed me. He was just playin'. He used to wrestle quite a bit. He taught me to bulldog...him and Red Allen. Now, there's a pair. If you didn't get down on your steer, they'd just reach over and grab your arm and put you down.

Lary was an announcer at the first WSU Intercollegiate Rodeo. Bob Hickman has programs of that rodeo in his museum upstairs. They had all of them for all three days. It was the spring of 1951, I believe. Lary and Red Allen always worked with the young group, especially around Lewiston. I was raised in Waitsburg, Washington. Fritz Zuger is my name. Z-U-G-E-R.

Lary used to work some racehorses for my dad before he passed away, so I've known Lary all my life. Truth was, we always rough-housed pretty hard. Holding a guy down and spurring him in the ribs was nothing unusual if you were man enough to do it. I didn't learn that in one of my college classes. It was extracurricular. But we had a lot of fun. We were growing up. There was seven members on that first rodeo team from Washington State College. There was Ron Taylor, Art Fulkerson, Roger Nielsen, Ernie Busek, Bill Brock, James Tippett, and myself. Bill is a vet in Ritzville, and Roger Neilsen is still around Walla Walla.

Rodeo was a lot different than it is now; it isn't as rough as it used to be in the old days. Like my father-in-law said in Pendleton, you used to ride bucking horses for a dollar a head, and if you got on twelve of 'em, that was good money. You lived in the barn. You had a lot more atmosphere than they do nowadays, riding around in campers and motor homes an' all.

We showed horses down around Pendleton in the early days. Dad was one of the early ones in quarter horses. We had a hundred head of our own, and we had something like 275 outside mares. It was a wheat ranch and a cattle operation with horses along with it. We run cows in the Wallowas and down on the Snake River at the Nine Mile Ranch.

I was raised in the Waitsburg area. The Walla Walla group and the group from Pendleton run around together. Curtis Tarwater from Walla Walla was an outstanding guy. I know he used to shoe horses here at Colfax for Les Riley. He shod a lot of horses on both sides of the river. He was my coach when I learned to rope. Curtis was a little different individual. He came out of the regular old horse cavalry. When he went to shoe a horse, it didn't matter if it was upside down or how, it got shod. He was helpful with college kids and young cowboys and cowgirls. I don't know how long he was coach at Walla Walla Community College—eight to ten years, I think.

Lary Daniels helped out on our first college rodeo. There were five of us kids that started it from nothing. Harley Tucker furnished the stock. Of course, we had run around with Lary at Lewiston already. I can't remember everyone who came out and helped us put on that rodeo. We used the old rodeo grounds at Lewiston. When the whole thing was over, we were short $5,000. I never will forget, Harley Tucker came in and asked us kids how we were doing. We said, "As near as we can tell, we're broke, and we're gonna have to sell the car and the whole works."

"Oh, I don't think so," he said. "You just give me what you got left, an' I'll take care of your loss."

How many people would do that for a bunch of kids? But he was an outstanding guy. He had quite a ranch out of Joseph, Oregon. I guess he had two or three ranches, but he had just the one left when he lived in a big brick house out towards the Imnaha.

Another guy on that rodeo team was Doug Tibbitt. He lives on a ranch out of Joseph-Enterprise. But at that time, he lived on the old homestead back on the Imnaha. It was on Chief Joseph Creek. But that group that came out of Hell's Canyon was a little different group too. They could ride a horse faster through the bluffs, faster

Harley Tucker.

than most people could ride 'em on the level. It was kind of outstanding to watch 'em work.

I worked mainly amateur, and I roped pretty good. It got to be that I had to go one way or the other, stay an amateur or turn pro. My father got sick, so I stayed with the horses and ranch. I used to rope against Dean Oliver and Harry Charters and some of them guys. I did fairly well. A fella by the name of Chuck Irwin, who was a generation ahead of me, who had been a pretty outstanding calf roper, would have put up the money if I had wanted to go, but my mother was left with that slug of horses, a bunch of cows, and a 2,000 acre ranch, so I chose to stay at home. I had two kids, and I didn't care to travel that much either.

We used to razz Harry Charters and tell him he ought to pack the horse in bulldoggin'. I'm pretty good size, but walking alongside him, I felt like a midget. He was twice as wide and another three or four inches taller.

Harry was a tough competitor. He kind of got himself all tore up. I don't remember where it happened, but it happened over a $200 watch. It was on a bull's horns. Harry was big and stout. That bull run into the calf chute, down in the barrier area. Harry was sitting there above him, so he thought he'd step down and get the watch. It put him in the hospital for something like six months. Just tore him to pieces. You'd think no man could think he could throw a Brahma bull and hold him. But it was a great inspiration and a heck of a record.

How many years have I known Les Riley? First time I seen him I came across the river with my dad. I don't even think I was school age yet. It was 53 years ago. I used to keep a Jack and a stallion down there. Les an' my dad used to trade horses back an' forth.

This is a funny story; I left it out when we were talking about college rodeo. I thought it was one of the funniest things I ever knew. Lary Daniels was talking about the kids riding bulls, and some hot shot up in the stands yells, "I'll bet you a thousand dollars you won't get on a bull!"

Lary says, "Bring the thousand dollars over here, friend. You're called."

He went down an' spurred the bull like you would a buckin' horse all the way out and went down and collected his bet.

Lary came to this country with "Puddin' Foot," a rope horse. He came up here and had a match race. I can't remember the figure they had on the race, but "Puddin' Foot" didn't look like he could run fast enough to settle anything. He had the matched race here in Colfax with Hugh Huntley, who had some pretty good race horses. "Puddin' Foot" run off and left him. This big old stout-lookin' horse, you wouldn't think he could run, but he sure could. He didn't look like a speed demon, I can tell you that.

Lary was always around helping that bunch of kids from Washington State College. He had the Harley Tucker string of bulls in there. They didn't start us off on any cream puffs.

I got on a bareback horse in Lewiston. I think her name was "Ginger Snap." She was chute balky. Harley leaned over an' said, "Now kid, this horse is gonna go out there an' jump an' turn back to the left real hard. You're never gonna see anything turn any harder."

Well, he hot-shotted her out of the chute, an' I'll guarantee she turned back hard. That's right where I got off. Jerked the riggin' right out of my hand. I didn't know I lost it. I was standing on my feet, and when she came around the next time, she kicked my hat off.

You know, that stuff went on all the time. You don't think too much of it.

I remember the first big college rodeo in Missoula, Montana. It was in 1951. That was quite a rodeo. We went to Missoula around the first of May if I remember right. It snowed fourteen inches. We hauled sawdust for the arena. I can remember this big old sorrel horse I had, his backbone stickin' way out; they run these horses in an' grain 'em for about two weeks and then stick 'em in there. You ever ride a bareback horse with his backbone showin'?

Another guy, Zebe Lewis was out of Cove, Oregon. He finally passed away up here in Idaho. Zebe's ranch ran from Oregon to New Mexico. It was the XIT. Zebe, along with Oren Four from Walla Walla, their dad's worked for the XIT ranch, and they were raised on the ranch. They used different methods on livestock than you've ever seen. Modern people don't even see that stuff anymore. They way you handle stock, you didn't mess with horses. You tied a leg up, sacked 'em out, and they was broke by the time you got done with 'em.

Fritz Allent won a Yakima Canutt trophy at LaCrosse, and, this could be hot air, but he told me it took him and his four brothers to carry it out of the arena. Everybody wanted it, and they had to fight for it. His sons have been champion bare back riders the last two years. The youngest one won it this year at the National Finals.

Demoss Bergevin used to put on rodeos below LaCrosse. He had an arena down by Fence Town. The creek behind the Bergevins place is still there where Tom Bergevin farms. He had rodeos for about ten years. He had a son by the name of Joe who was a real outstanding calf roper. He won at Pendleton a time or two. I think he won the steer roping there once and the calf roping. I would guess that was in the late '60s or early '70s.

I have something a lot of people would like to have, and it's funny, I got it as a kid. I would guess it is somewhere around the 1935-1938 period. It's a puzzle from the Let 'er Buck Horse at the

Pendleton Round-Up. I have no idea what it's worth, but it'll never leave my place as long as I'm alive. I keep it pretty well hid.

And I was gonna tell you about running horses with my father at the top of Cabbage Hill over near Pendleton.

People would say you're nuts, now, if you seen 30 to 40 head of horses runnin' across the highway on Cabbage Hill, but when I was a kid, it was nothing to see that at night and sometimes in the daytime. We went up to Meacham and back to the east, and in the brush there, the Indians had two or three big round pole corrals. Sometimes Dad would stay there an' mark horses. The Indians "Squaw" tied 'em, an' Dad just walked from one horse to the other an' marked em, an' he'd do that for two or three days in a row. How many head, it was hard to tell. And, of course, the Indians would get in the corral when this was going on an' ride those horses with mane holts. They'd get bucked into the timber an' the stumps that were in the corrals. And then the next one might ride a horse right over the top of him. It was quite an event. I was six or seven years old then. After that we'd go an' stay with the Indians. As long as you were there an' you were their friends, nobody bothered you. It was a strict code. For years, if you mentioned Dad's last name or even his first name on that reservation, you were welcome on the spot.

My Great Uncle Amery McCowen was a farmer in the horse days. He was a pretty good stockman too. He had a horse he could head out of Waitsburg with and ride up to just about Steptoe. He farmed another 2,000 acres up there with horses. It used to be the old Minnick place. He'd come up one day on this horse an' go back the next day. They talk about tough horses, he was tough. He would go up and across canyons an' up to the flats. It's a lot closer than following the highway, so in that way it was not so far, but there's draws runnin' all the way, an' he followed them, but you still gotta climb out of the Snake River going out both directions.

I run cattle from the Wallowa Mountains to Spokane an' different locations, all up an' down the Snake River, the Columbia, the Walla Walla. A lot of country was involved with it. It's kind of hard to believe when you tell somebody that when you move 100 miles in either direction, and stay in the same business, it changes.

The old Stockman cabin was still there when we run cattle there. It was right on the Forest Service line up the Minam River from the town of Minam. I guess it was eight or ten miles. That was a packline of this ranch we run out there. At that time it belonged to Swede Anderson out of Walla Walla. I've forgotten who owns it now, but they bought it from Swede. At that time there was a saw-mill at Minam and a store. That's what the Stockman cabin was for. It was a cow camp for people to stay at when they were running cattle on the Forest Service. At that time, from that ranch on the Minam River to the horse ranch, I think it was twenty-seven miles, and there was no road in between. It was all trail. We used to pack for fishing trips in the high Wallowas, and that was our vacation. We had pack stock on the Minam River, and we had all the horses we needed. You just took out the back gate to go fishing. It's a little different than now.

Maybe I shouldn't tell this story on myself, but I had a pretty bad time with my dad one year, and I went over to Joseph to the rodeo. I spent too much time at the bar, so they sent three people to get me. I guess I was so ornery that they just left me there. Anyway, an old guy by the name of Mose Tibedeau who was quite a Snake River cowboy, he thought, was the bouncer at this bar. I was back talkin' to him. I was just drinking my life away, I guess, and a fight started. Old Mose ran over an' grabbed this guy an' out the back door they went, an' I followed them out. It looked like this guy was gonna sandbag Mose from behind, so I just reached around from behind an' grabbed his arm an' jerked him off the sidewalk by the chin. A fella tapped me on the shoulder an' said, "Hey, fella, better put him down. He's the Deputy Sheriff."

I remember once old Tibedeau got on a bronc and stuck a spur in both shoulders an' said, "Now, go somewhere." It was over there in Hell's Canyon somewhere.

DON & JOANN GRIFFITH

Don Griffith and his wife Joann live in Spray, Oregon. Don is the older brother of Mac Griffith, a well known cowboy from Heppner, who was a top contender in bareback riding and bulldogging in the late '50s and early '60s. Mac's career as an all-around cowboy in the RCA was cut short when he was shot to death by an off-duty policeman. Don was a top-notch amateur rodeo competitor.

———————◆———————

Mac Griffith
as told by Don Griffith
Heppner, Oregon

My brother Mac Griffith went to all the big rodeos. He won the Big Four twice in a row. That was Ellensburg, Walla Walla, Lewiston, and Pendleton. He won the all-around in Pendleton in '63. He won the bulldoggin' and the all-around in Pendleton. I think he won the bull ridin' and the all-around in Calgary.

Mac won the Northwest Bronc Riding here at Heppner after they moved it from Pendleton. He won it the year before I did. He won it in '61. Norman Gory won it in 1959, the first year after they moved it here. He had trophies and saddles, but he hocked 'em all. After he got killed we tried to find one of his saddles. In Chicago, he won a saddle in the IRA, the International Rodeo Association, a world's champion saddle bronc riding saddle. We've got a picture of it with him here at Mom's house with him standing there with that saddle.

Mac never was big headed. He never cared about fame. He wanted the money. If he won a buckle, that was fine too. He had a pro attitude. He was kinda like me in a way. He didn't have any desire to be rich; he just wanted to make a livin', and that was it. He believed in keeping that money in circulation. Everybody's got to have a little bit of it.

Mac was good to help anybody if they needed help. Mac was tough on the outside and softer than hell on the inside. Very few people knew that, though. He loved kids. He used to baby-sit for entry fee money. He baby-sat with our little sister and a couple of twin girls that lived up here—Bill and Shirley Blake's twin daughters. For his high school graduation present, we paid his fees in bronc ridin' at Spray.

He went all through high school in Heppner, him and Neal Beamer. At home we've got a picture of Jan Beamer, Miss NRA. We have a picture of her presenting Mac one of his saddles. He pitched on the baseball team and played football. He was good sized for bull ridin'. He was 6 foot tall and weighed 190. He tried boxing once. He worked out and got in shape, but it didn't last long. He told me, "I'm gonna stick with rodeo. In boxing they can hit you any time they want from any direction."

We were always interested in rodeo. Dad rode a little bit when he was young, but he hated it. He hated for us to start. He stayed right there at the house in Fossil and wouldn't even go out to the arena and watch us ride. He just thought we were gonna grow up to be bums.

We had a ranch over there by Spray where we live now. The family bought the Caden Hotel in Enterprise, and we moved up there. We were always interested in horses. We started breaking horses up there for a guy named Gene Marr, and he got us started in Junior Rodeo. I rode race horses for Truman Poulson. I rode "Red Risk" in a match race at Enterprise.

Mac and I rode shotgun for Walter Brennan there at Joseph. He built that Rainbow Theater and Hotel. They had a big parade for the opening of that theater, and they had a stagecoach. Gene Marr's dad, Odel, drove the stagecoach, and he had the film up on the back of the stagecoach, and Mac and I rode shotgun for the stage. The name of the movie was "Curtain Call At Cactus Creek." It was the first movie at the Joseph Theater.

When we were in grade school at Spray, we had two horses that we were gettin' in shape, and we exercised 'em by riding 'em to school. The school bus would come just about the time we'd get to school, and we'd cut through and outrun the bus those last two miles to school. We could have gone to school in the bus.

That was kinda the way we got started, and then Mac joined the RCA and went to New York. I never was in the RCA. I remember ridin' in the finals in the NRA in Portland once. I stuck for thirteen seconds and he finally bucked me off and I got egged. The judge said, "I just wanted to see how long you could ride him."

I broke my leg in Lynn, Washington, in 1957. A bareback horse fell on me and broke it. Mac was there. Our daughter was just a baby. She was born in April, and that was in June. She was our first kid. They was loading me in the ambulance, a Chevy van, to take me to Ritzville. When I left, I told Mac not to turn my bronc loose because I'd be back. He said "Sure you will," and slammed the door.

He came to the hospital that night, him and his wife Marilyn, and they had our daughter. We had left her with them. That was when you couldn't take kids in hospitals.

Mac went by the nurse's desk, and the nurse hollered and said, "You can't take that baby in there!"

Mac said, "The hell I can't. Her dad's in there, and she wants to see him." He just walked right on by into the room and laid her on the bed with me.

Ed Ring and Bill Hudsell had the stock in Lynn, Washington. They came to the hospital to see me that night and give me $25. That horse had done that before. He just kicked too high. He couldn't stand up and just tipped on over and broke my leg. That's the first time any contractor ever gave me anything. Twenty-five dollars was a lot of money then. That was in the '50s.

The year Mac got killed they had started the new season for points, and he was in the world standings. He said that he might even go into training that year, and he said he was going to get serious and try to win the World's. He got killed in December of '64. He won a go-round in bronc riding in Deadwood, South Dakota, and he was pretty high in the standings. He went to the National Finals in 1963 in bull riding. We've heard a lot of times that if he hadn't got killed that Larry Mahan wouldn't have won near as many all-around's. Larry even said that himself. Mac worked four events.

Hank and Bob Christensen Sr. thought a lot of Mac. They put the chains on their Cadillac in Eugene and came up here for Mac's funeral. December 16, 1964, is when he got shot. He's buried here in Heppner right up on the hill. Ronnie Raymond was with Mac when he died. Jim Bothum was with Mac also.

240

One time Joann and I went somewhere, and we left little three-year-old John with a baby sitter. There was a picture of Mac on the table, and he pointed to the picture and told the baby sitter, "That's my uncle, and he's a big, tough son-of-a-bitch!"

L to R: Mac Griffith, Floyd Jones, Ralph Schwalbe
Photo by Hamley Co. From Howdyshell

REG KESLER

Reg Kesler is a stock contractor from the Calgary, Alberta area and is a regular supplier of livestock for the National Finals Rodeo. We interviewed Reg at the Aladdin Hotel & Casino during the National Finals in 1996. He's a busy man during the month of December, but he sat for two hours talking to us about his life with rodeo. Reg is a terrific emissary for rodeo, a promoter in every sense of the word.

———————————————

I was a stock contractor for 50 years. I didn't fall into stock contracting at all. I guess this is about 1946 when I first started supplyin' rodeo stock. I had a good friend up there, lived about five miles away from me. I said to him, "Clark, there's a lot of horses in this country. They're cannin' horses by the train load. Not the car load, but the train load. We ought to cull some of these horses out. There's four or five little rodeos around here. We ought to cull 'em out an' buy 'em. They're not eight to ten dollars apiece."

"Nah," he said. "We don't need to do anything like that."

"I think we should," I said.

"No," he said. "I'm not interested."

So I went to work along that line, cuttin' out the better horses, an' time went along, an' I trailed a bunch an' fed 'em in with an outfit from Gem. Mack McDonald was kind of a heads-up man that was takin' those horses to Calgary. It was about a hundred miles. So I threw my horses in with his an' sent 'em up there.

Well, they tried all those horses before the rodeo. Well, I'm rodeoin', an' I go to Calgary to see about my horses, an' out of the twenty head of horses, I had three left. They sent the rest to the cannery. They tried 'em out with those old dummy saddles. So I get in my car an' drove down to the plant, an' the horses hadn't been killed yet. So I got my horses back out of the plant. Would you believe I won the prize on one of those horses from the plant at the Calgary Stampede. It was the best buckin' horse there.

Those old flat saddles they put on 'em with the short trip, you know. If the horse bucks good, well, they kept him. If he didn't...

I don't even know if they put a flank strap on 'em cause I wasn't there. An old flat saddle with a trip on the side. A little 3/8 inch rope about 40 feet long, so they could give the horse lots of room. When they figured the horse had bucked long enough, they'd pull it off. Everything just fell off. They didn't have men ridin' 'em. They just used it at the Calgary Stampede to try those horses.

I been a rodeo contractor for a long time, and I like to see stock perform; but I never did get so far up that street that I wanted to see guys get hurt. I don't give a darn if I like you personally, or I didn't. I didn't want to see someone get hurt.

We had a bull or two that was bad. They jerked guys down. We had bull #6. He was a muley bull. There was no way those guys could ride that bull without getting jerked down. It was just the way he bucked. Well, I don't really believe the name of the game is to try to kill somebody.

I think, a case like that, they can criticize as much as they want. I didn't own "Bodacious." I might have felt differently if I did, but I don't think so. Some of these guys make just a damn big noise. They never got on a bull in their life. I been on lots of 'em, an' I sure don't want to get on one that's gonna smash my face in. There's lots of bulls that can buck you off, an' they won't smash your face in. I think that a cowboy, for cripes sake, is entitled to every break he can get up to a point. I don't think "Bodacious" has any business in rodeo if he smashes people in the face. He had that tendency to throw up his head when he dropped. Here comes the guy's head...you can't help it. I think rodeo has enough blood letting in it without built in things like that. And it's built in; I don't care what you say. It's a known fact that's gonna happen almost every time.

I was born an raised at a place called New Dayton, 50 or 60 miles across the border from Koots, an' a little bit northwest in Alberta, Canada. It's north of Montana. I stayed there an' rodeoed a little bit. I'll tell you how I got started in rodeo. When we were kids, there was no money. People today don't understand. I mean, if you went to town over once a month, you only got money to go once, and you got a nickel or a dime. That would buy a chocolate bar or a bottle of pop or a package of gum. Well, anyway, I went to this little town of Raymond, Alberta. It had the first recognized rodeo in Canada. I went there when I was eleven years old; course, I'd been going there before, an' I'd seen these guys ridin' these steers, these younger fellas.

So I found out if you rode a steer, you got a dollar. So I went over there an' asked 'em if I could ride a steer.

"Sure," they said. I rode the steer, an' they gave me a dollar. Well, sir, I rode two steers that time, an' I had two dollars.

The next year they put in a new rule. A boy couldn't ride a steer because they were keepin' the steers for those guys to supplement their income, those cowboys. They had calf ropin', bareback ridin', saddle bronc ridin', an' that was it. But if you went an' asked one of those guys, an' he said he didn't want to ride his steer, an most of 'em didn't, they was too high class for that, then you could ride the steer. Well, believe it or not, I rode thirteen steers that day. Talk about a guy bein' rich. That's what started me in the rodeo business. Boy, I thought, this is the life.

So the next break I had was I was goin' with a girl in the town of Raymond, an' her brother was a rodeo cowboy. He had four or five guys he rodeoed with all the time. I mentioned that I'd like to go to Calgary. "Well," he said, "I'll tell you what. If you can place in steer decoratin' here in Raymond, I'll take you."

Steer Decoratin' is putting a ribbon on the steer's horn. Would you believe, for cryin' out loud, I won the steer decorating. I put a ribbon on in four seconds flat. Not only did I have a chance to go to Calgary, but I had a little money.

When I got to Calgary, I placed a second in the first go-around in steer decorating. My bare back horse threw me off, an' that's the only two events I entered in.

The steers were four an' five years old, an' they had horns, maybe four feet, an' you didn't need to get down on 'em. They wouldn't flag you until your feet touched the ground or when you hit the ground. This guy was hazin' for me, an' he was cussin' at me "Get off!" At first I straightened up a little, what the heck, so then I fell off on the ground. An' that was when I put it on 'em in four seconds. No tellin' how fast I might have got 'em if I hadn't straightened up first before fallin' off. You don't try to stop those big old steers. They weighed 1000 to 1200 pounds.

Today it's an insult to a cowboy's intelligence, as far as I'm concerned, his manhood, an' everything else. Those cock-eyed steers don't weigh 450 pounds. I just don't identify with this nonsense. Most cowboys today are not cowboys; they're rodeo participants. They're not dumb, but they want to win that money as easy as they can. You don't see any real bad horses here at the NFR, unless it's an accident, I'll tell you that. They cull the real bad ones out. What do they do with 'em if they're too tough? I take 'em to my rodeos.

In my day, wagon trains were out of the picture. You have to have a good parade, a good Grand Entry, flags, an' gals dressed up pretty nice, things like that. That was the start of our rodeos. I put the whole rodeo on. I have a problem with *"I"*. If it weren't for *"We"*, there wouldn't be no *"I"*.

I put on rodeos nobody else even thought about, but at the same time, I couldn't have done it by myself. I had to have cowboys. I had to have management. I had to have a lot of things. So how in the heck can you look people in the face and say "I?" It's "We."

The first time I went to a rodeo across the line I went to Pendleton. Harley Tucker an' Mac Barbour an' Joe Kelsey were supplyin' the stock. It was somethin' else. Jim Shoulders was ridin' there. Harry Thompkins was riding there. All those good cowboys. I mean, the top of the line were there. An' they bucked 'em off with those bulls. A Harley Tucker bronc bucked Casey Tibbs off in bronc ridin'.

"Did you see it? Did you see it?" You could hear Harley Tucker yellin' an' hoppin' around, shakin' hands with everybody.

"We got the 'Buckle'! We got the 'Buckle'!"

Another time, Harley Tucker came into the Brown Palace in Denver. You could hear him all over that building. "Did you see it? Did you see it? We got that gold buckle! And right where you can have a good look at it!" The "Buckle" was Casey Tibbs.

A bareback rider from Canada, a good friend of mine, said, "You know, I drew one of Harley Tucker's bareback horses here in Pendleton."

"Oh, have you?" I said.

He asked me, "What do you think of him?"

I said, "I know one thing."

"What's that?"

"You better get your ridin' pants on, that's what I think," I said.

It was "Quick Change," or somethin' like that.

"He's a good one," Harley told him. "you'll like him."

He bucked off so quick, he didn't know whether he liked him or not.

The first time I ever went away from home to rodeo I took a gunny sack an' put my bareback riggin' an' my spurs in there. I guess that would be about 1949, maybe a little before that. I caught a ride to Lethridge, which was about 25 miles. I decided that I would hitchhike. Well, they got the longest, highest bridge in the world at Lethbridge. Across a coulee. So I decided, well, I'll walk across this bridge. The trains, they told me, always went slow. My dad had traveled an' talked about ridin' freights. So I'm gonna ride the freight to Carmangay, Alberta.

So I walked out onto that bridge, an' I looked across there, an' man, it was a long ways. Anyway, I went a walkin'. I got out in the middle of that bridge an' looked down an' there was a guy fordin' the river down below with a team o' horses an' a dog. I got across the other side, an here comes the freight. I threw my riggin' bag in an' jumped in. The door was open on this ol' boxcar. I'm sittin' there, going along, an' I hear somethin', an' lo an' behold, there's another guy there.

"Where are you goin'?" he asked.

"I'm goin' to Carmangay," I said.

"Well," he said, "You better hope this train is going to Carmangay."

"What are you talkin' about?" I asked.

"Up here a few miles, there's a Y in the road. One turns north to Carmangay. The other goes west to Fort Macleod."

Would you believe that cock-eyed thing went on to Fort Macleod? I don't know just how fast we were travelin', but we were goin' fairly good. The first thing I did when I realized we were past the turn was throw out my riggin' bag. Well, if I'd have known what was gonna happen, I never would have done it. That bag went out there an' bounced about thirty feet in the air an' rolled about twenty yards or maybe thirty. I could see what was gonna happen to me when I stepped off there.

Well, I stepped off that thing, an' I took the biggest step of my life. It must have been thirty feet at least. I ended up flat on my back. I laid there. It wasn't a matter of which bone was broke but how many. I finally gathered myself up an' walked up the road for about five or six miles. Not a soul around. It was towards evening an' I stopped at this old farmer's place. He was an old Swedish fella.

"There's hay in the barn; you can sleep there tonight," he said.

So, I built myself a nest in the hay, an' pretty quick here he comes. "Mama say, she is worried about you. She doesn't think you had anything to eat." So the old lady there, she fed me.

The next mornin' he was there bright an' early. "You come to de house," he said, "and you get more to eat. I have a horse here, and you can ride him to Carmangay."

When I took a look at that 1500 pound Clyde he had, I wasn't goin' to ride him to Carmangay. So I said I appreciated that, but I had some guys that I was gonna meet at Carmangay, and we were goin' on, so I wouldn't have any way of gettin' his horse back to him.

That was all right with him. Then he let out a yell an' started runnin' for the road. An' here comes his old neighbor puttin' along. He stopped him an said to me, "See that, I got you a ride right to Carmangay."

If I remember right, it cost me six dollars to enter the bareback ridin', the saddle bronc ridin', an' the calf ropin'. That's all they had.

I rode a bareback horse, an' this is the old era. These two old judges said, "You made a hell of a ride, boy, but you missed him out."

I got on the saddle bronc, a big brown horse. I borrowed the saddle from Carl Olson. He put the saddle on for me an' everything. This horse jumped out o' there an' turned back. There was no whistle in those days. They had a old horn hooked up to a battery. It blew, an' I was beamin'. These two old Indians were pickin' up there. Bad Eagle an' Plain Eagle were their names. Big braids down their necks. I flew out through there, an' this old boy reached out an' snared me, an' he held me out there an' he said, "By god, boy you ride like hell." I guess hell was good.

Well, I won third, but they didn't pay for third. They just paid for first an' second.

So, that was the end of that. I caught a ride back home. That was my first rodeo.

A friend of mine an' I went across the border an' rodeoed in some of those rodeos over there in the Okanogan Valley. We went to Omak. In the mornin' we went down to the rodeo grounds. There was just a little walk-in gate. We opened the gate, an' there was a contractor standin' there, talkin' to a cowboy.

Well, we knew this cowboy pretty good. He was Ken Browser. Kind of funny the way things turn out sometimes. He was talkin' to the contractor, who was Eddy Ring. He said, "You know, I'm entered in the bronc ridin' here, an' a guy wouldn't have a gol darn chance in the world winnin' any money. Gary Elders is entered here. Turk Greenough is entered here, and so on an' so on. They're all entered here. There's no chance."

I can remember the old contractor said, "Well, you know, winnin' depends on a lot of things. Some of those guys might get throwed off."

We turned an' walked away from there. This Wilf Gerlitz was a card. He nudged me in the ribs an says, "Say, you know what? He didn't mention us at all."

Wilf drew a bull they never had rode, an' he rode him an' won the bull ridin'. An' I had this gray horse, an' there was three gray horses this outfit had. One was "Whichway"; one was "Faraway"; an' the other one was "Mackiah." I don't recall which one I had, but anyway, it was a two day rodeo, an' I had this horse, an' I rode him. When I came back, I heard this Browser say, "Isn't that somethin'. That rubber boot irrigated farmer from Rosemary rode that horse. I heard so much about that plug, he can't do nothin'."

Well, I think Eddy Ring gave him that horse the next day. As I walked by the chutes there, I saw him gettin' on, an' I said, "Don't forget to spur that plug, or he won't buck at all."

Well, he did spur that horse. For about four jumps. When he landed, the paramedics came in, an' he was layin' there, tryin' to get a little air. I walked out there an' looked down at him. I said, "Ain't that awful, ain't that awful. That rubber boot farmer from up there at Rosemary spurred the heck out of that old gray plug, an' here a would-be bronc rider can't do nothin'!"

He wanted to fight. He wanted to do a lot of things, but he had no air. So that was the end of that. I won the bronc ridin', an' my friend, Wilf won the bull ridin'.

When we were at Omak, the river was floodin' real bad, right up in the corner of the arena. They had that suicide race. The guy that won that race won it three years in a row. His name was Mosse Sam. He rode a blind horse, a big bay horse that couldn't see at all.

An' they had a helicopter light in that arena. That was really somethin' back then. That was in the Deb Copenhaver era. An' there was an old boy downtown who had a bar, an' he sponsored him. You ask Deb whatever became of that picture of him ridin' "Snake," a Joe Kelsey horse. It was about three by five over the bar at that old boy's place in Omak.

That's one of the greatest pictures you'll ever see. That horse's head is throwed back on Deb's knee. The horse is kickin' way up here, an' you can see Deb's toes stickin' past that horse's head. It's really a good picture. It was taken in Penticton.

There's been a lot of rodeo participants but not too many down to earth cowboys anymore. But some of the guys, in my opinion, that were maybe cowboys...one was Mac Griffith. I don't remember where he was from, but let me tell you, this guy, this cowboy, this Mac Griffith...the first time I ever met this guy, he came to a little rodeo at Eastend, Saskatchewan. We didn't have any cowboys. I think we only had six, an' we put that rodeo on. Mac was the mainstay of that whole outfit. He was the guy that got the guys to get on those horses. We had the cock-eyedest rodeo you ever saw or could imagine with just six cowboys.

Mac Griffith, Pendleton.

249

I put the rodeo on, supplied the stock, everything. Carl Nasker, who trained a horse for the Kentucky Derby, was a bull rider. He was from somewhere down in the States.

The next rodeo we went to was about five hundred miles from there, a place called Rimbey, Alberta. Well, sir, the pickup man that I had hired didn't show up, so this Mac Griffith said, "Well, Reg, I'll help you."

He picked up buckin' horses, he rode buckin' horses, he rode bareback horses, he dogged, an' everything. But he had no doggin' horse. The guys entered in the doggin' wouldn't mount him. So he comes ridin' over to me on my pickup horse, an' he said, "I got nobody to mount me. Have you got a horse I could ride?"

I said he could use the sorrel horse we used for pickup.

"I'll just use him," he said.

So, I didn't pay no more attention to him. I was gettin' the guys ready in the buckin' chutes. Pretty quick he come over an' said, "I haven't got a hazer. Can you haze for me?"

He won both go-arounds. That was a two day rodeo, an' he rode that pickup horse, an' I hazed for him. Besides that, he picked up my buckin' horses an' everything else.

Not long after that he was in a bar someplace, an' he got in an argument with an off duty cop. The cop said, "I'll get my gun."

Mac said, "Go ahead."

The cop came in an' shot him square in the chest. He put a hand on his chest an' said, "You didn't do a very good job; you better shoot me again."

He shot him for the second time, an that was the end of Mac Griffith.

Mac Griffith was tough. The kind of guy I like. He didn't stir up trouble. That rumor was a lot of B.S. He could be tough if that's what you wanted. He didn't pick no fights that I heard of. Those people that didn't know the guy will tell you all kinds of things. But I knew the guy.

I'll never forget Lary Daniels came to this rodeo down in Regina, Saskatchewan, and I never seen a guy like him in my life. He couldn't just get up on a chute an' set on a horse. He had to take a run. That was the first time I saw Lary Daniels. He was a pretty good rodeo announcer, I'm gonna tell you, he was good. The next time I run into him was at Omak, Washington.

You seen the odd guy; we had the odd guy in rodeo history. He'd go through a bunch of acrobatics just before he'd get on a horse. This guy was jumpin' four feet high an' beating himself with his fists. I guess he was tryin' to get his motor runnin'. Lary would back off twenty or thirty feet an' take a run, an' up that chute an' onto that horse, an' right now, outside...

I rodeoed with some of the greatest cowboys in the world. I rodeoed with Carl Olson, the bronc ridin' champion of the world in 1947. We rodeoed together for five years until he quit. Things change.

I never rodeoed down in the States very much. We went to Omak; we went to Pendleton. I rode a bareback horse in Ellensburg. Carl Dodge was judging there. They had this picture of me ridin' this horse called "Up An' Over" splashed all over every cock-eyed newspaper in the country. Front page. I won a second or a go-around or somethin'. But, anyway, he comes to me after I rode this horse an' says, "Say, boy, are you gonna come to New York?"

Old "Stupid" went home to put up the hay!

I've thought about that a lot of times. You know, that could have been the difference, possibly. But you never know. It's the difference between being really well known in the rodeo business as a rider rather than a stock contractor.

I put the rodeo on at Cardston for quite a few years, but this one year, I was ridin' my horse down along the fence, an' I saw this little glitter, an' I thought, What's this?

I stopped my horse an' got off an' kicked the dirt back, an there's this watch. The watch is okay, there's nothin' wrong with it. Near as I know, anyway. On the back, somebody had tried to scratch the name off. Anyway, I could see the name was Guy Cash. Well, I knew that Guy Cash had rode in Calgary. That was the watch he won. In fact, I had watched him ride in Calgary. So I got explorin' an' found out he lived in Idaho. So I called him an' told him, "I think I got somethin' you might be interested in."

I worked for an old farmer for a whole week when I was a kid. He said, "See that pair of boots there? I'll either give you that pair of boots or $15.00 for the work."

This pair of boots was Hyres boots, 10 inch tops, an' square toes. I said, "I'll take the boots."

Well, now, I used those boots for several years. I went to Calgary an' got lucky, an' then I bought a new pair of boots from Irby

Munday, the second pair of boots I ever owned. They were Hyres style 100. I slept with 'em under my pillow for a month or so to make sure nobody stole 'em. But, anyway, the neighbor up there where I lived had a few cattle, an' he didn't have any boots. So I said, "Hey, you better take this pair of boots."

So, he took my first pair of boots. He finally sold out to move to Calgary. An' he died up there in Calgary. So I went to see his wife an' kids one day a year or so after he died. His wife said, "Say, you remember givin' Doug a pair of boots?"

"I sure do," I said.

"Would you like them back?"

"Sure," I told her. So she gave me the boots, an' I took 'em home an' put 'em in my basement. An' my mother-in-law come along one day an' said, "Whose boots are those?"

"They're mine. They're the first pair of boots I ever owned," I said.

"Can I have 'em?" she asked.

"Sure you can have 'em," I said.

They turned up setting on her mantle in Henrietta, Texas. She had 'em bronzed.

I'll tell you what...I'm a firm believer that the crowd is entitled to something. Rodeo hasn't but one thing in the world to sell, and that's entertainment an' excitement.

If there's one thing that kills a sport faster than repetition, I'd like to know what it is. If every guy stepped up an' knocked a home run in baseball, there'd be nobody in the stands. Okay. Every one of those horses loping slowly down the arena an' those guys movin' their arms an' their feet, it don't mean much. But you want to get a reaction from the crowd, have one of 'em really blow up an' see what happens. As far as I'm concerned, a cowboy, he's smart, an' dumb as H. e. double l. He wants to get his money easy, but in so doin', he's killin' the very thing he's got to sell.

I've seen this, an' I mean it. They would never have gotten Bull Riders Only approved by the PRCA if I had been on the board cause I don't believe in that. We had a fairly good sellin' point. Now they're gonna saturate this thing to the point where bull ridin' don't mean anything. I'm disappointed in a way that they approve of those things. I think they're jeopardizing the other events. The thing is like I told the President of this outfit not too many years ago. My card looks the same as his. I figured that everybody should be entitled to the same shake. You can't tell me that Bull Riders Only gives all cowboys in our Association a fair shake. It darn sure didn't.

They put a column in a paper up in Canada not too long ago about what I said about that. You'd be surprised how many I got agreein' with what I had to say. I think it's right, or I wouldn't say it.

I want to tell you about the rodeo movin' to Las Vegas from Oklahoma City. The move was bought, an' it wasn't by more money for the cowboys. It was bought by that circle of guys handlin' the PRCA business. I happened to be on that Board, an' I'll tell you what, I cannot prove it, but I'll tell you one thing that I do know. That you don't change my mind in fifteen minutes unless you have an awfully good reason. Money is one of the main reasons that I can think of in changin' some people's ideas. Not mine. But some people. The history of the guys involved: one guy owed the Internal Revenue Service quite a bit of money, and his bills went away. The other guy has never come to a rodeo since. So you just have to assume that somethin' went on. Shawn Davis was President, and Shawn Davis wanted the rodeo to come here to Las Vegas. I know why he wanted it to come here, an' so does he, but I'm not gonna say. But he knows why. So they held the vote, an' the vote was to stay in Oklahoma City. They called a fifteen minute recess, an' the vote was changed to come here to Vegas. An' that's how it came here. I know what I'm talkin' about. I was there. I'd like somebody that was there to stand up an' tell me any different.

Anyway, the reason I didn't want it to come here in the first place was this was not a place for women an' children. They've changed things a lot since then. You have to give concessions where concessions are due, an' they have since built some entertainment for younger kids. They didn't have anything at that time. All they were interested in at that particular time was the money. An' Benny Binion was the biggest instigator of the whole business comin' here to Vegas. And I can understand his point too. Naturally he wanted it here. I mean, bucks, bucks, bucks. An' that was the name of the game, an' it still is.

I understand politics. There's nothin' wrong with it. But when you do it for personal gain, then, I don't have any time for that nonsense. I sure don't.

I think rodeo could go a heck of a lot further than it has done. I expect it to go further because in the first place, football, hockey, baseball, basketball, anything like that...you have a clientele that goes and supports this thing. They seek out sponsorships, an' they make it possible to go to the Big House, so to speak. We have, in my opinion, an' I guess it's maybe because I don't know any better, the greatest sport in the world for excitement. Entertainment for every part of the family. Do we have brains enough to sell it? Uh, uh. If we'd a been workin' on the aspect of sellin' this thing, an' there's guys that will stand up an' say, "Well, how do you do that?" No one said anything about doin' it on your own, but that's the way cowboys think because they're on their own, you know. You just name me one part of the cock-eyed rodeo business, except for the team ropin', where the cowboy nods his head, an' he's not on his own. So there's lots of ways of lookin' at this thing, but I really believe it's gonna really take a-holt. They're talkin' about buildin' a big buildin' here. I don't know whether they will or not; they've been talkin' about it for several years. They really need it.

Not only that, any one of these cabbies, any one of these downtown merchants will tell you that this particular time of the year was the deadest time of the year. Until the rodeo came to town. It's no tellin' how many millions of dollars that this rodeo generates.

The younger generation doesn't understand what went on before. They think these things are just there. They don't know what created them. And there's one more thing. That's the life of a cowboy. As far as a participant is concerned, it's longer in the timed events, of course. But in the ridin' events your career is short.

The thing that I cannot identify with...if I was gonna play football tomorrow against a football team, and I could pick their players, who the heck do you think is gonna win? That's what's going on here today at the NFR. The cowboys are pickin' the stock that comes here. Absolutely. Showy, but not too tough. That's right. Once in awhile they make a mistake, an' one gets bad. Somebody hurt him with a spur or somethin'. We'll take him out. He can't be in the next go-around. He's too bad; he doesn't "match up"; or, "He's not even." That's what they call it.

"Even" is not rodeo. They still have the "Luck of the Draw."

What I'm interested in is the basic thing that's right. That's all. Right's right.

INDEX

Index